THIS BOOK
BELONGS TO

....

....

Copyright @2023

All rights reserved. No part of this publication may be reproduced, stored in a retrieval system, or transmitted in any form or by any means, electronic, mechanical, photocopying, recording or otherwise, without the prior written permission of the Publisher.

I can't tell you how grateful I am that you decided to read my book. My most heartfelt thanks that you took time out of your life to choose my work and I hope you find benefit within these pages.

There are so many books available today that offer similar content so that makes it even more humbling that you decided to buying mine.

Tell me what you thought! I am eager to hear your opinion and ideas on what you read as are others who are looking for a good book to buy. Leave a review on Amazon.com so others can benefit from your wisdom!

With much thanks.

Table of Contents

SUMMARY

Introduction	27
Yarn Fibres	29
Yarn Colours	34
Yarn Textures	38
Yarn Weights	42
Tools and Equipment	46
Gauge	48
Basic Stitches	53
More Complex Stitches	60
Following Crochet Patterns	65
Being Creative with Colour	74
Making Crochet Fabrics	80
Making Crochet Motifs	86
Joining Crochet Motifs	92
Flowers	103
Trims	184
Fabrics	247
Motifs	318

SUMMARY

What is the Crochet Flowers and Embellishments: Crochet Flowers and Embellishments refer to the various decorative elements that can be created using the art of crochet. Crochet is a technique of creating fabric by interlocking loops of yarn or thread using a crochet hook. It is a versatile craft that allows for the creation of a wide range of items, including garments, accessories, and home decor.

Crochet flowers and embellishments are small decorative elements that can be added to various crochet projects to enhance their visual appeal. These elements can be made in different shapes, sizes, and colors, allowing for endless possibilities in terms of design and creativity. They can be used to adorn hats, scarves, bags, blankets, and even clothing items like sweaters and cardigans.

One of the main advantages of crochet flowers and embellishments is that they can be easily customized to suit individual preferences and project requirements. They can be made using different types of yarn or thread, which can vary in thickness, texture, and color. This allows crocheters to create flowers and embellishments that perfectly match the overall aesthetic of their project.

Crochet flowers can be made in various styles, such as simple petals, layered petals, or even intricate designs that mimic real flowers. They can be attached to projects using stitches or sewn on separately. These flowers can be further embellished with beads, buttons, or sequins to add an extra touch of sparkle and dimension.

In addition to flowers, crochet embellishments can include other decorative elements like leaves, bows, butterflies, and even small animals or characters. These embellishments can be used to create unique and personalized designs, making each crochet project truly one-of-a-kind.

Crochet flowers and embellishments are not only visually appealing but also add a touch of elegance and charm to any crochet project. They can transform a simple hat or scarf into a stylish accessory or turn a plain blanket into a beautiful heirloom piece. They also provide an opportunity for crocheters to showcase their skills and creativity, as they require precision and attention to detail.

Overall, crochet flowers and embellishments are a wonderful way to add a decorative and artistic touch to crochet projects. They allow for endless possibilities in terms of design and customization, making them a favorite among crocheters of all skill levels. Whether you are a beginner or an experienced crocheter, incorporating crochet flowers and embellishments into your projects can elevate them to a whole new level of beauty and sophistication.

The Beauty of Handmade Floral Decor in Crochet Flower: Handmade floral decor in crochet flower is a beautiful and intricate art form that showcases the creativity and skill of the artist. Each piece is carefully crafted by hand, using a crochet hook and yarn to create delicate and lifelike flowers. The result is a stunning and unique decoration that adds a touch of elegance and charm to any space.

One of the most captivating aspects of handmade floral decor in crochet flower is the attention to detail. Every petal, leaf, and stem is meticulously crafted to mimic the natural beauty of real flowers. The artist carefully selects the colors and textures of the yarn to create a lifelike representation of the flower they are trying to recreate. This level of detail and precision is what sets handmade crochet flowers apart from mass-produced decorations.

Another remarkable feature of handmade floral decor in crochet flower is the versatility it offers. The artist can create a wide variety of flowers, from roses and daisies to sunflowers and orchids. They can also experiment with different sizes, colors, and patterns to create a truly unique and personalized piece. This allows individuals to find the perfect crochet flower decoration that matches their style and complements their home decor.

In addition to their aesthetic appeal, handmade crochet flowers also hold sentimental value. Each piece is a labor of love, with hours of time and effort invested in its creation. This makes them a meaningful and thoughtful gift for loved ones on special occasions such as birthdays, anniversaries, or weddings. Handmade crochet flowers can also be passed down through generations, becoming cherished family heirlooms that hold memories and stories.

Furthermore, handmade floral decor in crochet flower is an eco-friendly alternative to fresh flowers. While fresh flowers are beautiful, they have a limited lifespan and require constant maintenance. Handmade crochet flowers, on the other hand, can last for years with proper care. They do not require water or sunlight, making them a low-maintenance and sustainable option for those who want to bring the beauty of flowers into their homes without the hassle.

In conclusion, handmade floral decor in crochet flower is a stunning and versatile art form that showcases the creativity and skill of the artist. With their attention to detail, versatility, sentimental value, and eco-friendly nature, these handmade crochet flowers are a beautiful addition to any space. Whether used as a centerpiece, wall hanging, or gift, they bring a touch of elegance and charm that is sure to be admired by all who see them.

Understanding Crochet Hooks and Yarn of Crochet Flower: Crochet is a popular craft that involves creating fabric by interlocking loops of yarn or thread using a crochet hook. To successfully create a crochet flower, it is important to have a good understanding of the different types of crochet hooks and yarn available.

Crochet hooks come in various sizes and materials. The size of the crochet hook determines the size of the stitches and ultimately the size of the finished crochet flower. The most commonly used crochet hook sizes range from 2.25mm to 6.5mm, with smaller sizes producing tighter stitches and larger sizes creating looser stitches. It is important to choose the appropriate hook size for the desired outcome of the crochet flower.

Crochet hooks can be made from different materials such as aluminum, plastic, wood, or even bamboo. Each material has its own unique characteristics. Aluminum hooks are lightweight and glide smoothly through the yarn, making them a popular choice for beginners. Plastic hooks are also lightweight and affordable, but they may not be as durable as other materials. Wood and bamboo hooks have a warm and natural feel, providing a comfortable grip for longer crochet sessions.

Yarn selection is equally important when creating a crochet flower. Yarn comes in various weights, which determine the thickness of the yarn. The most common yarn weights used for crochet flowers are fingering, sport, and worsted. Fingering weight yarn is thin and delicate, creating dainty and intricate crochet flowers. Sport weight yarn is slightly thicker and provides a good balance between drape and stitch definition.

Worsted weight yarn is thicker and creates more substantial crochet flowers with a heavier feel.

In addition to weight, yarn is also categorized by fiber content. Common yarn fibers include acrylic, cotton, wool, and blends. Acrylic yarn is affordable, easy to care for, and comes in a wide range of colors. Cotton yarn is breathable and ideal for creating lightweight crochet flowers. Wool yarn provides warmth and elasticity, making it suitable for crochet flowers that require structure. Blends combine different fibers to create unique characteristics, such as the softness of acrylic with the breathability of cotton.

When selecting yarn for a crochet flower, it is important to consider the desired texture, drape, and appearance. Some yarns have a smooth and even texture, while others have a more textured or fuzzy appearance. The drape of the yarn refers to how the fabric hangs or falls, which can vary depending on the fiber content and weight of the yarn.

Essential Crochet Stitches for Flowers: Crocheting flowers is a popular and enjoyable craft that allows you to create beautiful and intricate designs. To successfully crochet flowers, it is important to have a good understanding of the essential crochet stitches that are commonly used in flower patterns. These stitches will help you create the various petals, leaves, and other elements that make up a crochet flower.

One of the most basic crochet stitches used in flower patterns is the chain stitch. This stitch is created by pulling the yarn through the loop on your hook, creating a new loop. The chain stitch is often used as the foundation for crochet flowers, as it provides a base for building upon.

Another important stitch for crocheting flowers is the slip stitch. This stitch is used to join rounds or to create a smooth edge. To make a slip stitch, insert your hook into the designated stitch, yarn over, and pull the yarn through both the stitch and the loop on your hook.

The single crochet stitch is another essential stitch for crocheting flowers. This stitch is created by inserting your hook into the designated stitch, yarn over, and pulling the yarn through the stitch. Then, yarn over again and pull through both loops on your hook. The single crochet stitch is often used to create the petals of a crochet flower, as it creates a tight and compact stitch.

The double crochet stitch is a taller stitch that is commonly used in flower patterns to create larger petals or leaves. To make a double crochet stitch, yarn over, insert your hook into the designated stitch, yarn over again, and pull the yarn through the stitch. Yarn over once more and pull through the first two loops on your hook, then yarn over again and pull through the remaining two loops. The double crochet stitch creates a looser and more open stitch than the single crochet stitch.

In addition to these basic stitches, there are also more advanced stitches that can be used to create more intricate and detailed crochet flowers. These stitches include the treble crochet stitch, the half double crochet stitch, and the popcorn stitch, among others. These stitches can be used to add texture and dimension to your crochet flowers, making them even more visually appealing.

Overall, having a good understanding of the essential crochet stitches for flowers is crucial for successfully creating beautiful and intricate crochet flower designs. By mastering these stitches, you will be able to create a wide variety of flowers, each with its own unique style and charm. So grab your crochet hook and yarn, and start exploring the world of crochet flowers!

Reading Crochet Patterns in Crochet Flower: When it comes to crocheting flowers, one of the most important skills to have is the ability to read crochet patterns. Crochet patterns are essentially a set of instructions that guide you through the process of creating a specific design. They provide you with all the necessary information, such as the type of stitches to use, the number of stitches to make, and the order in which to make them.

To successfully read crochet patterns in crochet flower making, it is essential to understand the various symbols and abbreviations used. These symbols and abbreviations represent different crochet stitches and techniques. For example, a chain stitch is often represented by the letter "ch," while a single crochet stitch is represented by the letter "sc." By familiarizing yourself with these symbols and abbreviations, you will be able to decipher the instructions in the pattern more easily.

In addition to symbols and abbreviations, crochet patterns also include written instructions. These instructions provide further details on how to complete each step of the pattern. It is important to read these instructions carefully and follow them precisely to ensure that your crochet flower turns out as intended.

When reading crochet patterns, it is also important to pay attention to any special instructions or notes that may be included. These instructions may provide additional guidance or tips to help you achieve the desired result. For example, the pattern may specify a specific type of yarn or hook size to use, or it may suggest a particular technique to create a certain effect. By following these special instructions, you can enhance the overall look and quality of your crochet flower.

Furthermore, crochet patterns often include a stitch diagram or chart. This visual representation of the pattern can be extremely helpful, especially for those who are more visual learners. The stitch diagram shows the pattern in a graphical format, with each stitch represented by a symbol or a box. By referring to the stitch diagram, you can easily see the pattern's structure and how the stitches are interconnected.

To effectively read crochet patterns in crochet flower making, it is important to practice and familiarize yourself with different patterns. Start with simpler patterns and gradually work your way up to more complex designs. As you gain experience, you will become more comfortable with interpreting the instructions and understanding the various symbols and abbreviations used.

In conclusion, reading crochet patterns is an essential skill for crocheting flowers. By understanding the symbols, abbreviations, written instructions, special notes, and stitch diagrams, you will be able to successfully create beautiful crochet flowers.

Choosing the Right Colors for Your Flowers in Crochet Flower: When it comes to crochet flowers, choosing the right colors can make all the difference in the final result. The colors you select can enhance the overall design, create a specific mood, or even evoke certain emotions. Therefore, it is important to carefully consider your color choices to ensure that your crochet flowers turn out exactly as you envision them.

One of the first things to consider when choosing colors for your crochet flowers is the purpose or theme of your project. Are you creating a bouquet of flowers for a wedding? Or perhaps you are making a spring-inspired wreath? Understanding the purpose or theme will help guide your color choices. For a wedding bouquet, you may want to stick to traditional white or pastel shades, while for a spring wreath, you can experiment with vibrant and cheerful colors.

Another factor to consider is the color scheme or palette you want to work with. There are various color schemes to choose from, such as monochromatic, complementary, analogous, or even a rainbow palette. Each color scheme creates a different visual impact and can convey a different mood. For example, a monochromatic color scheme using different shades of pink can create a soft and romantic feel, while a complementary color scheme using purple and yellow can create a bold and vibrant look.

Additionally, it is important to consider the color intensity or saturation. Some crochet flowers may look best with bold and saturated colors, while others may benefit from softer and more muted tones. The intensity of the colors can also affect the overall visual impact of your crochet flowers. Bright and intense colors can create a lively and eye-catching effect, while softer and pastel shades can create a more delicate and subtle look.

Furthermore, it is essential to consider the color placement within your crochet flower design. You can choose to have a single color for the entire flower, or you can incorporate multiple colors to create a more intricate and detailed look. The way you arrange the colors can also create different effects. For example, using a gradient effect where the colors transition from light to dark can create a sense of depth and dimension in your crochet flowers.

Lastly, don't be afraid to experiment and play around with different color combinations. Crochet flowers offer endless possibilities when it comes to color choices, so don't limit yourself to traditional or expected color combinations. Try mixing unexpected colors together or incorporating different shades and tones to create unique and eye-catching crochet flowers.

Adding Crochet Flowers to Garments and Accessories: Adding crochet flowers to garments and accessories is a creative and versatile way to enhance their overall appearance. Crochet flowers can be used to add a touch of femininity, elegance, or even a bohemian vibe to any outfit or accessory. Whether you are a seasoned crocheter or a beginner, incorporating crochet flowers into your projects can be a fun and rewarding experience.

One of the great things about crochet flowers is that they can be made in various sizes, shapes, and colors, allowing you to customize them to suit your personal style and the specific garment or accessory you are working on. You can choose to make small delicate flowers for a subtle and understated look, or opt for larger, more intricate designs to make a bold statement.

When it comes to attaching crochet flowers to garments, there are several methods you can use. One popular technique is to sew the flowers onto the fabric using a needle and thread. This method provides a secure and permanent attachment, ensuring that the flowers will stay in place even with regular wear and washing. Another option is to use a crochet hook to slip stitch the flowers directly onto the fabric. This method is particularly useful when working with delicate or lightweight fabrics that may be damaged by sewing needles.

In addition to garments, crochet flowers can also be added to various accessories such as hats, bags, scarves, and even shoes. By attaching crochet flowers to these items, you can instantly transform them into unique and eye-catching pieces. For example, a plain straw hat can be instantly elevated with the addition of a few crochet flowers in vibrant colors. Similarly, a simple tote bag can be given a bohemian twist by attaching crochet flowers along the straps or on the front.

The possibilities for incorporating crochet flowers into your projects are endless. You can experiment with different yarns, stitches, and patterns to create flowers that are as unique as you are. Additionally, you can mix and match different flower designs to create a bouquet-like effect or create a cohesive look by using the same flower design throughout your project.

Adding crochet flowers to garments and accessories not only enhances their aesthetic appeal but also allows you to showcase your crochet skills and creativity. Whether you are looking to add a subtle embellishment or make a bold fashion statement, crochet flowers are a versatile and beautiful option. So why not give it a try and see how crochet flowers can elevate your next project?

Enhancing Home Decor with Floral Embellishments of Crochet Flower: One way to enhance the overall aesthetic of your home decor is by incorporating floral embellishments, specifically crochet flowers. Crochet flowers are a versatile and charming addition that can instantly add a touch of elegance and whimsy to any room.

Crochet flowers come in various shapes, sizes, and colors, allowing you to customize them to match your existing decor or create a unique focal point. Whether you prefer a more traditional or contemporary style, there is a crochet flower design that will suit your taste.

One of the benefits of using crochet flowers as embellishments is their versatility. They can be used in a multitude of ways to enhance different areas of your home. For instance, you can attach them to curtains, lampshades, or throw pillows to instantly transform these everyday items into eye-catching pieces. You can also use crochet flowers to create beautiful wall hangings or wreaths that will add a pop of color and texture to your walls.

Another advantage of crochet flowers is that they can be easily made at home, even if you have limited crochet skills. There are numerous patterns and tutorials available online that provide step-by-step instructions on how to create various crochet flower designs. This allows you to unleash your creativity and make unique embellishments that perfectly complement your home decor.

In addition to their decorative appeal, crochet flowers can also evoke a sense of nostalgia and warmth. The handmade nature of crochet adds a personal touch to your home, making it feel more inviting and cozy. Guests will surely appreciate the attention to detail and the unique character that crochet flowers bring to your space.

Furthermore, crochet flowers can be a cost-effective way to update your home decor. Instead of purchasing expensive floral arrangements that will eventually wither, crochet flowers offer a long-lasting alternative. With proper care, they can maintain their beauty for years to come, saving you money in the long run.

In conclusion, enhancing your home decor with floral embellishments, specifically crochet flowers, is a wonderful way to add charm and personality to your space. Their versatility, handmade appeal, and cost-effectiveness make them an excellent choice for anyone looking to elevate their home's aesthetic. So why not give crochet flowers a try and see how they can transform your living space into a beautiful and inviting haven?

Crafting Unique Gifts with Crocheted Flowers: Crafting unique gifts with crocheted flowers is a creative and thoughtful way to show your loved ones how much you care. Crocheting flowers allows you to add a personal touch to any gift, making it truly one-of-a-kind. Whether you're making a blanket, a hat, or even a piece of jewelry, adding crocheted flowers can instantly elevate the item and make it extra special.

One of the great things about crocheting flowers is that there are endless possibilities when it comes to design. You can choose from a wide variety of flower patterns, each with its own unique shape, size, and texture. From delicate roses to vibrant sunflowers, there's a flower pattern out there to suit every taste and occasion.

Not only are crocheted flowers beautiful, but they also add a touch of nature and whimsy to any gift. They can be used to create a stunning centerpiece on a blanket or a hat, or they can be attached to a pin or a hair clip for a more versatile accessory. The possibilities are truly endless.

Crocheting flowers also allows you to experiment with different colors and yarns. You can choose to use a single color for a more classic and elegant look, or you can mix and match different colors to create a vibrant and eye-catching design. The choice is yours, and that's what makes crocheting flowers so exciting.

In addition to being visually appealing, crocheted flowers also have a tactile quality that adds to their charm. The texture of the yarn and the stitches used to create the flowers give them a three-dimensional quality that makes them stand out. When you give a gift with crocheted flowers, the recipient will not only see the beauty of the flowers but also feel their softness and warmth.

Another great thing about crocheting flowers is that it's a relatively easy skill to learn. With some basic crochet stitches and a little practice, you'll be able to create beautiful flowers in no time. There are plenty of online tutorials and patterns available to help you get started, so even if you're a beginner, you can still create stunning gifts with crocheted flowers.

In conclusion, crafting unique gifts with crocheted flowers is a wonderful way to express your creativity and show your loved ones how much you care. Whether you're making a blanket, a hat, or a piece of jewelry, adding crocheted flowers will instantly elevate the item and make it extra special.

Mixing and Matching Flower Patterns for Versatility of Crochet Flower: When it comes to crochet flowers, the possibilities are endless. With a wide variety of flower patterns available, you can mix and match different designs to create a versatile range of crochet flowers. This allows you to add a unique touch to your crochet projects, whether you're making a blanket, a hat, or a scarf.

One of the advantages of mixing and matching flower patterns is the ability to create different sizes and shapes. By combining different patterns, you can create flowers of varying sizes, from small and delicate to large and bold. This allows you to customize your crochet projects and add dimension and visual interest.

Another benefit of mixing and matching flower patterns is the opportunity to experiment with different color combinations. Flowers are often associated with vibrant and beautiful colors, and by using different patterns, you can create flowers in a wide range of hues. This allows you to play with color and create unique and eye-catching crochet flowers.

Furthermore, mixing and matching flower patterns allows you to incorporate different crochet techniques into your projects. Each flower pattern may use different stitches and techniques, such as puff stitches, popcorn stitches, or picot stitches. By combining these patterns, you can practice and showcase your crochet skills while creating beautiful flowers.

In addition to versatility in size, shape, color, and technique, mixing and matching flower patterns also offers the opportunity to create themed crochet projects. For example, you can combine patterns of different flowers to create a bouquet or a garden-themed blanket. This adds a cohesive and thematic element to your crochet projects, making them even more special and meaningful.

Lastly, mixing and matching flower patterns allows you to express your creativity and personal style. With so many patterns available, you can choose the ones that resonate with you and reflect your unique taste. By combining these patterns, you can create crochet flowers that are truly one-of-a-kind and showcase your individuality.

In conclusion, mixing and matching flower patterns for crochet projects offers a world of possibilities. From creating different sizes and shapes to experimenting with color combinations and crochet techniques, the versatility of crochet flowers knows no bounds. So go ahead, explore the vast array of flower patterns available, and let your creativity bloom.

Crochet Flower Trims for Clothing and Bags: Crochet flower trims are a popular and versatile accessory that can be used to enhance the look of clothing and bags. These delicate and intricate designs add a touch of femininity and charm to any outfit or accessory.

When it comes to clothing, crochet flower trims can be used in a variety of ways. They can be sewn onto the hemline of a dress or skirt to create a whimsical and bohemian look. They can also be added to the neckline or sleeves of a top to give it a unique and eye-catching detail. Crochet flower trims can even be used to create a beautiful and intricate pattern on the back of a cardigan or sweater, adding a touch of elegance and sophistication.

In addition to clothing, crochet flower trims can also be used to embellish bags. Whether it's a tote bag, a clutch, or a backpack, adding crochet flower trims can instantly transform a plain and ordinary bag into a stylish and fashionable accessory. These trims can be sewn onto the edges of the bag, creating a beautiful and intricate border. They can also be used to create a pattern or design on the front or back of the bag, making it truly unique and one-of-a-kind.

One of the great things about crochet flower trims is that they can be made in a wide variety of colors and sizes. This allows for endless possibilities when it comes to incorporating them into your clothing or bags. Whether you prefer a subtle and understated look or a bold and vibrant statement, there is a crochet flower trim out there for you.

Furthermore, crochet flower trims can be made using different types of yarn, giving them a different texture and feel. From soft and fluffy yarns to more structured and sturdy ones, you can choose the type of yarn that best suits your desired look and feel. This versatility allows for even more creativity and customization when it comes to incorporating crochet flower trims into your wardrobe.

In conclusion, crochet flower trims are a beautiful and versatile accessory that can be used to enhance the look of clothing and bags. Whether you're looking to add a touch of femininity to a dress or skirt, create a unique and eye-catching detail on a top, or transform a plain bag into a stylish accessory, crochet flower trims are the perfect choice. With endless possibilities in terms of colors, sizes, and yarn types, you can truly make these trims your own and add a personal touch to your wardrobe.

Pro Tips for Crocheting Perfect Flowers: Crocheting flowers can be a fun and creative way to add a touch of beauty to your projects. Whether you're making a decorative accessory, embellishing a garment, or creating a floral arrangement, crocheted flowers can bring a unique and personalized touch to your work. To help you achieve perfect crocheted flowers, here are some pro tips to keep in mind:

1. Choose the right yarn: The type of yarn you use can greatly affect the outcome of your crocheted flowers. Opt for a lightweight yarn with good stitch definition, such as cotton or bamboo, to ensure that the intricate details of your flower design are clearly visible.

2. Use the appropriate hook size: The size of your crochet hook should match the weight of your yarn. Using a hook that is too small can result in a tight and stiff flower, while using a hook that is too large can create

a loose and floppy flower. Experiment with different hook sizes to find the perfect balance for your desired flower shape and size.

3. Start with a magic ring: When crocheting flowers, starting with a magic ring can give you a seamless and tight center. This technique allows you to adjust the size of the center hole by pulling the yarn tail, ensuring that your flower petals are evenly spaced and securely attached.

4. Pay attention to tension: Consistent tension is key to achieving a professional-looking crocheted flower. Make sure to maintain an even tension throughout your work, neither too tight nor too loose. This will ensure that your stitches are uniform and your flower maintains its shape.

5. Experiment with stitch combinations: Crocheted flowers can be made using a variety of stitches, such as single crochet, double crochet, and treble crochet. Experiment with different stitch combinations to create unique textures and patterns in your flowers. You can also incorporate techniques like picots or clusters to add extra flair to your designs.

6. Block your flowers: Blocking is a technique used to shape and set your crocheted pieces. After completing your flower, gently wet it and shape it into the desired form. Pin it down on a blocking board or use a foam mat to hold its shape while it dries. This will give your flower a polished and professional finish.

7. Embellish with beads or buttons: Adding beads or buttons to the center of your crocheted flowers can enhance their visual appeal and give them a more realistic look.

Troubleshooting Common Flower-Making Issues of Crochet Flower: Crochet flowers are a popular and versatile craft project that can be used to embellish various items such as hats, scarves, bags, and even home decor. However, like any craft, there can be some common issues that arise during the flower-making process. In this guide, we will explore some troubleshooting tips for these common flower-making issues in crochet.

One common issue that crocheters may encounter is the flower not turning out the way they envisioned. This can be due to a variety of factors, such as using the wrong yarn weight or hook size. It is important to follow the pattern instructions carefully and use the recommended materials to achieve the desired result. If the flower is too small or too large, adjusting the hook size can help achieve the desired size. Additionally, experimenting with different yarn weights can also alter the size and appearance of the flower.

Another issue that may arise is the petals of the flower not lying flat or curling up. This can be caused by tension issues while crocheting. If the tension is too tight, the petals may curl up, while if the tension is too loose, the petals may not lie flat. It is important to maintain consistent tension throughout the project to ensure that the petals are uniform and lie flat. Practicing and experimenting with different tension techniques can help achieve the desired result.

Crocheters may also encounter issues with the flower shape not being symmetrical or even. This can be due to inconsistencies in stitch counts or uneven tension. It is important to count stitches carefully and ensure that each round or row has the correct number of stitches. Using stitch markers can help keep track of stitch counts and ensure even shaping.

Additionally, paying attention to tension and maintaining consistent tension throughout the project can help achieve a symmetrical and even flower shape.

Another common issue is the flower not holding its shape or appearing floppy. This can be caused by using a yarn that is too soft or not stiffening the flower properly. Choosing a yarn with more structure or adding a stiffening agent, such as fabric stiffener or glue, can help the flower hold its shape. Additionally, blocking the flower by wetting it and shaping it while it dries can also help achieve a more structured and defined shape.

Lastly, crocheters may encounter issues with the flower unraveling or coming apart. This can be caused by not securing the ends properly or not weaving in the ends securely.

Blocking and Finishing Your Crocheted Flowers: Blocking and finishing your crocheted flowers is an important step in the process of creating a polished and professional-looking finished product. While it may seem like an extra step that can be skipped, taking the time to block and finish your flowers can greatly enhance their appearance and durability.

Blocking is the process of shaping and stretching your crocheted flowers to ensure that they lay flat and have a uniform shape. This is especially important if you are using a yarn that tends to curl or if your stitches are uneven. Blocking can help to even out the tension in your stitches and create a more symmetrical and visually appealing flower.

To block your crocheted flowers, you will need a blocking board or mat, rust-proof pins, and a spray bottle filled with water. Start by laying your flower flat on the blocking board or mat, making sure that it is in the desired shape and position. Use the rust-proof pins to secure the edges of the flower to the board, gently stretching and shaping it as needed. Once the flower is pinned in place, lightly mist it with water using the spray bottle. Allow the flower to dry completely before removing the pins. This process will help to set the shape of the flower and give it a more professional finish.

Finishing your crocheted flowers involves adding any additional embellishments or details that you desire. This can include sewing on buttons, attaching beads or sequins, or adding embroidery stitches. Finishing touches can really elevate the look of your crocheted flowers and make them stand out.

When adding embellishments, it is important to consider the overall design and aesthetic of your flower. Choose embellishments that complement the colors and style of the flower, and be mindful of not overcrowding or overpowering the design. Sew on buttons or beads securely, making sure that they are firmly attached and will not come loose with wear.

If you choose to add embroidery stitches, consider using a contrasting color of thread to create a striking effect. Embroidery stitches can be used to add texture, outline the petals, or create intricate designs within the flower. Take your time and carefully plan out your embroidery stitches before starting, as they can greatly enhance the overall look of your crocheted flower.

In conclusion, blocking and finishing your crocheted flowers is a crucial step in creating a polished and professional-looking finished product. Blocking helps to shape and even out the tension in your stitches, while finishing adds embellishments and details that enhance the overall design.

Introduction

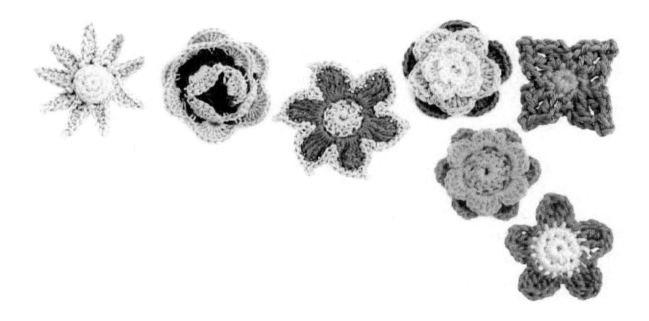

This book offers a comprehensive collection of crochet stitches, ranging from the very simple to the most complex; the traditional to the innovative. Use it as an inspirational guide to making your own unique crocheted pieces, whether you are creating beautiful garments and accessories for yourself, or stylish adornments for your home.

The book is divided into four sections: **Flowers, Trims, Fabrics and Motifs**. Each section has its own colour palette to inspire you.

> There is a great range of designs in the Flowers section, from the natural to the more flamboyant. Add these to garments and interior items, or use them to make jewellery.
>
> Use the edgings and borders in the Trims section to add an individual touch to your next crocheted or knitted

garment or a crocheted trim to ready-made clothing.

Included in the Fabrics section are texture, lace and colour patterns; make them into panels to add to ready-made items or make a patchwork throw of your favourites.

There are three shapes of Motifs: squares, circles and hexagons; traditional alongside new. Ideas for joining motifs to make different items are given later in this section.

Each section starts with a showcase of inspirational projects that offer you different ideas about how to use the designs; use these as a springboard for designing your own versions. For example, the Cushion Panel could be worked in texture or colour stitches. The Patchwork Scarf shows you how to combine any number of stitches together; this uses lace fabrics but you could mix in motifs too.

Each design has a title to help identification. You may recognize some of these and know them by a different name. Neither is right or wrong; it's just that different countries have different ways of naming the stitches. For each design there are both written instructions and a chart, making it easier to see how to work each row or round.

If you are unfamiliar with working with charts, you will find some advice later in this section. We also give guidance on how to work from written instructions; understanding abbreviations and shorthand phrases; how to make the correct number in a foundation chain, and how to work more complex stitches such as shells, clusters and popcorns. We also provide a full key to the symbols used in the charts.

Yarn Fibres

There is a huge range of yarns available to inspire the creative crocheter. Yarn can be categorized in various ways, and over the next few pages we'll discuss colours, textures and weights. When choosing the yarn to use for your project, you should first consider whether it needs to be made of tough fibres to resist wear and tear, such as cotton or wool, or is suitable to be worked in softer fibres, such as silk, because it is more decorative than practical. A child's garment that needs frequent washing should be made in a hard-wearing, machine-washable yarn. Alternatively, a throw that isn't laundered as frequently can be made in less robust yarn, such as handwash-only wool, cashmere or silk. A rug should be worked in tough, thick wool to withstand wear from feet, but a necklace could be made in the most delicate yarns, such as laceweight wools, metallics or fine linen threads. Some fibres cost more than others; throws take a lot of yarn so reserve expensive fibres for smaller items or combine them in stripes or blocks with less costly yarns.

Natural Fibres

Alpaca is spun from the coat of the alpaca, a close relation of the llama. It is a wonderfully soft and lustrous yarn, which has many of the qualities of cashmere but at a more affordable price. It can shed hairs so may be unsuitable for high-use items.

Angora yarn comes from the angora rabbit. A yarn with a high content of angora is very fluffy and sheds hairs. It is usually blended with another fibre to give it stability, making a super-soft yarn.

Cashmere is spun from the hair of the cashmere goat. Pure cashmere yarn is very expensive and best kept for luxury items.

When it is blended with another fibre, such as wool, it becomes much more affordable.

Cotton comes from the ball of the cotton plant. It is a heavy fibre, very hard-wearing and is available in a great range of colours. Cotton can be mercerized; this process gives it greater lustre and helps it to take brighter dyes. Matt cotton tends to be more loosely spun.

Mercerized cotton glows with colour, makes crisp, clear stitches and is hard-wearing.

Linen comes from the stem of the flax plant. It is often blended with cotton to soften it. In its natural colour, it has rustic simplicity; when it is dyed it produces soft, dusty shades for understated elegance.

Mohair is spun from the coat of the angora goat. The softer kid mohair is the first or second shearing of a kid goat and is finer than the mohair from the adult goat. It is usually blended with another fibre to give it strength. It is light and airy, but can shed fine hairs.

Silk is a continuous filament secreted by the silkworm larva, which it spins around itself to form a cocoon. This cocoon is unwound and many of these fibres are spun together to form a yarn. Silk has a lustre; it is soft and has a dry feel. Use it blended with cotton or wool to make it harder-wearing.

Wool is spun from the fleece of a sheep; different breeds of sheep give different qualities. Merino wool is very soft, for example, whereas Shetland wool is more hard-wearing. Wensleydale is very lustrous, while Jacob wool is spun in fantastic natural colours. Wool has excellent insulating qualities; it is warm in winter and cool in summer. Wool works up beautifully and can be pulled back and recycled without loss of quality. Wool can be tweed with flecks of contrasting colours, dyed in a solid colour, or kept in its natural shades. Look out for organic or locally produced wool too.

As a fibre, wool cannot be beaten for its warmth, durability and timeless feel.

Blended and Synthetic Fibres

Blended yarns of natural and synthetic fibres combine the natural yarn's qualities with the hard-wearing and stable features of the synthetic. Synthetic yarns are hard-wearing and can be spun into wonderful fancy yarns, such as eyelash and ribbon. They take dyes well, especially vibrant and bright colours.

Yarn Colours

Colour is a great inspiration for the creative crocheter. Experiment with vibrant colours together for a striking look, or try a sophisticated palette of natural, muted colours. In this book, each of the four design sections uses a main palette with either contrasting or harmonious highlights. The Flowers section uses the natural contrasts of green, yellow and orange to support the range of dark purple to soft pink. The warm palette of the Trims section uses oranges and yellows, with a sharp contrast of hot pink and lime green. The Fabrics section is designed with a cool palette of greens mixed with harmonious blues. The Motifs are predominantly blue with contrasts worked in lilac and aqua.

Choose a simple palette of blues and greens to create a deep, rich panel of sea-inspired crochet

Warm palette

Warm colours are mixed with red or yellow, so think hot pink, orange and orange-yellow. Fiery and bright, they add warmth to winter clothes or a glow to accessories like the Lavender Sachets. Mix shades of red, or spicy orange and tangerine. For contrast, add a trim of lime to a combination of citrus lemon, orange and hot pink.

Cool palette

Cool colours are based on blue, so include green, blue and blue-violet as well as mixes of these shades, such as blue-green, turquoise and purple. Use shades of one colour; oceanic blues including aqua, grey-blue and pale turquoise, or shades of green from mint to sage. The olive green Skirt project is trimmed with a matching khaki. The Skirt Pocket blends three shades of indigo.

Natural palette

A calm, restful and sophisticated palette of wood, stone and terracotta, and the colours of nature: earthy ochre and sand; woodland browns; pebbles and stone greys, or organic shades of undyed wool. The dark brown Cushion is embellished with a flamboyant copper swirl.

Rich palette

To add luxury and opulence, think of jewel colours such as ruby, amethyst and emerald. These colours add drama and mystery and look fantastic in metallic fibres or silk and ribbon yarns. Deep rich red is used for the Heart roses and dark royal purple for the Necklace.

Adding colour

Contrast brings colours alive, while toning colours are harmonious. Greens can be toned with blues or contrasted with plum. Purples and violets go together well but are lifted by a small trim of yellow-green.

Yarn Textures

Yarns are made in a wide range of textures, from plain, plied yarns to extravagant concoctions of ribbon, bouclé or eyelash. These tassels illustrate the diversity of yarn textures. Each shows the qualities of the yarn and what type of fabric it makes when crocheted. Simple single or double crochet fabrics reveal how fabulous textured yarns are; small patterned crochet stitches would be lost in the texture. However an open lacy fabric or motif would look fantastic worked in mohair.

This garment combines two textures, chenille and mohair.

1 Bouclé has a texture of short tight snarls that curl across the surface of the fabric. This cotton bouclé is crisp and produces a dense texture like a towel. Softer bouclés in mohair and wool make a luxurious deep fabric. Use as a simple stripe or edging to contrast with smoother yarns.

2 Chenille is a short-pile yarn; it produces a wonderfully rich, velvety fabric. This chunky version would be great on its own worked on a large hook in an open lace or as a dense solid fabric. Combine it with another texture such as the Appliqué Flowers.

3 Cord is a smooth, round yarn that can be worked on a large hook for an open fabric or worked more tightly on a small hook for a stiff, structured fabric.

4 Eyelash yarn looks like a frayed ribbon. It can be difficult to crochet with and the stitches are hard to see; keep it for the last row of a trim or a simple single-crochet edging.

5 Matt cotton has a fantastic dry texture; this is a yarn that has weight and will add strength and structure when worked together with other yarns. The colours can be beautifully dusty like painted plaster, or zingy like citrus fruit.

1 Bouclé
2 Chenille
3 Cord
4 Eyelash
5 Matt cotton

6 Mercerized cotton is a tight, lustrous yarn that makes a very clean, crisp fabric. It is available in a wide range of bright, intense colours. Any stitch looks great in it, looking even better when worked on a small hook to make structured, upright stitches. It is used to make the fantastically colourful flower Bunting project as well as the funky Necklace.

7 Metallic yarns are crunchy, modern and full of light. This is a mix of viscose and metallic elements that adds a sharp highlight in a soft fluid fabric. Use for jewellery, or as a single stripe to add sparkle to a matt yarn.

8 Mohair is a soft, fluffy yarn; the fibres trap air and light to produce a feather-soft fabric. Use a large hook to create open fabrics or make soft flowers like the roses used to embellish the willow Heart project.

9 Ribbon is a woven version of tape. It is flat and varies in width from narrow to wide, and is available in any fibre from wool to modern synthetics. This ladder ribbon has a strong structure punctuated with sharp stabs of precise colour. Ribbons can be multicoloured; stranded with metallic; open or solid structures; fluffy or crisp; slinky or hard.

10 Tape is a fluid knitted flat yarn that rarely produces a completely flat fabric; it twists and folds on the hook. It folds in half for one stitch and then opens out for the next. This cotton version will make a fabric with structure, but a viscose version produces a wonderfully slinky fabric.

11 Tweed yarn is a combination of two or more colours, spun together or introduced as slubs or knots of colour. A crocheted tweed fabric looks warm, cosy and sturdy. Contrast it with metallic or cotton for an exciting twist. Two shades of tweed wool were used for the Crochet Hook Holder.

Yarn Weights

The weight of a yarn refers to its thickness; a lightweight yarn crochets up into a soft, delicate fabric, while a medium-weight (aran) yarn is thicker and makes a chunkier fabric. Try new yarns and discover how a fabric can be changed by altering the weight of yarn used. Thick yarns such as bulky and super-bulky are ideal for making rugs and other large projects. Light- and medium-weight yarns can be used for finer projects such as a, Cushion Panel, floral Bag Decorations, or garment trims such as the Skirt Pocket project. Several strands of fine or lightweight yarns can be held together to make up a thicker yarn.

A medium-weight cotton makes a firm but lacy edging on a cotton skirt.

Bulky-weight tweed wool is worked on a large hook to make a thick, dense fabric.

Plies

Yarns are sometimes described by a number of ply – for example, 2ply, 4ply or 6ply. A ply is a single twisted strand. As a general rule, the more plies that are twisted together, the thicker the yarn. However, just to confuse things, plies can be different thicknesses themselves. A tightly spun ply will be thinner than a loosely spun one. For example, a 2ply Shetland wool yarn crochets up to fine-weight (or 4ply) gauge, but a thick Lopi yarn (a type of wool traditionally sourced from Iceland) is a single ply.

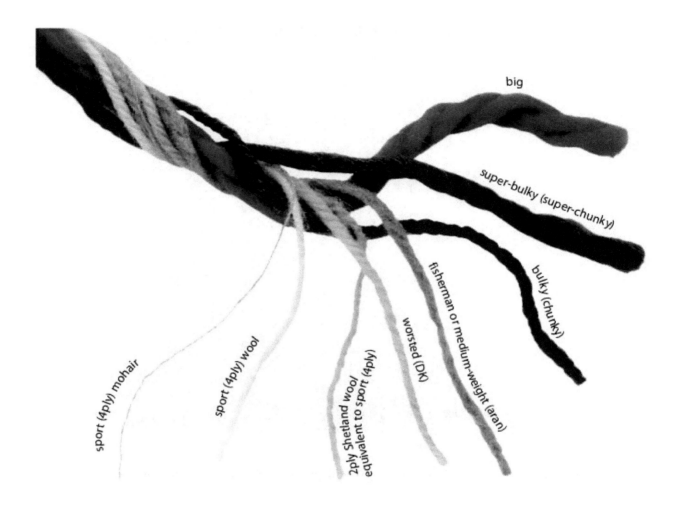

Yarn Weight Standards

In this book, we refer to weight using the standard developed by the Craft Yarn Council of America, which divides yarns into weight rather than number of plies. The projects in this book are included to inspire your own ideas, so the yarn references are kept only to the weight rather than mentioning specific yarns. This means that you can use any yarn that is the same weight to make a similar project. Yarn manufacturers in the US and in the UK sometimes use different names to identify the same weight of yarn. Where they differ, I have included both in the following table. Throughout this book, we give the US weight first, with the UK equivalent following in brackets.

Craft Council of America's Standard Yarn Weights

Weight	Crochet gauge*	Hook size**	Yarn type***
Lace	32-42 sc	Steel 6-8 and B1 (1.4-1.6mm)	Crochet thread
Super-fine	21-32 sc	B1-E4 (2.25-3.50mm)	Sock, fingering (2ply, 3ply)
Fine	16-20 sc	E4-7 (3.50-4.50mm)	Sport, baby (4ply)
Light	12-17 sc	7-I9 (4.50-5.50mm)	Light worsted (DK)
Medium	11-14 sc	I9-K10½ (5.50-6.50mm)	Worsted, afghan (aran)
Bulky	8-11 sc	K10½-M13 (6.50-9.00mm)	Chunky, craft, rug
Super-bulky	5-9 sc	M13 and larger (9.00mm and larger)	Super-chunky, roving

* Gauge (known as 'tension' in the UK) is measured over 4in (10cm) in single crochet (abbreviated to 'sc'). This is a guide only and is the most commonly used gauge.

** US hook sizes are given first, with UK/metric equivalents in brackets.

*** Alternative US yarn types are given first with UK equivalents in brackets.

Tools and Equipment

Crochet is a very versatile craft, requiring very little equipment: if you have some yarn and an appropriate size hook to work that yarn, you have pretty much everything you need! Here we discuss the range of hooks available and the two main sizing systems: US and metric.

Hooks

Crochet hooks are available in a variety of materials including metal, plastic, wood and bamboo. The size of the hook is directly related to the thickness of the yarn being used; a fine yarn requires a small hook, while a thick yarn needs a much chunkier hook. Crochet hooks are sized according to the diameter of the shaft. There are two main sizing systems in use: the US system and the metric system (used in the UK and Europe).

Crochet hook conversion chart

US	METRIC
B1	2.25mm
C2	2.75mm
D3	3.25mm
E4	3.50mm
F5	3.75mm
G6	4.00mm
7	4.50mm
H8	5.00mm
I9	5.50mm
J10	6.00mm
K10½	6.50mm
L11	8.00mm
M/N1	9.00mm

3
N/P15 10.00mm
O16 12.00mm
P/Q 15.00mm
Q   16.00mm
S   19.00mm

> You only need a few simple tools: yarn, a crochet hook, and a pattern to follow (although you can try making up your own stitches and designs!). You'll also need a few crafting basics: scissors to snip off yarn ends, a darning needle to sew in loose ends, and a tape measure and pins for measuring gauge (tension).

Gauge

Gauge (tension) is the number of stitches and rows of a crochet fabric, or the finished dimensions of a motif, and is vital if you are following a pattern and have to achieve a stated size. However, the collection of patterns in this book are to be used to create your own items and can be worked in any yarn weight with a suitable sized hook. To create your own designs, such as making a trim to fit the hem of a skirt, measure your own gauge and use it as a guide to achieve satisfactory results. If you are working without the need to achieve a certain size, you won't need to know the gauge. Simply stop when the item is the size you want it.

Choosing Yarn

The weight of the yarn will determine the finished size of the stitches. A fabric worked in a fine-weight cotton will be smaller than the same fabric (using the same number of stitches) worked in a bulky-weight yarn. An afghan made in thin crochet thread will be more delicate and light than the same afghan made in the same motifs made from medium-weight wool.

Fabrics

Making a Gauge Swatch

Using your yarn and the relevant hook, make a foundation chain of three pattern repeats, not forgetting to add any additional chain as stated in the instructions. Work through the stitch instructions until the swatch is 6in (15cm) long.

Measuring the Gauge

Lay the swatch out flat. Using pins, mark the start and end of one pattern repeat of stitches across a row. If it is a small pattern repeat, mark out at least 2in (5cm) of pattern repeats. Lay a ruler on to the crochet, starting at one pin, and measure the distance between the pins. If this is one pattern repeat, the measurement will be the width of one pattern repeat. If you have marked out two or three pattern repeats, this will be the width for that number of repeats.

Using the Gauge

Now you know the width of one pattern repeat you can work out how many pattern repeats are needed to make a panel of fabric a certain size. To do this, divide the width that you want by the width of one pattern repeat. For example, a panel needs to be 10in (25cm) wide and one pattern repeat is 2in (5cm). 10in (25cm) divided by 2in (5cm) gives the answer 5. Therefore you need to make a foundation chain of 5 pattern repeats (plus any additional chain as stated in the instructions).

Flowers

Gauge is harder to measure for flowers; often the only way of working out the finished size of a flower is to make it. Starting with the correct yarn will give some idea of the size; thin yarns will make small flowers, while thick yarns will make bigger flowers.

Trims

Making a Gauge Swatch

Trims worked horizontally: Using your yarn and the relevant hook, make a foundation chain of three pattern repeats, adding any additional chain as stated in the instructions. Work through the stitch instructions to make the trim.

Trims worked vertically: Using your yarn and the relevant hook, make the number of chain stated in the stitch instructions. Work though the stitch instructions until the trim measures 6in (15cm).

Measuring the Gauge

Horizontal Trims: Follow the instructions for Fabrics. The measurement will be the width of one pattern repeat.

Vertical Trims: Lay the trim out flat. Using a ruler, measure the trim across its width at the widest point. This measurement will be its full width. You don't need to measure the length, as the trim will be worked until it is the correct length for your project.

Using the Gauge

Horizontal Trims: Follow the instructions above for Fabrics.

Vertical Trims: If you want the trim to be wider, use a size larger hook or use thicker yarn. If you want it to be smaller, use a smaller hook or thinner yarn.

Motifs

Making a Gauge Swatch

Using your yarn and the relevant hook, make the chosen motif.

Measuring the Gauge

Lay the motif out flat. Place a ruler horizontally across the motif to measure the width. Square motifs can be measured in two ways, depending on how you are going to arrange them. Using them as squares, measure across the width from side to side. Using them as diamonds (rotated on to one corner), measure them across from corner to corner along the diagonal. This measurement will be the width of one motif. Circular motifs are measured from side to side across the diameter. This measurement will be the width of one motif. Hexagonal motifs can be measured from one flat side to the opposite flat side, or from point to point, depending on how you are going to arrange them.

Using the Gauge

Now you know the width of one motif you can work out how many motifs are needed to make an item a certain size. To do this, divide the width that you want by the width of one motif. For example, an afghan of square motifs needs to be 60in (152cm) wide and one motif is 4in (10cm) wide. 60in (152cm) divided by 4in (10cm) gives the answer 15. Therefore you need to make a row of 15 motifs to begin the afghan. If the finished afghan is square, it will need a total of 225 motifs.

Altering the size

The size of a panel of any of the fabric stitches can be altered by adding more pattern repeats to the width and working in the pattern until it is the correct length. However, motifs, trims and flowers that are a set number of stitches or rows cannot be altered in this way. You can only alter the size by using a different size hook or another weight of yarn. The three Decoration projects have been made using the same cotton but at three different sizes by using successively smaller hooks. To make something smaller or narrower, use a smaller hook. To make something bigger or wider, use a bigger hook. Make gauge swatches, altering the hook by one size bigger or smaller. Using the same yarn, you can alter the hook by a few sizes but eventually the fabric made will become too dense and hard (by using a smaller hook) or too open and floppy (by using a bigger hook). Then you will have to use a different weight of yarn, decreasing the thickness to make something smaller or increasing the thickness to make something bigger.

Basic Stitches

The designs in this book are created using only the basic crochet stitches. In this section we include useful reminders for how to make each stitch as well as ways they have been used in this book to generate different effects. We use US crochet terms here; for UK terms see the conversion table in the Following Crochet Patterns

Chain

(abbreviation = ch)

Every design in this book starts with a length of foundation chain. To make a motif, the length of chain is joined into a circle with a slip stitch. Chain stitches are also used to create lacy effects like those for Star Lattice and the Trefoil Loops edging. The Snowflake motif is made entirely of chain lengths fixed with single crochet stitches.

Chain lengths can make large spaces to be worked into, as seen in the Daisy Hexagon or the Large Fan Lace.

Wrap the yarn around the hook from back to front. Pull the yarn through the loop on the hook. One chain stitch made. The pattern instructions will tell you how many to make; don't forget that the slip knot at the beginning doesn't count as a stitch.

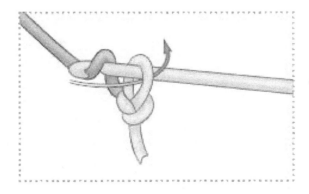

Single crochet

(abbreviation = sc)

This is the shortest crochet stitch; by itself, it makes a dense fabric, such as the Solid Circle motif. It can be worked in rows to create a dense fabric stripe between lacier areas such as Square Stripes or combined with chain lengths as illustrated by Buttonhole Fabric. Single crochet is often combined with taller stitches to create wave or zigzag effects, such as in the Zig Zag Stripe.

There will already be a loop on the hook, either from the foundation chain or from another stitch. Following the stitch instructions, insert the hook into the work at the correct position. Wrap the yarn around the hook from back to front and pull the yarn through the work on the hook.

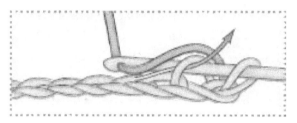

Wrap the yarn around the hook from back to front again and pull through both loops on the hook. One single crochet made.

Double crochet

(abbreviation = dc)

This stitch is taller than the single crochet; it can make a dense fabric when several stitches are worked together such as Building Blocks, or a more open fabric when combined with chain stitches like Simple Filet Crochet. Double crochet forms a solid base for the more lacy elements in Clover Border. It also creates the famous Granny crochet stitch, which can be used as a fabric or a motif.

There will already be a loop on the hook, either from the foundation chain or from another stitch. Wrap the yarn around the hook from back to front then insert the hook into the work at the correct position. Wrap the yarn around the hook from back to front and pull the yarn through the work on the hook. There are now three loops on the hook.

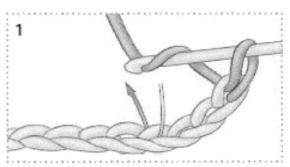

Wrap the yarn around the hook from back to front and pull through the first two loops on the hook.

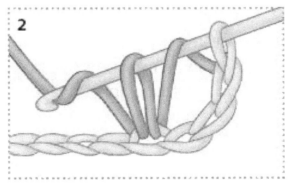

Wrap the yarn around the hook from back to front and pull through the remaining two loops on the hook. One double crochet made.

Half double crochet

(abbreviation = hdc)

The height of this stitch is halfway between the single and double crochet stitches. It isn't often used to make a fabric by itself but is effective when combined with other stitches. Sawtooth Fabric combines several heights of stitches together to create triangular blocks. Half double crochet is often used to shape flower petals such as the Large Simple Flower and the Four-Layer Flower, among many examples in this book.

Follow the instructions for the double crochet until there are three loops on the hook. Wrap the yarn around the hook from back to front and pull the yarn through all three loops. One half double crochet made.

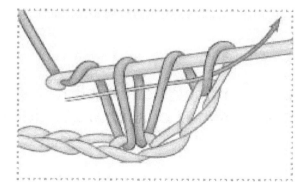

Treble

(abbreviation = tr)

This stitch is taller than a double crochet and begins a series of very tall stitches that are used most effectively in lace fabrics or to create large open spaces. Mexican Edging combines trebles into clusters to create oversized fans of stitches, while V Stitch Lattice uses trebles as an easy way to make a lace fabric. The contrast in height can be seen in the petals of the Small Rose; the short ones worked in double crochet and the taller ones in treble stitches.

Wrap the yarn twice around the hook then insert the hook into the work at the correct position.

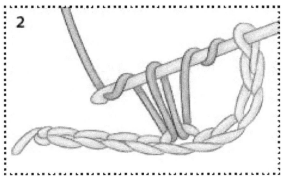

Wrap the yarn around the hook and pull through the work – there are now four loops on the hook. Wrap the yarn around the hook and pull through the first two loops on the hook.

There are now three loops on the hook. Wrap the yarn around the hook and pull through the first two loops, leaving two loops on the hook.

Finally, wrap the yarn around the hook from back to front and pull through the remaining two loops on the hook. One treble stitch made.

Taller treble variations

Double treble (abbreviation = dtr)

Triple treble (abbreviation = tr tr)

Taller stitches are made by wrapping the yarn around the hook more times before inserting it into the work. These tall stitches are used as fans like the Large Fan Braid, or to make long pointed petals for the Pointed Daisy.

Double treble

Wrap the yarn three times around the hook before inserting it into the work. Follow the instructions for the treble stitch, starting by pulling the yarn through the work and then pulling it through two loops on the hook each time. You will do this one more time than the treble.

Triple treble

Wrap the yarn four times around the hook before inserting it into the work. Follow the instructions for the treble stitch, starting by pulling the yarn through the work and then pulling it through two loops on the hook each time. You will do this twice more than the treble.

Slip stitch

(abbreviation = sl st)

A working stitch with no height but many unseen uses. It is used to join the foundation chain into a circle to begin a motif, and close each round in a motif. It is used to move the hook to a new place without cutting yarn or adding height, such as with the Snowflake; to close picots; or to fix long loops of chain stitches in place such as in the Loop Daisy.

There will already be a loop on the hook, either from the foundation chain or from another stitch. Insert the hook into the work at the correct position. Wrap the yarn around the hook from back to front and pull the yarn through both the work and the loop on the hook. One slip stitch made.

More Complex Stitches

The basic stitches worked plainly on their own can create many varied crochet fabrics. But worked together into more complex stitches such as clusters, shells, fans and popcorns, they widen out the range of textures, lacy fabrics and colour effects that can be created and that are all featured in this book. Read the individual design instructions carefully, as a shell in one fabric may be different from a shell in another.

Shells and fans

These are two names for the same crochet element: a group of tall stitches spreading out from a single point. Both terms are used in the design instructions in this book. Fabrics can be made up entirely from shells, like the Treble Fans, or combined with other elements, such as with chain loops to make Shell and Net. A scalloped edging can be created along the edge of a garment by working the Simple Shell Edging or the Picot Shell edging, which has the extra frill of picots. The Damask Rose has petals made from shells, while the Patchwork Square uses shells of increasing size to form the corners of a square.

Following the design instructions, make the required number of stitches into one point, usually a stitch or a chain.

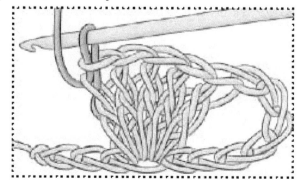

Clusters

Clusters are the opposite of shells; a group of almost completed tall stitches spread across several points and then drawn together with a closing stitch. This creates an upside-down shell. Each stitch within the cluster is called a leg; the design instructions will tell you where to work each leg. A cluster can be made up of just a few stitches, like those used to make the petals on the Cluster Flower or the Gothic Flower Edging. Other clusters within this book use up to five legs, like those in the Large Sunflower Square, or as many as six legs to create the dense blocks of the Clam Fabric.

To make a cluster, work the individual stitches (or legs) up to the point where there are two loop on the hook – just before the stitch is completed. When all the individual legs have been made (three legs are shown in the artwork above), close the cluster by wrapping the yarn around the hook from back to front and pulling through all the loops on the hook.

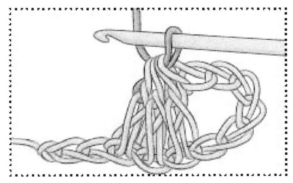

If each leg is made up of a couple of stitches, such as the Large Daisy Fabric, the instructions may use a special abbreviation, such as '3 trnc'. This is explained in the written instructions.

Anywhere you see 'tog' in the written instructions or in the symbol key indicates a cluster; several stitches pulled together. A wide range of different 'tog' stitches are used in the stitch patterns, including sc2tog and sc3tog and tr2tog, tr3tog and tr4tog. The stitch type means you are working in sc (or tr), while the number is the number of stitches in the cluster (2, 3 or 4), and 'tog' shows it is a cluster.

'Tog' stitches are also used to make decreases to shape crochet fabric.

Puff stitches

This is a small bobble of stitches: a group of half-completed stitches worked in one point and then drawn together with a closing stitch. Puff stitches make very effective petals to a simple flower. Puff stitches are usually made from half double crochet stitches so they are short and dense, but always check the design instructions for variations.

There will already be a loop on the hook, either from the foundation chain or from another stitch. Wrap the yarn around the hook from back to front, then insert the hook into the work at the correct position. Wrap the yarn around the hook from back to front and pull the yarn through the work on the hook. There are now three loops on the hook. Make more stitches in the same way at the same point, according to the design instructions.

Wrap the yarn around the hook from back to front and pull through all the loops on the hook.

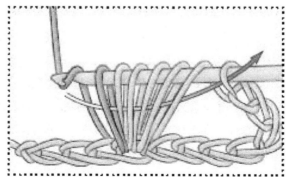

One puff stitch made. Sometimes an extra chain stitch is worked to further close the puff stitch; check the design instructions.

Popcorns

These are worked in the same way as a shell, but when the shell is completed another closing stitch is worked to draw the shell up into a bobble. Although both elements create texture, a popcorn is different from a puff stitch in that it can be made from taller stitches and is larger. The Popcorn Hexagon uses popcorns at each corner of the shape; the Baltic Square uses popcorns to make a three-dimensional motif.

Following the design instructions, work the required number of stitches in one point. Pull the last loop so it is bigger than usual and remove the hook. Carefully insert the hook through the top of the first stitch of the popcorn and then back into the enlarged end stitch. Pull the yarn to tighten this stitch again.

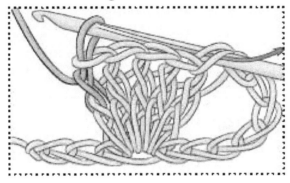

Wrap the yarn around the hook from back to front. Pull the yarn through both loops on the hook. One popcorn completed.

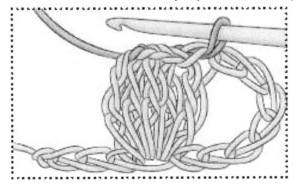

Picots

Picots are small decorative loops of chain stitches; they are a simple way to add a frill edge to any crocheted item. The simplest form is the Simple Picot Edging, which can be added to a plain crochet garment or to woven fabric as a decorative frill. Many of the edgings in this book are finished with picots; for example, the Chain Loop Ruffle has three large picots on each point, and the Teardrop Edging has picots grouped around a lacy shell.

Following the design instructions, work to the point where the picot is to be made. Work the required number of chain. Insert the hook into the stitch at the beginning of the chain.

Wrap the yarn around the hook from back to front. To close with a slip stitch, pull the yarn through the work and the loop on the hook. To close with a single crochet, pull the yarn through the work on the hook, wrap the yarn around the hook from back to front and pull the yarn through both loops on the hook.

Following Crochet Patterns

The stitch patterns in this book have both written instructions and a chart. The instructions and diagrams can be used independently of each other, but referring to both can make it easier to work the design. Here we give some advice on following written crochet instructions; later we give advice on following charts.

Abbreviations

Abbreviations are used in crochet patterns to shorten commonly used terms so that the instructions are easier to read and a manageable length. The following is a list of all the abbreviations used in this book.

beg	beginning
ch	chain
ch sp(s)	chain space(s)
cm	centimetre(s)
dc	double crochet
dtr	double treble
foll	following
hdc	half double crochet
in	inch(es)
mm	millimeter
rep	repeat
rnd	round
RS	right side
sc	single crochet
sl st	slip stitch
sp(s)	space(s)

st(s)	stitch(es)
tch	turning chain
tog	together
tr	treble
trnc	treble not completed
tr tr	triple treble
WS	wrong side
yoh	yarn over hook

Written Patterns

Each row or round (for the motifs) of the stitch patterns is written out; shorthand phrases are used to shorten the instructions and make them clearer. They refer to a set of instructions that must be repeated across a row or round.

Brackets

The repeated instructions may appear inside a set of round brackets: ( ). The number of times the instructions are repeated appears after the closing bracket.

For example: '(1 dc into next dc, 2 ch) 15 times.'

Asterisk

Sometimes for a long set of instructions an asterisk * is used. This marks the beginning of the repeat and is ended by the words 'rep from * to …' This means you work across the instructions and then return to the asterisk and repeat them. You may be told how many times to do this or told to repeat to the end of the row or round, or to repeat to the last few stitches. The instructions may also tell you to repeat a certain number of times more. This means that you have already completed one repeat and so must repeat it that number of times again.

For example: '* 1 sc into each of next 5 dc, (1 sc, 3 ch, sl st into 3rd ch from hook, 1 sc) all into 2 ch sp; rep from * 7 times.'

OR: '* 1 sc into each of next 3 dc, 2 ch, miss 1 dc; rep from * 4 times more.'

OR: '* 2 sc into next 2 ch sp, 1 sc into next dc; rep from * to end.'

OR: '* 2 ch, miss 4 ch, 1 sc into next ch; rep from * to last 3 ch.'

Ending last repeat with…

Sometimes this is written as 'rep from * to end, ending with…' This means that the last repeat may be shorter or end differently than the previous repeats. Instead of writing out a lot of repeated instructions, this phrase is used to tell you how to end the last repeat.

For example: '* 1 sc into next ch, 5 ch, 1 sc into each of next 3 sc; rep from * to end, ending with 1 sc into each of last 2 sc.'

Into each of…

This phrase is used to replace writing out that the same stitch is worked into the next few stitches or chains below.

For example: '1 sc into next dc, 1 sc into next dc, 1 sc into next dc' is replaced by: '1 sc into each of next 3 dc.'

All into…

This is used to clarify that a lot of stitches are all going to be worked in the same place. Sometimes this is quite a lot of different stitches; they are written in brackets, so it is important to read to the end of the brackets to check where they will be worked.

For example: '(1 dc, 1 ch, 1 dc, 2 ch, 1 tr, 2 ch, 1 dc, 1 ch, 1 dc) all into next dc.'

Foundation chain

The stitch patterns are written in pattern repeats. The number of foundation chain you must make to begin the pattern is also written in pattern repeats; these are called multiples. Many of the stitch patterns also have an extra few chain that you must add after the multiples have been made.

For example: 'Make a foundation chain of a multiple of 16 ch plus an extra 9 ch.'

This means that for the pattern to work correctly, you must make a foundation chain of a multiple of 16; so 32, or 48, or 64, or 80, and so on. Then make an extra 9 chain to complete the foundation chain.

IMPORTANT: The slipknot does not count as one of the chain. So to begin, make a slipknot on your hook and then begin counting the foundation chain as you make them. The final chain will be the one on your hook.

If you are a beginner start with small projects, such as trimming a pair of gloves, to boost your pattern-reading confidence.

US and UK crochet terms

The stitch patterns in this book are written in US terms. These differ quite significantly from UK terms so care must be taken by UK and European crocheters that they work the correct stitches. Translating between the two can be confusing, as the same term can refer to different stitches under the different systems. One way to tell where you are is that the American system starts with a single crochet, which the UK system doesn't have; therefore any pattern with 'sc' in it can be identified as an American pattern. (To cause further confusion, some US patterns use the term 'triple' rather than 'treble', but we use 'treble' in this book.)

US	UK
single crochet (sc)	double crochet (dc)
half double crochet (hdc)	half treble (htr)
double crochet (dc)	treble (tr)s
treble (tr)	double treble (dtr)
double treble (dtr)	triple treble (tr tr)
triple treble (tr tr)	quadruple treble (qtr)

Crochet Charts

Each design in this book has its own chart. This is a visual representation of the stitch pattern; those worked in rows have a horizontal diagram of rows, while the motifs are a circle, square or hexagon. Each stitch is drawn and it is easy to see in which position it should be worked. The diagrams are read from the bottom to the top; the foundation chain is on the bottom edge, or, for motifs, the foundation ring will be in the centre. The charts are also printed in two colours. This makes the diagram easier to read, but doesn't mean that you have to change colour on every row or round.

Each type of stitch is represented by a different symbol. This symbol shows the height of the stitch, so the symbol for an sc is shorter than the symbol for a tr. With each diagram, there is a key to explain what each symbol means. The same symbol is used to represent the most commonly used stitches in every diagram. Special or unusual stitches have their own symbols; similar symbols may mean slightly different things in different diagrams, so always check the key to make sure you work the stitch correctly. Stitches such as clusters or popcorns are drawn as they appear when you crochet them.

The rows or rounds are numbered and the pattern repeat is drawn along the foundation chain to show which part needs to be repeated. But always check with the written instructions, as the repeat can move to the left or right on different rows.

Crochet Chart Symbols

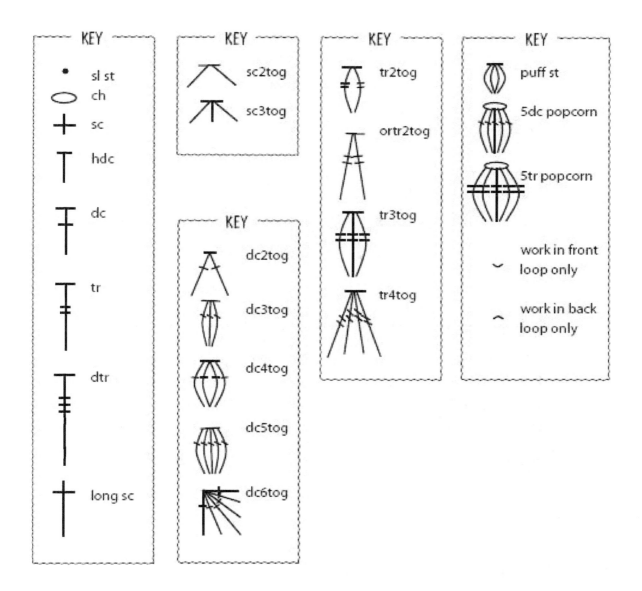

Charts for Fabrics and Trims

Charts for the designs in the Fabrics and Trims sections are drawn in rows, beginning with the foundation chain at the bottom. The arrows indicate the direction each row is worked. Each row starts with a turning chain. Here we show the Seafoam Fabric as an example of a design worked in rows.

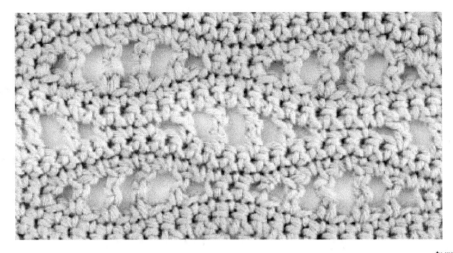

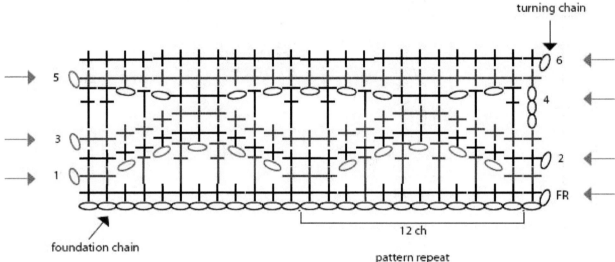

Charts for Motifs and Flowers

Charts for the Motifs and for many of the designs in the Flowers section are drawn in rounds, beginning with the foundation chain in the centre. Each round starts with a turning chain and is worked anti-clockwise round to the beginning. It is joined with a slip stitch. Here we show the Granny Square as an example of a design worked in rounds.

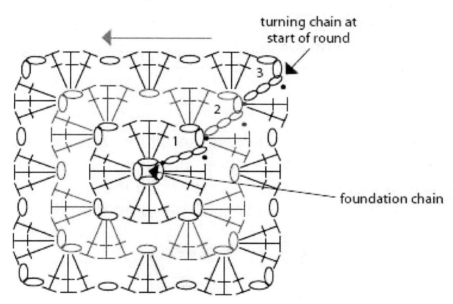

turning chain at start of round

foundation chain

Being Creative with Colour

The design swatches in each chapter of the stitch library have been worked in a limited palette. The colours have been used in imaginative ways to illustrate the different effects that working with colour can give, but also demonstrate the many ways in which each design can be reworked. Taking Motifs as an example, these designs could be worked in a single colour; with a different-colour centre; or with a different colour for each round. An item made from motifs can have each motif worked in the same colourway or as individuals. Every length of yarn can be used – keep the short lengths for the centres and longer lengths for outer rounds.

Inspiration for colour

The design swatches for Motifs illustrate all the variations mentioned above; the Moorish Square uses three shades of blue from light blue in the centre to dark on the outer edge, while the flower in the centre of the Flower Hexagon is highlighted in aqua against dark blue.

The Flower designs are shown mostly in natural colours, but also in some surprising shades. The names are purely descriptive and shouldn't stop you interpreting the form and shape in the 'wrong' colours. The Damask Rose is presented in dark purple edged with soft mauve, but would look totally different in rich red with a plum edge or gold with an olive green edge.

Trims can also be worked in different combinations of colours; single, stripes, or the last edging row picked out in a contrasting colour. The Flower Garland shows how picking out the flower row has highlighted the key element of this trim. The Braid has been worked in two colours, but would look striking worked all in gold with the final picot row worked in ruby red.

The Fabric designs have one or two rows highlighted in different colours to illustrate the effect of working the fabric in stripes. Solid stitches like the Square Stripes could have a pattern of two colours or more, using a different colour for each pattern repeat. However, using multiple colours breaks up the overall blend of stitches so may not be appropriate for lace fabrics.

Changing colour at the beginning of a row or round

The nature of crochet means that the final loop of the last stitch of a row becomes part of the first stitch of the next row. Working in one colour doesn't highlight this, but as soon as you change colour it becomes obvious. To get a neat change of colour, the last stitch of a row should be completed in the new colour.

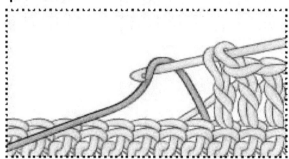

To do this, work the final stitch in the old colour up to just before the last step. Pick up the new colour and complete the stitch.

Working in stripes

Any number of colours can be used to make a motif that is worked in rounds. The rounds start and finish in the same place, so any unused colours are always in the correct place to begin the next round. Colours can be used for single rows, two rows, or more, with unused colours being carried up the wrong side of the work. Although fabrics can use many colours in any stripe combination, there are a couple of rules regarding the number of colours that can be used without there being a need to constantly cut and rejoin yarn.

Single or odd row stripes for fabric

Use an odd number of colours to make single-row stripes in fabric. Both the Crochet Hook Holder and the Lavender Sachets alternate three colours, working one row in each. Seed Stitch shows the effect of working a simple stitch in three colours. The unused yarn is carried up the side of the work. Using an odd number of colours means that there is always a yarn ready to be picked up for the next row. If these pieces of fabric were made in two colours, the yarn would have to be cut and rejoined at the beginning of each row. So to work single- or odd-row stripes without cutting yarns, always use an odd number of colours.

Even row stripes for fabric

Working two, four or six rows in one colour means that the colour is always returned to the same edge of the fabric, so there is always a new colour in the correct place to be picked up for the next row. So to work in an even number of colours without cutting yarns, always work an even number of rows.

Multiple Yarn Ends

Working with different colours in one piece will make multiple yarn ends that need to be sewn in. A quicker method of finishing these yarn ends is to work over them and enclose them in the crochet as you work. To do this, lay the cut end along the top of the stitches of the previous row or round and continue to crochet as per the design instructions, enclosing the yarn ends into the base of the new stitches. Work a few stitches over it and then trim off any excess neatly.

Making Crochet Fabrics

All the designs in this book rely on the correct placement of the stitches to work properly. Each set of instructions tells you where to work the stitches, but don't tell you how. Here are a few reminders about how to work each technique properly so that each design will be successful.

Starting with foundation chain

Each design is begun with a foundation chain. Working into this length of chain creates a neat edge to a project. Sometimes the foundation chain can become tight and it will draw in the bottom edge of the fabric or trim. I often use a size bigger hook so the foundation chain remains elastic and not too tight. This is especially important when making lace that may have large lengths of unworked foundation chain, such as the Large Clam Shell or the Fan and Filet Edging. Motifs are started in a different way from fabrics; see the Making Crochet Motifs section.

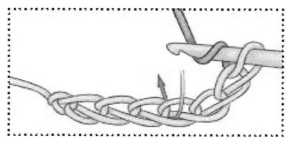

Following the design instructions, prepare for the first stitch and then insert the hook through the middle of the chain specified in the instructions. The hook will go below two strands of the chain stitch. Complete the stitch as per the design instructions.

Working into the top of stitches

This is how most stitches are placed; the design instructions will tell you if you need to do it in a different way. The tops of crochet stitches are flat; look along a row of stitches and each one is connected into a length of chain stitches. These chain stitches are what you work into.

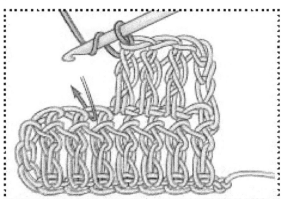

Following the design instructions, prepare for the first stitch and insert the hook under the two strands at the top of the stitch (the chain stitch) and complete the stitch as per the instructions.

Working into one loop only

By working into both the back and the front loops of a stitch, two layers of crochet can be made. This technique has been used for several of the flowers in this book, such as the Ruffle Rose, where the stitches in the last row of the centre disc are used twice, while the Trumpet Flower has a trumpet and the petals both worked from the same stitches. The design instructions will tell you when to do this and the charts show it by a special symbol. Sometimes it is difficult to illustrate this layering in a chart so it is especially important to use the chart and instructions together.

Back of loop only

Following the design instructions, prepare for the first stitch and then insert the hook from front to back under the back strand of the stitch below. Complete the stitch as per instructions.

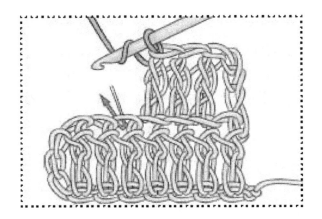

Front of loop only

Following the design instructions, prepare for the first stitch and then insert the hook from front to back under the front strand of the top of the stitch below. Complete the stitch as per instructions.

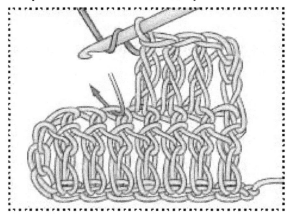

Working into chain spaces

Many of the lace fabrics in this book are made up of solid stitches and areas of chain spaces. By working into these chain spaces instead of into solid fabric, a more open lacy fabric is made. Small Spreading Fans uses chain spaces to create a hole at the base of a fan, while smaller spaces of just one chain stitch are used in the Seafoam Fabric to reintroduce stitches lost to create holes. Many of the Motifs are also constructed in this way. The chain spaces can form corners to accommodate a large number of stitches such as the Four-Petal Square and the Diamond Square. Trims often use chain spaces as the base for a design element, such as the scallops on the Sunrise Braid or the arches of Picot Arch edging.

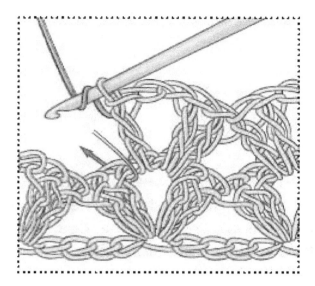

Following the design instructions, prepare for the first stitch and then insert the hook from front to back into the chain space. Complete the stitch as per instructions. The stitch is not worked into the chain but into the clear space beneath it. The new stitch encloses the chain.

Working fabric in rows

All the Fabric designs in this book and some of the Trims and Flowers are worked flat by working one row of stitches on top of another and turning at the end of each row. The first row worked along the foundation chain is called the foundation row and isn't repeated again in the design instructions. To begin the next row, a short length of chain needs to be made to raise the hook up to the height of the first stitch. This is called a turning chain (abbreviated to 'tch'). The number of chain depends on the height of the stitch to be worked. This turning chain sometimes counts as the first stitch. The design instructions will tell you what it replaces; this could be a single stitch or a stitch and a length of chain. For example, for the Large Daisy Fabric, one turning chain replaces a part of a cluster, while in Spreading Fans a turning chain replaces one double crochet and three chain. The design instructions will also tell you how to work into this turning chain at the end of the row above it.

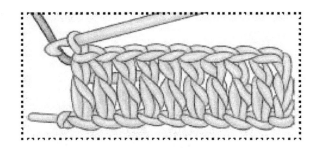

Following the design instructions, make a foundation chain and work the first row along this length of chain. The turning chain has been included in the foundation chain, so the design instructions will tell you which chain to work the first stitch into.

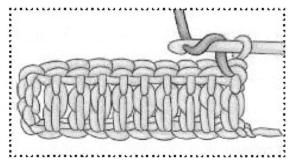

Turn the work to begin the next row. Make the turning chain as per the instructions.

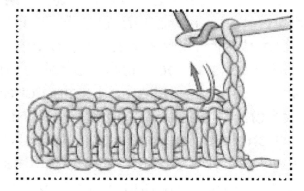

If the turning chain is counted as the first stitch, the next stitch of the pattern is worked into the top of the next stitch below. To work it in the correct place, miss the stitch at the base of the turning chain and then insert the hook from front to back into the next stitch. If the turning chain isn't counted as a stitch, the design instructions will tell you to work the next stitch into the same place.

Making Crochet Motifs

The Motifs and Flowers sections illustrate the many ways that a crochet motif can be made and varied by different arrangements of stitches. The next few pages explain how motifs are made, how the different shapes are created, and how they can be joined together. Motifs are fantastic building blocks for making all types of projects. There are several ideas included at the beginning of each chapter and these should be used as inspiration for your own designs.

Inspiration for motifs

Consider altering the scale of the motif; these designs don't only have to be small. Try a large hook and bulky-weight yarn to create sculptural pieces; these are especially effective in three-dimensional motifs such as the Irish Crochet Rose or Popcorn Hexagon. Experiment with colour too; the Patchwork Square could be worked in four different colours or would be just as effective worked in a colour-change yarn. Don't forget the classic Granny Square; easy to make and open to interpretation as vintage crochet using oddments of yarn or as innovative fashion accessory using the latest trend colours.

Motif centres

Every piece of crochet is started with a length of foundation chain. The Fabrics, Trims, and several of the Flowers are worked straight from the foundation chain, but Motifs (and the remainder of the Flowers) are worked from a ring of chain. For motifs, the foundation chain is made into a ring by joining the ends together with a slip stitch. Motifs are made from rounds of crochet rather than rows; the stitches are worked into the ring for the first round and every round from then on is worked on top of the previous round. The end of each round is joined to the first stitch of that round by a slip stitch.

Each round is started with a short length of chain stitches to raise the hook up to the correct level for the height of the first stitch.

First you need to join your chain stitches into a ring. There will already be a loop on the hook, from the foundation chain. Insert the hook into the first stitch of the chain. Wrap the yarn around the hook from back to front and pull the yarn through both the work and the loop on the hook. One slip stitch made and foundation chain joined into a ring.

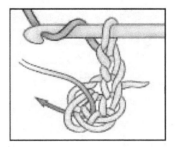

To work the first round, follow the design instructions to make the correct number of chain and to prepare for the first stitch. Insert the hook into the centre of the ring and complete the stitch as per the design instructions. Make sure the hook goes through the ring and not through one of the chain stitches. Work the first round of stitches evenly into the ring until the last stitch rests against the first stitch. Join with a slip stitch.

The foundation chain consists of fewer chain stitches than the first round. This is so that the centre of the motif is tight and any hole created by working into the ring is kept small.

If the hole has widened too much and you want to close it up, use the yarn end at the beginning to thread through the base of the first round stitches and draw up tightly. This will close the hole and also sews in the yarn end at the same time.

Some of the Flowers designs in this book are started in a different way. They begin with a length of chain but it isn't joined into a ring; instead, the first round of stitches is worked into the first chain. The Six-Petal Daisy begins in this way, as do the Ruffle Rose and Orchid, among others. When the flower has been completed, the yarn end at the beginning is pulled tight, which tightens the first chain stitch and eliminates any hole at the centre of the flower. This yarn end needs to be sewn in securely to stop the chain from working loose again.

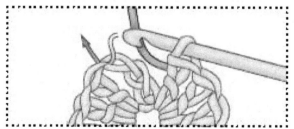

The end of each round is joined to the beginning by working a slip stitch into the top of the first stitch.

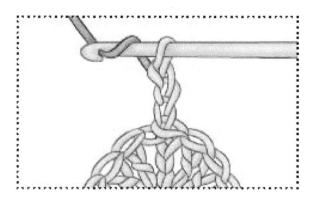

A length of chain is worked at the beginning of each round before the first stitch is made. The design instructions will tell you if this counts as a stitch or not.

Shapes of motifs

Although all motifs start in more or less the same way, different shapes are created by the arrangement of stitches in a round. The final shape of the motif may only become apparent as the final round is being worked. Within this book are three shapes of motifs: square, circle and hexagon.

The square and hexagon motifs have corners; the square has four and the hexagon has six. These corners are created by working a group of stitches into one place; sometimes this group is split into two by a short length of chain. For example, the Granny Square has two sets of three double crochet at each corner separated by two chain stitches. This creates a corner.

The circle motifs have no corners and the different arrangement of stitches are worked evenly around the centre. The Double Crochet Circle, for example, uses the same stitches as the Granny Square, but they are repeated throughout the round; no corners are made.

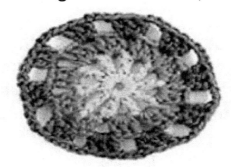

Shapes of flower motifs

Although Flowers form a separate chapter in this book, many of them are worked in the same way as motifs. Most of them are circle motifs; the Small Sunflower, for example, could easily be repeated as a motif and joined to create a large panel of floral fabric, as could the Simple Loop Flower. Both of these have a final round of chain loops and can be joined together as they are worked by making half the required number of chain, inserting the hook into a corresponding chain loop on another motif and then working the remainder of the chain.

Joining Crochet Motifs

Single motifs can be used as decorations, trimmed with beads, or worked in metallic yarns. They can be used as three-dimensional embellishments on bags, accessories or garments. However, a strip of motifs can be joined to form a simple scarf or a border on a ready-made afghan. Joining several strips together could make a cushion or a rug. A loop of motifs could make a jewellery cuff or even a necklace using fine wire worked on a small hook. There are several ways to join motifs depending on their shape and the stitches used in the final round.

How to join motifs

There are two ways to join motifs: one after all the motifs have been completed, and one while the motifs are being made. The Skirt Pocket project is made from three hexagons and illustrates how well this shape of motif fits together. Putting more of these together could make an afghan reminiscent of patchwork quilts. The motifs for the pocket were completed before being sewn together; they could also be crocheted together. The Collar project uses circles to create a curved strip that can be added to the neckline of a ready-made garment. These motifs were joined as they were made because the last round of the motif had lengths of chain that could be joined from one motif to another.

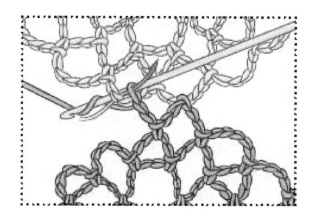

This is the method to use when the final round of a motif has chains or picots that can be worked into. Complete the first motif. Work the second motif up to the beginning of the final round. Place the two motifs together side by side.

Work half the required number of chain, insert the hook into the corresponding chain space on the first motif and then complete the chain length. The two motifs will be joined. The second motif can then be worked until another chain space is reached that can be joined to the first motif.

It is easy to see where square and hexagon motifs can be joined – they have straight sides and can be joined along the length of one side. With circle motifs, joining points are not so obvious. Place the two circles together and they will touch along a short length of the curved edge. Depending on how far apart the chain spaces are, the two motifs may only be joined in two or three places. Lay them down flat as you join them to make sure that you are not joining too much; each motif in the collar was joined in two places.

Arranging motifs

As described in the introduction, a strip of motifs can be used to make a simple scarf, belt or border. If you have completed all the motifs, lay them out in position and sew or crochet them together along opposite sides. If you are joining them as they are made, complete the first motif and then join the second motif to it along one side. Add a third motif in the same way to the second motif and so on until the strip is the required length.

Joining motifs into a loop

Once a strip has been made, it is easy to join it into a loop. This could be made into a shoulder wrap, a cowl, or an extremely fine jewellery ring. Simply join the last motif on two opposite sides; one to the penultimate motif and one to the first motif.

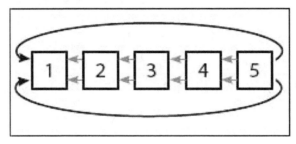

Joining motifs into a rectangle

Putting several strips together makes a rectangle or a square. This could be used to make a cushion, table runner or place mat, or it could be used to form a wider scarf or wrap. A rectangle could be folded in half to make a bag. Garments are often made completely from motifs; look at existing patterns for ideas about the arrangement of motifs for different styles. Find a pattern that has a clear diagram of the layout of the motifs and make sure that your chosen motif is the same size as that used in the pattern.

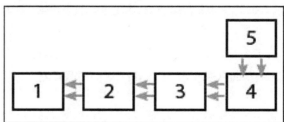

Complete the first strip of motifs. The first motif of the second strip is joined to the motif in the strip below.

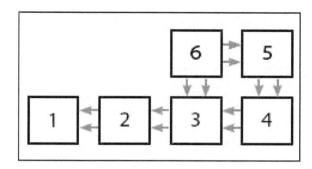

From now on, each motif of the second strip will be joined to the motif below in the first strip and to the previous motif in the second strip. Lay the pieces out flat as you are joining them to make sure that you are joining the correct edges together.

Sewing Seams

Use a large blunt-ended tapestry needle to sew up with, and the same yarn as was used for the crochet. If you used a textured or hairy yarn, it is easier to use a smooth yarn in a matching colour.

Over-sewing

This produces a flat seam with almost no bulk and is stitched with the right side of the work facing you.

Joining stitch to stitch: motifs or the top edges of fabric

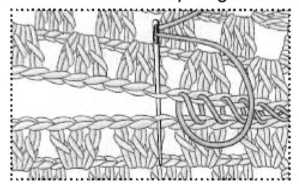

Lay the two pieces to be joined edge to edge with the right sides facing upwards. Thread the needle with yarn and secure it at one end of the seam. There is a line of chain stitches along each edge; these are the stitches that are sewn together to make the seam.

However, only one strand is used, not the whole chain stitch. This is the strand that lies at the bottom. In one scooping movement, insert the needle downwards under the bottom strand of the chain that is at the top of the first stitch on one edge and then upwards under the bottom strand of the chain that is at the top of the first stitch on the opposite edge. Pull the yarn through both stitches to pull the edges together. Go back to the first edge and repeat this scooping movement to join the second stitches together. Complete the seam in the same way, joining each stitch to the opposite stitch. By carefully joining stitch to stitch, the pattern of stitches can be matched, making the seam almost invisible.

Joining row to row: edges of fabric

To over-sew row ends together, place the two pieces to be joined side by side with the right sides facing upwards. Thread the needle with yarn and secure it at one end of the seam. In one scooping movement, insert the needle downwards through the base of the first stitch on one edge and then upwards through the base of the first stitch on the opposite edge. Pull the yarn through both stitches to pull the edges together. Go back to the first edge and repeat this scooping movement to join the middle of the two stitches together and then repeat to join the tops of the same two stitches together. Complete the seam in the same way, joining each row end to the opposite row end. By carefully joining row to row, the pattern of stitches can be matched, making the seam almost invisible.

Crocheting Seams

This is quicker than sewing, but it adds bulk to the seam and is more visible. These seams can be worked on the right side of the work or on the wrong side. If worked on the right side, the crochet edge will show and can be featured as part of the finished design. If worked on the wrong side, it is hardly visible on the right side. Use the same hook and yarn as were used for the crochet pieces. Two stitches can be used: slip stitch or single crochet.

Joining seams with slip stitch

The slip stitches form a tight line of chain stitches along the seam. Sometimes they can be worked too tightly and can pucker the seam. If this happens, use a size larger hook to loosen the stitches.

Joining stitch to stitch: motifs or the top edges of fabric

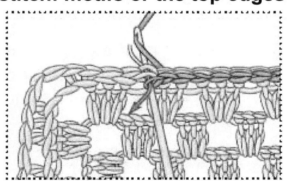

Place the two pieces to be joined together with either right sides facing (seam on inside) or wrong sides facing (seam on outside). There is a line of chain stitches along each edge; these are the stitches that are used to crochet the seam. Only one strand is used, not the whole chain stitch. These are the strands that lie on the outer edges of the chain stitches. Insert the hook from front to back under the front strand of the first stitch on the piece closest to you and then under the back strand of the first stitch on the other piece.

Wrap the yarn around the hook from back to front and pull the yarn under both strands on the hook. Insert the hook in the same way from front to back through the second stitch of both pieces. Wrap the yarn around the hook from back to front and pull the yarn under both strands and the loop on the hook. Complete the seam in the same way, joining each stitch to the opposite stitch. By carefully joining stitch to stitch, the pattern of stitches can be matched, making the seam neater.

Joining row to row: edges of fabric

Place the two pieces to be joined together with either right sides facing (seam on inside) or wrong sides facing (seam on outside). Join with slip stitches as described above, but insert the hook through the bottom of the first stitches, then through the middles, and then through the tops of the stitches. By carefully joining row to row, the pattern of stitches can be matched, making the seam neater.

Joining seams with single crochet

This makes a more flexible seam than slip stitch but adds more bulk. It is best used as a decorative seam to join motifs.

Joining stitch to stitch: motifs or the top edges of fabric

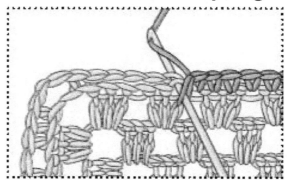

Work in the same way as joining with slip stitches, but work a single crochet instead.

Joining row to row: edges of fabric

Work in the same way as joining with slip stitches, but work a single crochet instead.

Joining with a decorative seam

This is particularly effective for joining motifs, especially lacy ones. It is a row of chain lengths worked in a zig zag between two motifs. The chain lengths are connected to the motifs by either slip stitches or single crochets. If you have made the motifs in one colour, using the same yarn will blend the motifs together into one piece of fabric. If the motifs are multi-coloured, use one contrasting colour for the seam as a frame around each motif.

Place the two pieces to be joined together with right sides facing upwards. There is a line of chain stitches along each edge; these are used to crochet the seam. The whole chain stitch is used (unlike the other types of seams).

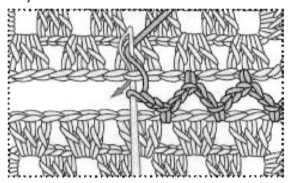

Insert the hook from front to back under the chain loop at the top of the first stitch on the first edge. Wrap the yarn around the hook from back to front and pull the yarn under both strands on the hook. Make a length of chain of the required number of stitches. Insert the hook in the same way from front to back under the chain loop of the required stitch on the opposite edge. Make either a slip stitch or a single crochet. Make a length of chain of the required number of stitches.

Insert the hook in the same way from front to back under the chain loop of the required stitch on the first edge. Complete the seam in the same way, spacing out the stitches evenly to form a zig zag by connecting groups of stitches, as shown in the diagram.

Attaching crochet to woven and stretch fabric

Many of the projects featured in this book use ready-made items as the base for the crochet fabrics, trims or motifs. A trim is added to the hem of a shirt and used as a decorative feature on a cushion. Fabric can be worked in a panel and sewn onto a cushion or to make a curtain panel. Motifs can be used singly, like on the pincushion, or in a group to create a pocket. It is better to hand-sew the crochet in place rather than using a sewing machine, which may stretch the crochet too much. Press both the crochet and the ready-made item before joining them together.

Place the two pieces to be joined together with right sides facing upwards. There is a line of chain stitches along each edge; these are used to crochet the seam. The whole chain stitch is used (unlike the other types of seams).

To sew on a crochet trim

The trim should be made long enough to fit along the edge to be trimmed without being stretched. If the trim is too short and is stretched to fit, it will gather in the edge. This will be especially problematic around a garment hem or sleeve. Divide the edge up into quarters and pin the trim into place, making sure that there are the same number of pattern repeats in each section. The trim will then be even all along the edge. If you are adding a trim to a garment, use the seams as a guide to getting the trim even. Sew on using slip stitch and a strong sewing cotton.

To sew on a crochet motif

Pin the motif onto the ready-made item, making sure the fabric isn't creased beneath the motif. Sew on securely using slip stitch and strong sewing cotton.

To sew on a panel of crochet fabric

The crochet panel should be long enough to fit over the ready-made item without stretching. Pin the panel into place, making sure it is centralized. Sew on securely using slip stitch and strong sewing cotton. When adding a crochet panel along the edge of the woven fabric or between two pieces of woven fabric, make sure that the crochet is long enough to fit without stretching. Divide the woven fabric edge into quarters. Lay the two pieces to be joined so the edges are touching and pin the crochet into place, making sure that there are the same number of pattern repeats in each section. The panel will then be even. Carefully slip stitch into place, catching a small amount of woven fabric into each stitch and then a small amount of crochet fabric. Make the stitches small and even. Do not pull the stitches too tight or the seam will be gathered.

Flowers

Bunting

Floral bunting is easy to make and you can be really creative with yarns and colours. This project can be worked in one flower, or you could try mixing different flowers for a garland effect. This bunting is made in brightly coloured fine-weight mercerized cotton with a D3 (3.00mm) hook, using the Loop Daisy pattern. Join the flowers as you make them by working half a petal, inserting the hook through a petal of the previous flower, and then completing the petal.

Heart

A gift for Valentine's Day, this willow heart is decorated with two Small Roses and a Rose Bud made using two strands of dark red fine-weight mohair yarn and a D3 (3.00mm) hook. The three Leaves are made in a dark green lightweight silk and wool mix yarn with a G6 (4.00mm) hook. Sew the leaves onto the heart.

Corsage

A glitzy ready-made evening top is given even more sparkle with a corsage of three Open Roses. Refer to the pattern and use a lightweight metallic yarn in a toning shade with a D3 (3.00mm) hook. Sew the roses onto the neck edge. Alternatively, sew brooch pins onto the back of the flowers so they can be removed.

Necklace

Crochet flowers can be used to make simple but effective jewellery. This necklace is made from the Six-Petal Daisy pattern in three shades of lightweight purple wool using a D3 (3.00mm) hook. Cut a piece of waxed cord the length of necklace required. Make enough flowers to fit around the length; they can be grouped close together or spaced wider apart. Using a blunt needle, thread the flowers onto the cord, tying a knot at each side of the flower to prevent it slipping.

Bag decorations

Here a plain summer bag is brightened up with the addition of raffia flowers worked in shades of gold and green. Use a G6 (4.00mm) hook and the Ruffle Rose pattern. Work some of the flowers with two layers of petals and others with only one layer. Sew the flowers onto the bag.

Six-Petal Daisy

Make 2 ch.

Rnd 1 5 sc into 2nd ch from hook, sl st into 2nd of 2 ch to form a ring. 6 sc.

Rnd 2 (5 ch, 1 sc into 2nd ch from hook, 1 dc into each of next 2 ch, 1 hdc into last ch, sl st into next sc of rnd 1) 6 times.

Fasten off.

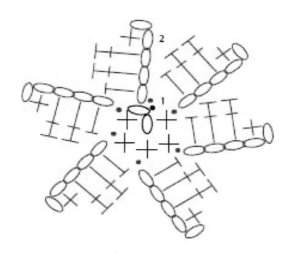

```
---- KEY ----
  ·   sl st
  ⌒   ch
  +   sc
  T   hdc
  ┼   dc
```

Small Sunflower

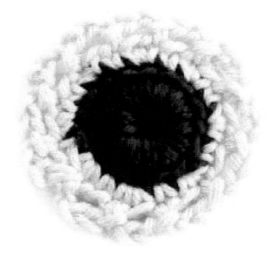

Make 4 ch and join with sl st to form a ring.

Rnd 1 1 ch, 12 sc into ring, sl st into first sc.

Rnd 2 16 long sc into ring over scs of rnd 1, sl st into first sc.

Rnd 3 Working into back of loop only, 1 ch, 2 sc into same sc, 1 sc into next sc, (2 sc into next sc, 1 sc into next sc) 7 times, sl st into 1st sc. 24 sc.

Rnd 4 (3 ch, miss 1 sc, sl st into next sc) 12 times.

Fasten off.

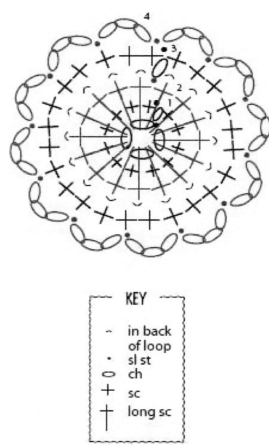

KEY
- ~ in back of loop
- • sl st
- ○ ch
- + sc
- † long sc

Loop Daisy

Make 2 ch.

Rnd 1 8 sc into 2nd ch from hook, sl st into 2nd of 2 ch to form a ring. 9 sc.

Rnd 2 2 ch (counts as 1 sc), 1 sc into same place, 2 sc into every sc to end, sl st into 2nd of 2 ch at beg of rnd. 18 sc.

Rnd 3 (10 ch, sl st into next sc) 18 times.

Fasten off.

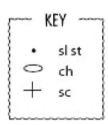

Ruffle Rose

Make 3 ch.

Rnd 1 11 dc into 3rd ch from hook, sl st into 3rd of 3 ch to form a ring. 12 dc.

Rnd 2 2 ch (counts as 1 sc), 1 sc into same sp, 2 sc into each of next 11 dc, sl st into 2nd of 2 ch. 24 sc.

Back layer of petals

Rnd 3 Working into back of loop only, 4 ch. 1 tr into same place, 2 tr into next sc, 1 tr into next sc, 4 ch, sl st into same sc, sl st into next sc, (4 ch, 1 tr into same sc, 2 tr into next sc, 1 tr into next sc, 4 ch, sl st into same sc, sl st into next sc) 7 times, working last sl st into first sc of rnd 2.

Front layer of petals

Rnd 4 Working into front of loop only, 3 ch, 1 dc into same place, 1 dc into next sc, 3 ch, sl st into same sc, sl st into next sc, (3 ch, 1 dc into same sc, 1 dc into next sc, 3 ch, sl st into same sc, sl st into next sc) 11 times, working last sl st into first sc of rnd 2.

Fasten off.

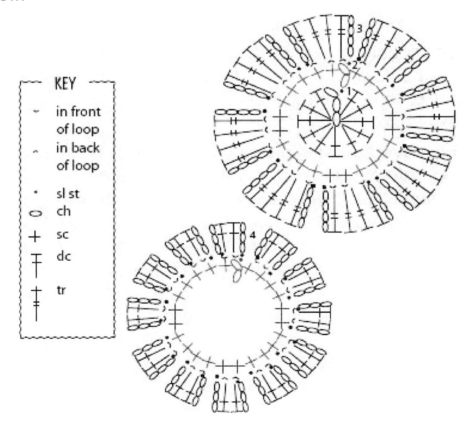

KEY
- ⁻ in front of loop
- ⌃ in back of loop
- • sl st
- ○ ch
- + sc
- ┬ dc
- ┼ tr

Open Rose

Make 4 ch and join with sl st to form a ring.

Rnd 1 2 ch (counts as 1 sc), 7 sc into ring, continue working in a spiral as follows: 2 sc into front of loop of 2nd of 2 ch at beg of rnd, 2 sc into front of loop of each of next 7 sc, 1 sc into front of loop of each of next 16 sc. 40 sc in total.

Turn work to reverse direction so WS is facing. Working into empty front of loop only and in a spiral from outer edge to centre, make a total of 20 petals [NB: chart shows first 8 petals only for guidance] as follows: 1 ch, (1 hdc, 3 dc, 1 hdc) into first sc, * 1 sc into next sc, (1 hdc, 3 dc, 1 hdc) into next sc; rep from * 18 times more, 1 sc into last sc.

Fasten off.

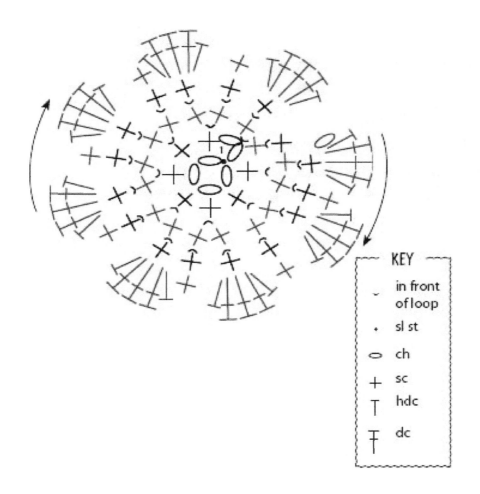

KEY
- in front of loop
- · sl st
- ○ ch
- + sc
- T hdc
- ┼ dc

Small Rose

Make 36 ch.

Row 1 1 sc into 2nd ch from hook, 1 sc into each ch to end. 35 sc.

Row 2 3 ch, 3 dc into same sc, 3 ch, sl st into next sc, (3 ch, 3 dc into next sc, 3 ch, sl st into next sc) twice, (3 ch, 2 dc into each of next 2 sc, 3 ch, sl st into next sc) 3 times, (4 ch, 2 tr into each of next 3 sc, 4 ch, sl st into next sc) 5 times.

Fasten off.

Roll the strip up starting with the small petals at the centre. Secure with a few stitches sewn through all thicknesses.

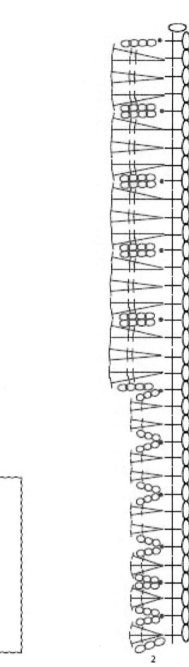

Rose Bud

Make 16 ch.

Row 1 1 sc into 2nd ch from hook, 1 sc into each ch to end. 15 sc.

Row 2 3 ch, 3 dc into same sc, 3 ch, sl st into next sc, (3 ch, 3 dc into next sc, 3 ch, sl st into next sc) twice, (3 ch, 2 dc into each of next 2 sc, 3 ch, sl st into next sc) 3 times.

Fasten off.

Roll the strip up starting with the small petals at the centre. Secure with a few stitches sewn through all thicknesses.

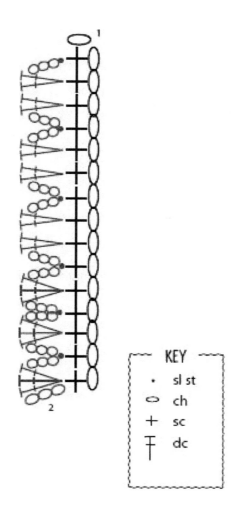

Leaf

Make 10 ch.

Rnd 1 1 sc into 2nd ch from hook, 1 hdc into next ch, 1 dc into next ch, 1 tr into each of next 3 ch, 1 dc into next ch, 1 hdc into next ch, 3 sc into last ch, continue back along other side of foundation ch as follows: 1 hdc into next ch, 1 dc into next ch, 1 tr into each of next 3 ch, 1 dc into next ch, 1 hdc into next ch, 1 sc into last ch.

Fasten off.

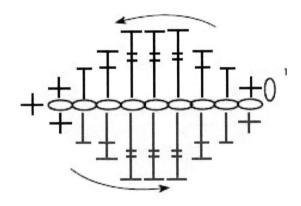

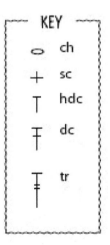

Irish Crochet Rose

Make 4 ch and join with sl st to form a ring.

Rnd 1 3 ch (counts as 1 dc), 11 dc into ring, sl st to 3rd of 3 ch.

Rnd 2 1 ch, 1 sc into same place, 3 ch, * miss 1 dc, 1 sc into next dc, 3 ch; rep from * to end, sl st into first sc.

Rnd 3 * sl st into next 3 ch sp, (1 ch, 2 hdc, 1 dc, 2 hdc, 1 ch, sl st) all into same 3 ch sp; rep from * 5 times more.

Rnd 4 2 ch, sl st into first missed dc of rnd 2, 1 ch, 1 sc into same place, 4 ch, * 1 sc into next missed dc, 4 ch; rep from * to end, sl st into first sc.

Rnd 5 * sl st into next 4 ch sp, (1 ch, 1 hdc, 3 dc, 1 hdc, 1 ch, sl st) all into same 4 ch sp; rep from * 5 times more.

Fasten off.

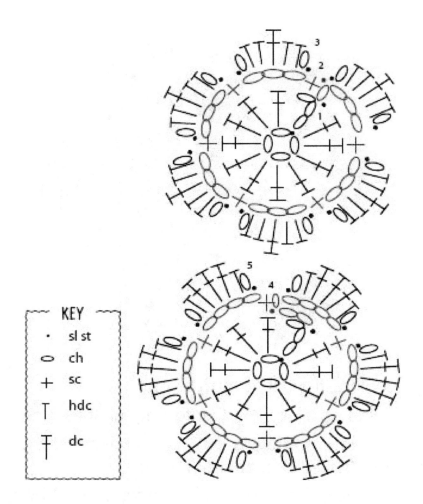

Large Simple Flower

Make 4 ch and join with sl st to form a ring.

Rnd 1 3 ch (counts as 1 dc), 11 dc into ring, sl st to 3rd of 3 ch.

Rnd 2 * (1 ch, 1 hdc, 2 dc, 2 tr, 2 dc, 1 hdc, 1 ch) all into same place as sl st, miss next dc, sl st into next dc; rep from * 5 times more, working last sl st into first sl st.

Fasten off.

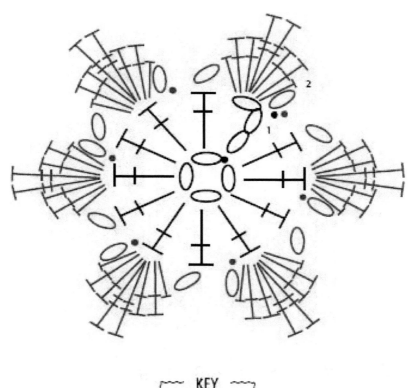

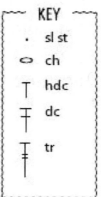

Star Flower

Make 5 ch and join with sl st to form a ring.

Rnd 1 1 ch, 10 sc into ring, sl st to first sc.

Rnd 2 1 ch, 2 sc into each sc, sl st into first sc.

Rnd 3 (7 ch, 1 sc into 2nd ch from hook, 1 sc into next ch, 1 hdc into each of next 2 ch, 1 dc into each of next 2 ch, miss 1 sc of ring, sl st into next sc, turn work, 1 ch, 1 sc into each of next 2 dc, 1 sc into each of next 2 hdc, 1 sc into each of next 2 sc, turn, 1 ch, 1 sc into each of next 2 sc, 1 hdc into each of next 2 sc, 1 dc into each of next 2 sc, miss 1 sc of ring, sl st into next st) 5 times.

Fasten off.

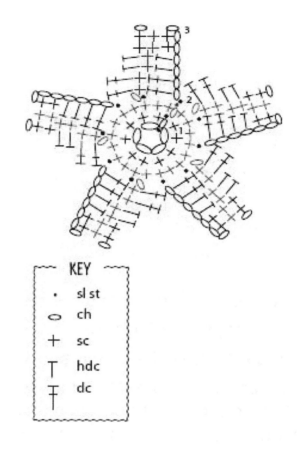

KEY
- · sl st
- ○ ch
- + sc
- T hdc
- ☦ dc

Pansy

Make 4 ch and join with sl st to form a ring.

Rnd 1 2 ch (counts as 1 hdc), 9 hdc into ring, sl st into first hdc.

Rnd 2 1 ch, 1 sc into same place, (3 ch, miss 1 hdc, 1 sc into next hdc) 4 times, 3 ch, miss 1 hdc, sl st to first sc.

Rnd 3 (sl st, 2 ch, 9 tr, 2 ch, sl st) all into each of first and second 3 ch sps, (sl st, 2 ch, 7 dc, 2 ch, sl st) all

into each of next three 3 ch sps.

Fasten off.

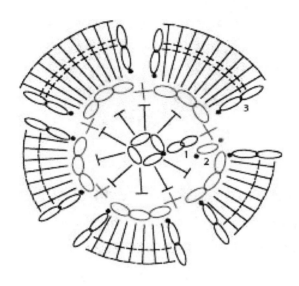

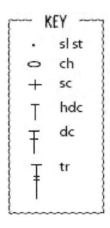

Dahlia

Make 2 ch.

Rnd 1 9 sc in 2nd ch from hook, join with sl st into first sc.

Rnd 2 4 ch, sl st into front of loop of first sc, (4 ch, sl st into front of loop of next sc) 8 times, sl st into first sl st.

Rnd 3 1 ch, 2 sc into back of loop of first sc, 2 sc into back of loop of each of next 8 sc, sl st into first sc.

Rnd 4 6 ch, sl st into front of loop of first sc, (6 ch, sl st into front of loop of next sc) 17 times more, sl st into first sl st.

Rnd 5 [NB: this rnd is not shown on chart but should be worked behind rnd 4] 8 ch, sl st into back of loop of first sc, (8 ch, sl st into back of loop of next sc) 17 times more.

Fasten off.

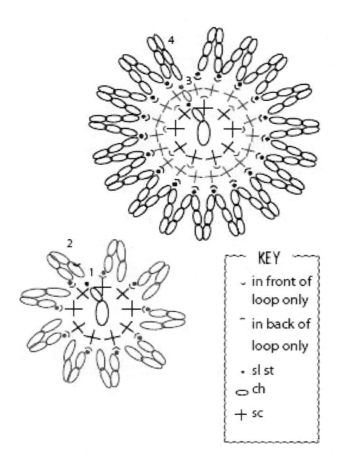

KEY
- in front of loop only
- in back of loop only
• sl st
◯ ch
+ sc

Four-Layer Flower

Make 2 ch.
Rnd 1 5 sc into 2nd ch from hook, sl st into front of loop of first sc.

Rnd 2 (1 sc, 1 ch, 1 sc, sl st) all into front of loop of first sc, (1 sc, 1 ch, 1 sc, sl st) all into front of loop of each of next 4 sc, working last sl st into back of loop of first sc.

Rnd 3 (2 ch, sl st in back of loop of next sc) 5 times.

Rnd 4 (sl st, 1 ch, 4 hdc, 1 ch, sl st) all into first 2 ch sp and into each of next four 2 ch sps.

Rnd 5 3 ch, sl st into back of petal between second and third hdc of first petal, (3 ch, sl st into back of next petal between second and third hdc) 5 times, ending with last sl st worked in first 3 ch sp.

Rnd 6 (1 ch, 1 hdc, 4 dc, 1 hdc, 1 ch, sl st) all into first 3 ch sp, (sl st, 1 ch, 1 hdc, 4 dc, 1 hdc, 1 ch, sl st) all into each of next four 3 ch sps.

Rnd 7 3 ch, sl st into back of petal between second and third dc of first petal, (4 ch, sl st into back of next petal between second and third dc) 5 times, ending with last sl st worked in first 4 ch sp.

Rnd 8 (sl st, 1 ch, 1 hdc, 6 dc, 1 hdc, 1 ch, sl st) all into first 4 ch sp, (sl st, 1 ch, 1 hdc, 6 dc, 1 hdc, 1 ch, sl st) all into each of next four 4 ch sps.

Fasten off.

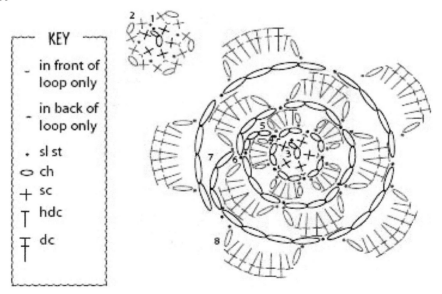

KEY
- in front of loop only
- in back of loop only
- sl st
- ch
- sc
- hdc
- dc

Trumpet Flower

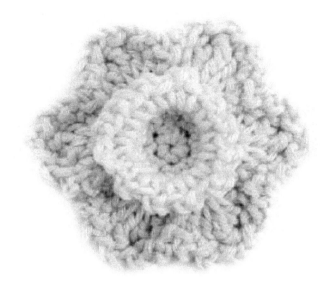

Centre

Make 2 ch.

Rnd 1 6 sc into 2nd ch from hook, sl st to first sc.

Rnd 2 1 ch, 2 sc into each sc, sl st into first sc. 12 sc.

Rnd 3 1 ch, 1 sc into front of loop of each sc, sl st into first sc.

Rnd 4 1 ch, 1 sc into each sc, sl st into first sc.

Rnd 5 1 ch, 1 sc into first sc, 2 ch, (1 sc into next sc, 2 ch) 11 times, sl st to first sc.

Fasten off.

Petals

Rejoin yarn to back loop of any dc on row 3.

Rnd 6 1 ch, 1 sc into same place, (2 ch, 1 sc into back of loop of each of next 2 sc) 5 times, 2 ch, 1 sc into back of loop of last sc, sl st to first sc.

Rnd 7 Sl st into first 2 ch sp, * (1 ch, 1 hdc, 1 dc, 1 tr, 1 dc, 1 hdc, 1 ch) all into 2 ch sp, sl st between next 2 sc; rep from * 5 times more.

Rnd 8 * Sl st into 1 ch sp of petal, (2 ch, sl st into next st) 5 times, 2 ch, sl st into last 1 ch sp of petal; rep from * 5 times more.

Fasten off.

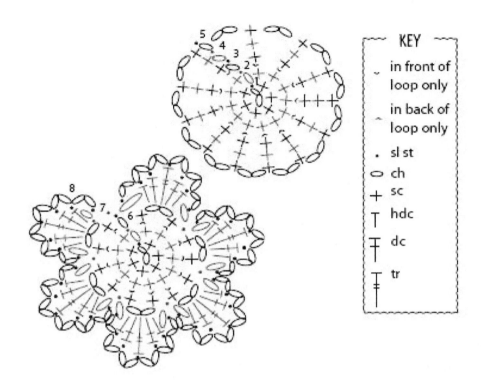

Frilly Rosette

Make 4 ch and join with sl st to form a ring.

Rnd 1 1 ch, 6 sc into ring, sl st into back of loop of 1st sc.

Rnd 2 1 ch, 2 sc into back of loop of each sc, sl st into back of loop of 1st sc. 12 sc.

Rnd 3 1 ch, 2 sc into back of loop of each sc, sl st into back of loop of 1st sc. 24 sc.

Rnd 4 1 ch, 1 sc into back of loop of each sc, sl st into back of loop of 1st sc.

Rnd 5 (14 ch, 1 sc into back of loop of next sc) 24 times, (10 ch, 1 sc into front of loop of next sc) 24 times. Two layers of petals on outer rnd [NB: only the first layer of petals is shown on the chart].

Rnd 6 1 ch, 1 sc into front of loop of next sc on rnd 3, (6 ch, 1 sc into front of loop of next sc) 24 times.

Fasten off.

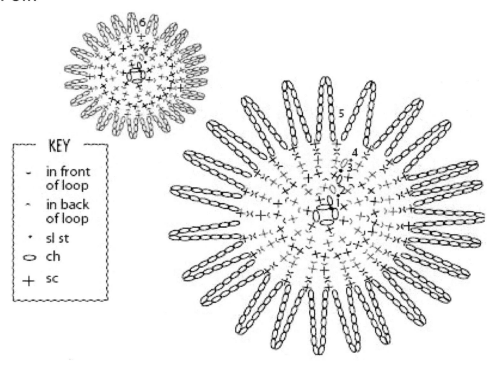

KEY
- in front of loop
- in back of loop
- sl st
- ch
- sc

Quick Flower

Make 4 ch and join with sl st to form a ring.

Rnd 1 3 ch (counts as 1 dc), 11 dc into ring, sl st to 3rd of 3 ch. 12 dc.

Rnd 2 1 ch, 1 sc into same place, (4 ch, 1 dc into 4th ch from hook, miss 1 dc, 1 sc into next dc) 6 times, omitting last sc, instead ending with sl st into first sc.

Fasten off.

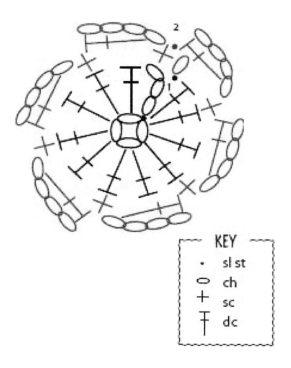

KEY
- sl st
- ch
- sc
- dc

Button Carnation

Make 2 ch.

Rnd 1 6 sc into 2nd ch from hook, sl st into first sc.

Rnd 2 1 ch, 2 sc into each of 6 sc, sl st into first sc. 12 sc.

Rnd 3 1 ch, 1 sc into each of next 12 sc, sl st into first sc.

Rnd 4 1 ch, (1 sc into each of next 2 sc, sc2tog) 3 times, sl st into first sc. 9 sc.

Rnd 5 (2 ch, 1 dc, 1 ch, 1 tr, 1 ch, 1 dc, 2 ch, sl st into same sc, sl st into next sc) 9 times.

Fasten off.

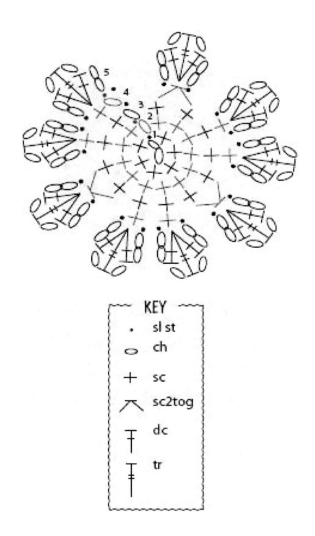

Pointed Daisy

Make 4 ch and join with sl st to form a ring.

Rnd 1 3 ch (counts as 1 dc), 11 dc into ring, sl st into first dc. 12 dc.

Rnd 2 1 ch, 1 sc into same place, (2 ch, miss 1 dc, 1 sc into next dc) 5 times, 2 ch, sl st into first dc.

Rnd 3 Sl st in 1st 2 ch sp, *(1 ch, 1 sc, 2 ch, 1 tr, 3 dtr, 1 tr, 2 ch, 1 sc, 1 ch) all into same 2 ch sp, sl st into next 2 ch sp; rep from * 5 times more, sl st to first sc.

Rnd 4 * Sl st into first 2 ch sp, 2 sc into same 2 ch sp, 1 sc into each of next 2 sts, (1 sc, 3 ch, sl st into 3rd ch from hook, 1 sc) all into next st, 1 sc into each of next 2 sts, 2 sc into 2 ch sp, sl st into ch between petals; rep from * 5 times more.

Fasten off.

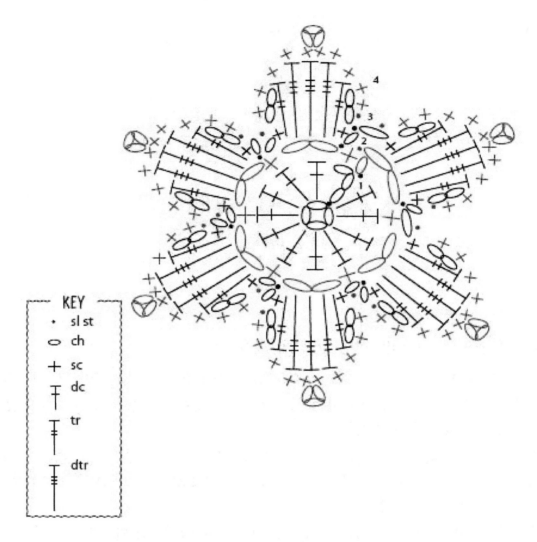

Traditional Crochet Flower

Make 4 ch and join with sl st to form a ring.

Rnd 1 1 ch, 8 sc into ring, sl st into front of loop of first sc.

Rnd 2 (3 ch, sl st into front of loop of next sc) 8 times.

Rnd 3 (1 ch, 2 sc, 1 ch, sl st) all into first 3 ch sp, (sl st, 1 ch, 2 sc, 1 ch, sl st) all into each of next seven 3 ch sps.

Rnd 4 2 ch, 2 dc into back of loop of first sc on rnd 3, 2 dc into back of loop of each sc, sl st to first dc.

Rnd 5 (3 ch, sl st into next dc) 16 times.

Rnd 6 (1 ch, 2 sc, 1 ch, sl st) all into first 3 ch sp, (sl st, 1 ch, 2 sc, 1 ch, sl st) all into each of next fifteen 3 ch sps.

Fasten off.

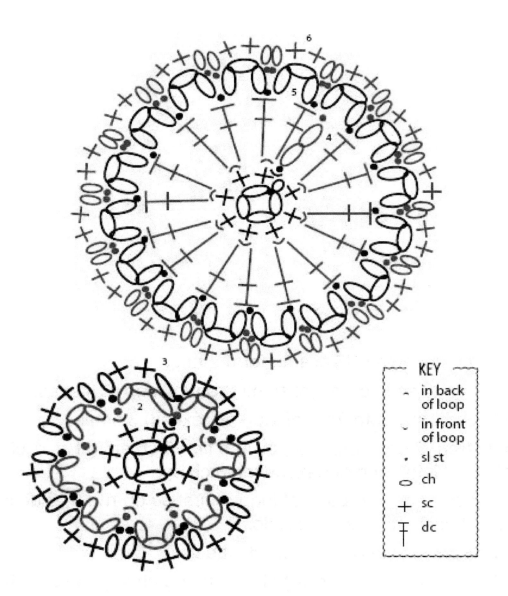

Gerbera

Make 6 ch and join with sl st to form a ring.

Rnd 1 1 ch, 12 sc into ring, sl st to first sc.

Rnd 2 1 ch, 1 sc into first sc, (16 ch, 1 sc into next sc) 11 times, 16 ch, sl st to first sc.

Rnd 3 Into each 16 ch loop work as follows: 1 sl st into each of first 3 ch, 1 sc into each of next 4 ch, 2 sc into each of next 2 ch, 1 sc into each of next 4 ch, 1 sl st into each of next 3 ch.

Fasten off.

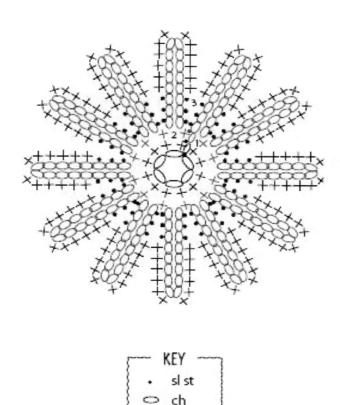

KEY
- sl st
○ ch
+ sc

Button Daisy

Make 2 ch.

Rnd 1 6 sc into 2nd ch from hook, sl st into first sc.

Rnd 2 1 ch, 2 sc into each of next 6 sc, sl st into first sc. 12 sc.

Rnd 3 1 ch, 1 sc into each of next 12 sc, sl st into first sc.

Rnd 4 1 ch, (1 sc into each of next 2 sc, sc2tog) 3 times, sl st to first sc. 9 sc.

Rnd 5 (6 ch, sl st into 2nd ch from hook, 1 sc into each of next 2 ch, 1 hdc into next ch, 1 dc into next ch, sl st into next sc or sc2tog) 9 times.

Fasten off.

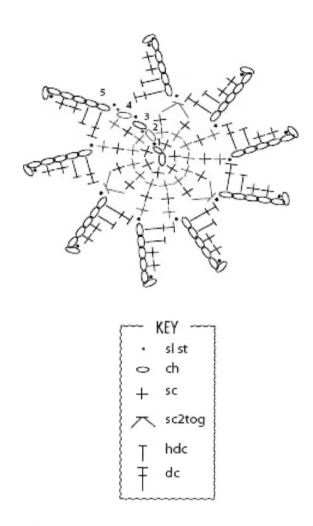

Open Flower

Make 4 ch and join with sl st to form a ring.

Rnd 1 1 ch, 7 sc into ring, sl st into first sc.

Rnd 2 1 ch, 2 sc into each of next 7 sc, sl st to first sc. 14 sc.

Rnd 3 1 ch, (1 sc into next sc, 2 ch, 1 dc into next sc, 2 ch) 7 times, sl st to first sc.

Fasten off.

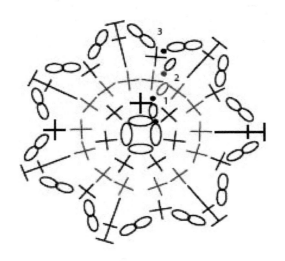

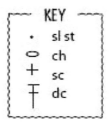

KEY
- • sl st
- ○ ch
- + sc
- ┬ dc

Small Orchid

Make 2 ch.

Rnd 1 6 sc into 2nd ch from hook, sl st into first sc. 6 sc.

Rnd 2 (4 ch, 1 sc into 2nd ch from hook, 1 hdc into next ch, 1 sc into next ch, sl st into front of loop of next sc) 6 times, ending by working sl st into back of loop of first sc.

Rnd 3 1 ch, 2 sc into back of loop of each of next 6 sc, sl st into first sc. 12 sc.

Rnd 4 (5 ch, 1 sc into 2nd ch from hook, 1 hdc into next ch, 1 dc into next ch, 1 tr into next ch, miss 1 sc of rnd 3, sl st into back of loop of next sc) 6 times.

Fasten off.

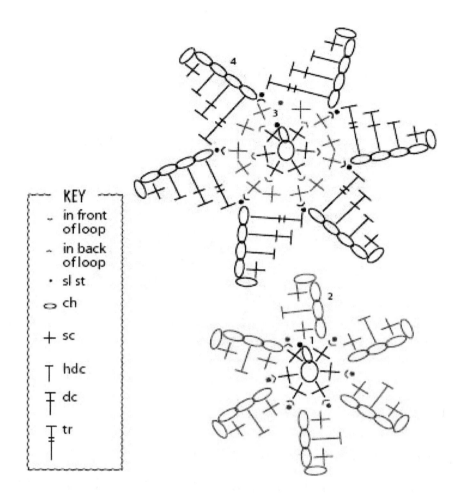

Orchid

Make 3 ch.

Rnd 1 7 dc into 3rd ch from hook, sl st into 3rd of 3 ch to form a ring. 8 dc.

Rnd 2 (4 ch, 1 sc into 2nd ch from hook, 1 hdc into next ch, 1 sc into next ch, sl st into front of loop of next dc) 8 times, ending by working sl st into back of loop of first dc.

Rnd 3 3 ch (counts as 1 dc), 1 dc into same place, 2 dc into back of loop of each of next 7 dc, sl st into first dc. 16 dc.

Rnd 4 (5 ch, 1 sc into 2nd ch from hook, 1 hdc into next ch, 1 dc into next ch, 1 tr into next ch, miss 1 dc of rnd 3, sl st into next dc) 8 times.

Fasten off.

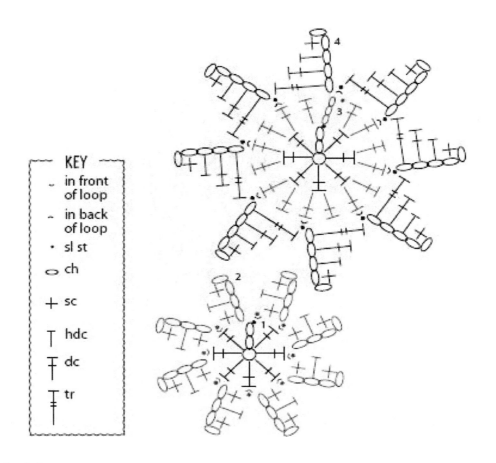

Periwinkle

Make 4 ch and join with sl st to form a ring.

Rnd 1 1 ch, 5 sc into ring, sl st to first sc.

Rnd 2 1 ch, (1 sc, 1 ch, 2 dc, 1 ch) all into each of next 5 sc, sl st to first sc.

Fasten off.

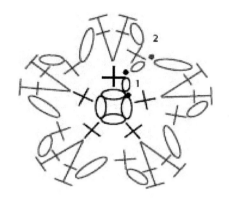

```
┌─ KEY ─┐
  •   sl st
  o   ch
  +   sc
  ┬   dc
└──────┘
```

Cluster Flower

Make 6 ch and join with sl st to form a ring.
Rnd 1 (3 ch, tr3tog, 3 ch, sl st into ring) 5 times.
Fasten off.

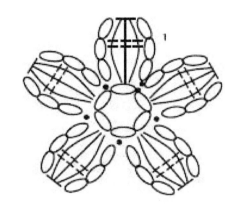

Picot Daisy

Make 5 ch and join with sl st to form a ring.

Rnd 1 1 ch, (1 sc into ring, 5 ch) 5 times, sl st to first sc.

Rnd 2 * 3 ch, 4 tr into 5 ch sp, 3 ch, sl st into sc; rep from * 4 times more.

Rnd 3 * 2 ch, sl st into 3 ch sp, (3 ch, sl st into 3rd ch from hook, sl st into next tr) 4 times, 3 ch, sl st into 3rd ch from hook, sl st into 3 ch sp, 2 ch, sl st into sl st between petals; rep from * 4 times more.

Fasten off.

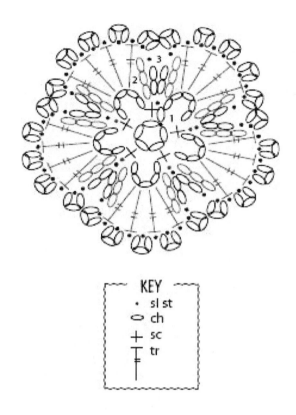

Large Gerbera

Make 6 ch and join with sl st to form a ring.
Rnd 1 1 ch, 14 sc into ring, sl st to first sc.

Rnd 2 1 ch, in front of loop of each sc work (1 sc, 6 ch, 1 sc), sl st to first sc.

Rnd 3 1 ch, in back of loop of each sc work (1 sc, 8 ch, 1 sc), sl st to first sc.

Fasten off.

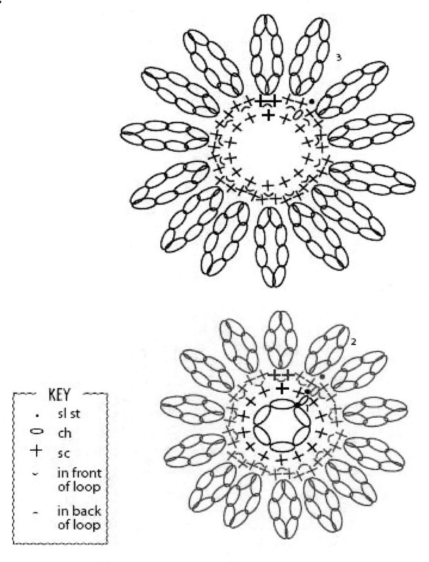

KEY
- . sl st
- o ch
- + sc
- ~ in front of loop
- - in back of loop

Damask Rose

Make 39 ch.

Row 1 1 dc into 6th ch from hook, * 1 ch, miss 2 ch, (1 dc, 2 ch, 1 dc) all into next ch; rep from * to end.

Row 2 3 ch (counts as 1 dc), (1 dc, 2 ch, 2 dc) all into 1st 2 ch sp, * 2 ch, (2 dc, 2 ch, 2 dc) all into next 2 ch sp; rep from * to end.

Row 3 3 ch (counts as 1 dc), 5 dc into first 2 ch sp, (1 sc into next 2 ch sp, 6 dc into next 2 ch sp) twice, (1 sc into next 2 ch sp, 8 dc into next 2 ch sp) 4 times, (1 sc into next 2 ch sp, 10 dc into next 2 ch sp) 5 times.

Fasten off, leaving a long tail for sewing up.

Thread the long tail onto a needle. Roll the petals up from the centre, beginning with the small petals. Sew through all layers at the base to secure.

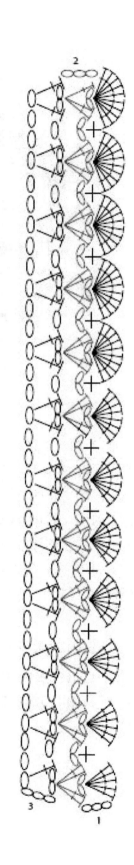

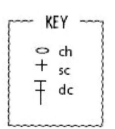

KEY
- ○ ch
- + sc
- ┬ dc

Long Star Flower

Make 3 ch.

Rnd 1 19 dc into 3rd ch from hook, sl st to top of 3 ch to form a ring.

Rnd 2 * 10 ch, 1 sc into 2nd ch from hook, 1 sc into each of next 8 ch, 1 sc into each of next 2 dc; rep from * to end, sl st to first sc.

Fasten off.

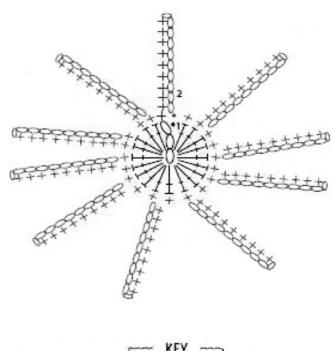

KEY
- . sl st
- ○ ch
- + sc
- ⊤ dc

Blossom

Make 5 ch and join with sl st to form a ring.

Rnd 1 2 ch, dc2tog into same place (counts as 1 dc3tog), 5 dc3tog into ring, sl st to top of first dc3tog.

Rnd 2 (1 ch, 3 dc, 1 ch, sl st all into top of dc3tog, sl st into top of next dc3tog) 6 times.

Fasten off.

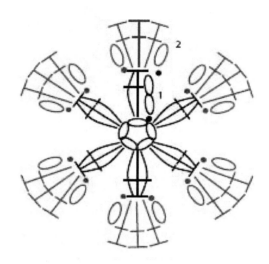

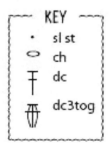

KEY
- sl st
- ch
- dc
- dc3tog

Simple Picot Flower

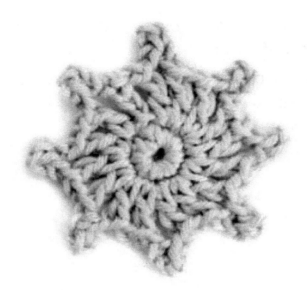

Make 4 ch and join with sl st to form a ring.

Rnd 1 1 ch, 8 sc into ring, sl st to first sc.

Rnd 2 7 ch, sl st into 3rd ch from hook, 1 ch, 1 dc into sc at base of 7 ch, 1 ch, (1 dc, 4 ch, sl st into 3rd ch from hook, 1 ch, 1 dc, 1 ch) all into each of next 7 sc, sl st to 3rd of 7 ch.

Fasten off.

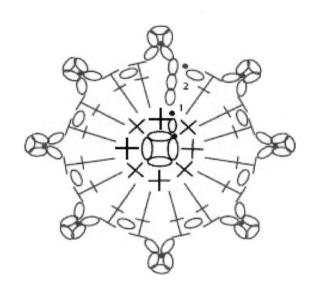

KEY
. sl st
◯ ch
+ sc
⊤ dc

Four-Petal Flower

Make 2 ch.

Rnd 1 7 sc into 2nd ch from hook, sl st into 2nd of 2 ch to form a ring. 8 sc.

Rnd 2 * 2 ch, (1 dc, 3 ch, sl st into 3rd ch from hook, 1 dc) all into next sc, 2 ch, sl st into next sc; rep from * 3 times more.

Fasten off.

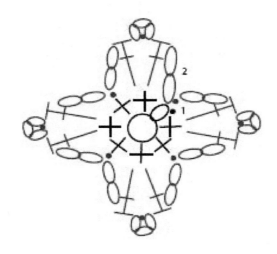

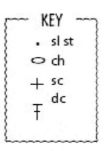

Five-Petal Flower

Make 2 ch.

Rnd 1 9 sc into 2nd ch from hook, sl st into 2nd of 2 ch to form a ring. 10 sc.

Rnd 2 1 ch, 1 sc into same place, 2 sc into each of next 9 sc, 1 sc into same place as first sc, sl st to first sc. 20 sc.

Rnd 3 (3 ch, tr2tog worked over next 2 sc, 3 ch, sl st into each of next 2 sc) 5 times, ending with 1 sl st into first sc.

Fasten off.

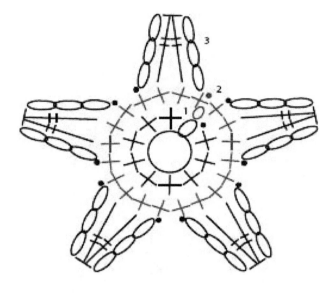

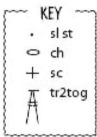

Eight-Petal Flower

Make 4 ch and join with sl st to form a ring.

Rnd 1 1 ch, 1 sc into ring, (3 ch, 1 sc) 7 times into ring, 1 ch, 1 dc into first 3 ch sp.

Rnd 2 1 ch, 1 sc into top of dc, (4 ch, sl st into 3rd ch from hook, 1 ch,

1 sc into next 3 ch sp) 8 times, ending with sl st into first sc. Fasten off.

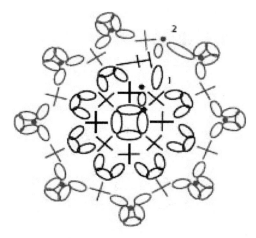

KEY
. sl st
◯ ch
+ sc
T dc

Large Cluster Flower

Make 4 ch and join with sl st to form a ring.

Rnd 1 3 ch, 1 tr into ring (counts as 1 tr2tog), (3 ch, 1 tr2tog into ring) 5 times, 3 ch, sl st into top of first tr.

Rnd 2 1 ch, (1 sc, 1 hdc, 3 dc, 1 hdc, 1 sc) all into first 3 ch sp and into each of next five 3 ch sps. Fasten off.

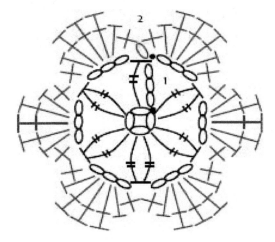

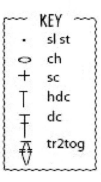

Button Gerbera

Make 4 ch and join with sl st to form a ring.

Rnd 1 2 ch, dc2tog into ring (counts as 1 dc3tog), five dc3tog into ring,

sl st to first dc3tog.

Rnd 2 (4 ch, 1 sc into 2nd ch from hook, 1 hdc into next ch, 1 dc into next ch, sl st to top of next dc3tog) 6 times.

Fasten off.

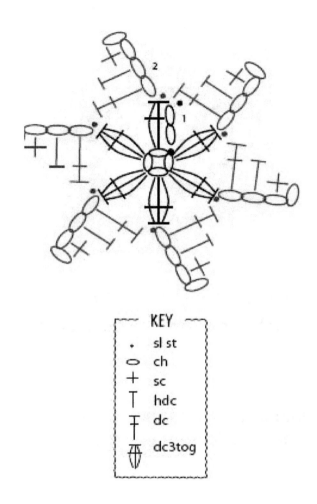

Hellebore

Make 5 ch and join with sl st to form a ring.

Rnd 1 3 ch (counts as 1 dc), 14 dc into ring, sl st to first dc.

Rnd 2 * 2 ch, 1 dc into same place, 3 dc into next dc, (1 dc, 2 ch, sl st) all into next dc, sl st into next dc; rep from * 4 times more.

Fasten off.

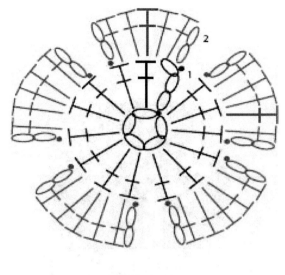

KEY
- sl st
- ch
- dc

Traditional Crochet Rose

Make 4 ch and join with sl st to form a ring.

Rnd 1 1 ch, 6 sc into ring, sl st to first sc.

Rnd 2 1 ch, 1 sc into same sc, (3 ch, 1 sc into next sc) 5 times, 3 ch, sl st into first sc.

Rnd 3 Sl st into first 3 ch sp, (1 sc, 3 hdc, 1 sc, sl st) all into same 3 ch sp, (sl st, 1 sc, 3 hdc, 1 sc, sl st) all into each of next five 3 ch sps. Fasten off.

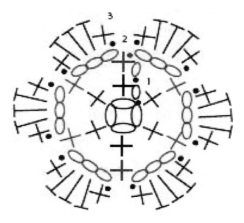

KEY
. sl st
○ ch
+ sc
T hdc

Sunflower

Make 4 ch and join with sl st to form a ring.

Rnd 1 3 ch (counts as 1 dc), 9 dc into ring, sl st to 3rd of 3 ch. 10 dc.

Rnd 2 1 ch, (1 sc, 3 ch, sl st into 3rd ch from hook, 1 sc) all into first dc, * 3 ch, sl st into 3rd ch from hook, (1 sc, 3 ch, sl st into 3rd ch from hook, 1 sc) all into next sc; rep from * 9 times more, sl st to first sc.

Fasten off.

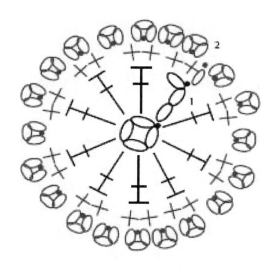

```
    KEY
  . sl st
  ◦ ch
  + sc
  ┬ dc
```

Irish Crochet Leaf

Make 8 ch.

Row 1 1 sc into 2nd ch from hook, 1 sc into each of next 5 ch, 5 sc into last ch, working along other side of foundation ch, 1 sc into each of next 6 ch, 3 sc into next ch, 1 sc into each of next 5 sc.

Row 2 1 ch, 1 sc into each of next 6 sc, 3 sc into next sc, 1 sc into each of next 6 sc.

Row 3 1 ch, 1 sc into each of next 7 sc, 3 sc into next sc, 1 sc into each of next 5 sc.

Row 4 1 ch, 1 sc into each of next 6 sc, 3 sc into next sc, 1 sc into each of next 6 sc.

Fasten off.

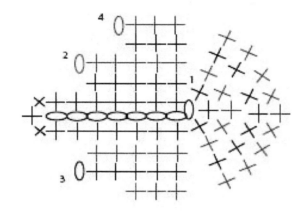

KEY
o ch
+ sc

Four-Leaf Sprig

Make 5 ch.

Row 1 1 ch, 1 sc into 2nd ch from hook, 1 sc into each of next 3 ch, (6 ch, 1 sc into 2nd ch from hook, 1 hdc into next ch, 1 dc into next ch, 1 hdc into next ch, 1 sc into next ch, sl st into next ch) 3 times.

Fasten off.

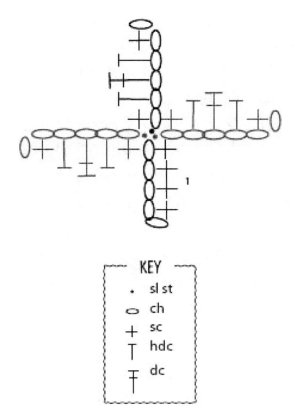

Fern Leaf

Make 8 ch.

1st leaf 1 sc into 2nd ch from hook, 1 hdc into next ch, 1 dc into next ch, 2 ch, sl st into next ch.

2nd leaf 6 ch, 1 sc into 2nd ch from hook, 1 hdc into next ch, 1 dc into next ch, 2 ch, sl st into next ch.

3rd leaf 4 ch, 1 sc into 2nd ch from hook, 1 hdc into next ch, 1 dc into next ch, 2 ch, sl st into same ch at end of previous leaf.

4th leaf 4 ch, 1 sc into 2nd ch from hook, 1 hdc into next ch, 1 dc into next ch, 2 ch, sl st into same ch at end of previous leaf.

5th leaf Sl st into each of next 2 ch, sl st into same ch as first leaf, 4 ch, 1 sc into 2nd ch from hook, 1 hdc into next ch, 1 dc into next ch, 2 ch, sl st into same ch as first leaf, sl st into each of next 4 ch.

Fasten off.

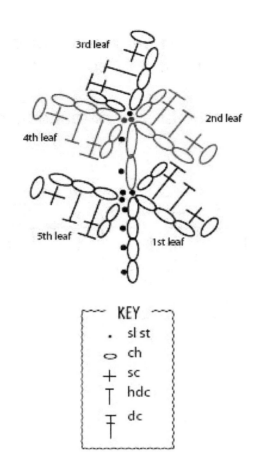

Picot Leaf

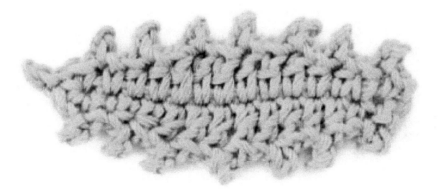

Picot 3 ch, sl st into 3rd ch from hook

Make 15 ch.

Row 1 1 sc into 2nd ch from hook, * make a picot, 1 sc into next ch, 1 hdc into next ch, make a picot, 1 hdc into next ch, 1 dc into next ch, (make a picot, 1 dc into each of next 2 ch) twice, make a picot, 1 dc into next ch, 1 hdc into next ch, make a picot, 1 hdc into next ch, 1 sc into next ch, make a picot, * (2 sc, make a picot, 2 sc) into last ch.

Row 2 Working along the other side of foundation ch, rep from * to *, 1 sc into last ch.

Fasten off.

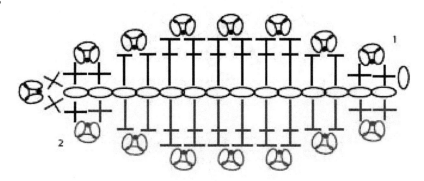

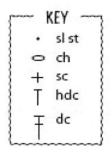

KEY
- • sl st
- ◦ ch
- + sc
- T hdc
- ₸ dc

Puff Stitch Flower

Make 4 ch and join with sl st to form a ring.

Rnd 1 * 2 ch, work a puff st as follows: (yoh, insert hook into ring, yoh, pull a loop through) 4 times, yoh, pull through all 9 loops on hook, 2 ch, sl st into ring; rep from * 4 times more.

Fasten off.

KEY
- sl st
- ch
- puff st

Simple Loop Flower

Make 4 ch and join with sl st to form a ring.

Rnd 1 1 ch, 8 sc into ring, sl st into first sc. 8 sc.

Rnd 2 (3 ch, sl st into next sc) 8 times.

Fasten off.

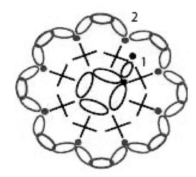

```
┌─── KEY ───┐
.    sl st
◯    ch
+    sc
└───────────┘
```

Six-Petal Flower

Make 6 ch and join with sl st to form a ring.

Rnd 1 1 ch, (1 sc, 4 ch, 1 sc into ring) 6 times, sl st into first sc.

Rnd 2 1 ch, (6 sc into 4 ch sp, sl st between 2 sc of previous rnd) 6 times.

Fasten off.

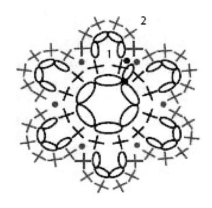

KEY
- • sl st
- ◌ ch
- + sc

Carnation

Make 6 ch and join with sl st to form a ring.

Rnd 1 1 ch, 15 sc into ring, sl st into first sc. 15 sc.

Rnd 2 3 ch (counts as 1 dc), 2 dc into same sc, 3 dc into each of next 14 sc, sl st into 3rd of 3 ch at beg of rnd. 45 tr.

Rnd 3 3 ch (counts as 1 dc), 2 dc into same dc, 3 dc into each of next 44 dc, sl st into 3rd of 3 ch at beg of rnd. 135 dc.

Rnd 4 * 4 ch, sl st into next dc; rep from * to end.

Fasten off.

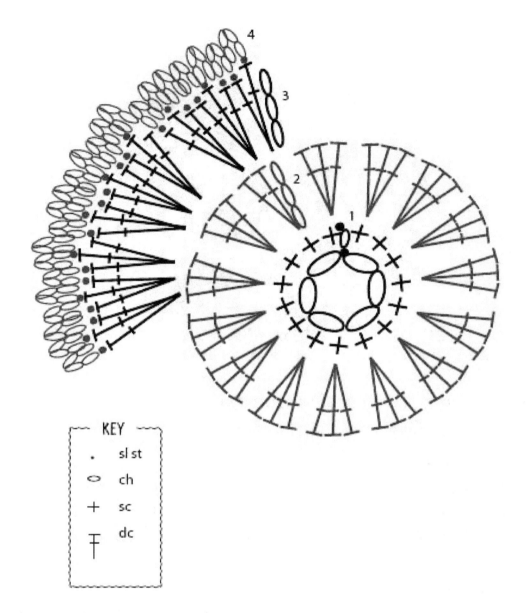

Chrysanthemum

Make 6 ch and join with sl st to form a ring.

Rnd 1 1 ch, 15 sc into ring, sl st into first dc. 15 sc.

Front layer of petals

Rnd 2 Working into front of loop only, (8 ch, sl st into 2nd ch from hook, sl st into each of next 6 ch, sl st into next sc) 14 times, 8 ch, sl st into 2nd ch from hook, sl st into each of next 6 ch, sl st into back of next sc.

Back layer of petals

Rnd 3 Working into back of loop only, 1 ch, 2 sc into each of next 15 sc, sl st to first sc. 30 sc.

Rnd 4 (8 ch, sl st into 2nd ch from hook, sl st into each of next 6 ch, sl st into next sc) 30 times.

Fasten off.

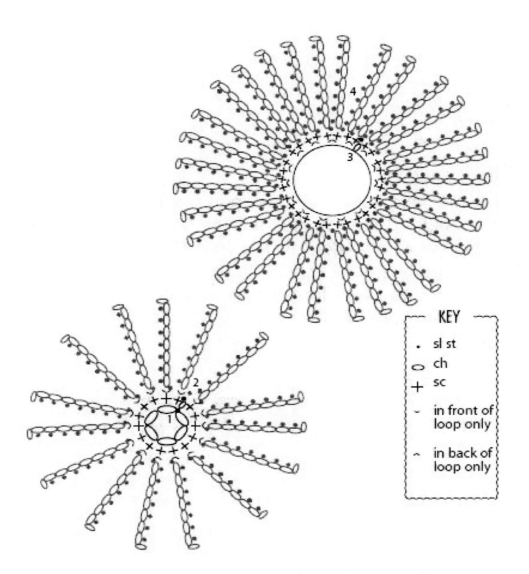

Trims

Necklace

Worked in precious fibres such as linen or silk, or in metallic or self-beaded threads, trims make unique jewellery. This 60in-long (150cm) necklace is worked in Ric Rac Braid in linen sportweight (4ply) using a B1 (2.00mm) hook. Make a sample to work out how many chains to start with for your chosen length. Be generous and add more than you think you need; any unused can easily be unravelled.

Scarf edging

Lacy Fan Braid adds a flamboyant touch to a fleece scarf worked in worsted (DK) yarn using a G6 (4.00mm) hook. Work until the trim is long enough to fit the edge. Sew one onto each end of the scarf. If using a horizontally worked trims, make a foundation of a multiple of whole pattern repeats (plus any extra chain) to fit across the scarf.

Blouse

Any garment can be updated with trims. This blouse is with a length of Daisy Chain sewn down each front. Use a yarn to match the garment material for trouble-free laundering; mercerized cotton on cotton, wool on wool, and so on. Try adding trims in different ways too; around collars, around cuffs (especially on short sleeves) or across pocket tops.

Skirt

Rejuvenate last season's skirt or add length to a short one by adding a trim around the hem. This is Large Fan Braid worked in an olive-green cotton worsted (DK) using a G6 (4.00mm) hook. Work a length to fit around the hem and sew on to the skirt. To add length, position the trim so it hangs below the edge of the skirt. If you choose one of the horizontal trims, make a foundation of a multiple of whole pattern repeats (plus any extra chain) to fit around the hem.

Cushion

This cushion has been embellished with a spiral made from a length of Simple Shell Edging using a silk worsted (DK) yarn and a E4 (3.50mm) hook. From the centre of the cushion front, mark a series of concentric circles ¾in (2cm) apart, using chalk. Work a length of chain in multiples of whole pattern repeats (plus any extra chain) that fits around these circles from the centre to the outer edge. Make more than you think you need, as the trim will be gathered slightly. Make the trim, then run a gathering stitch along the edge to gently gather the trim. This helps it lie around the curves. Attach the trim, starting at the centre.

Simple Shell Edging

Make a foundation chain of a multiple of 6 ch plus an extra 1 ch.

Row 1 4 dc in 3rd ch from hook, miss 2 ch, sc into next ch, * miss 2 ch, 5 dc into next ch, miss 2 ch, sc into next ch; rep from * to end.

Fasten off.

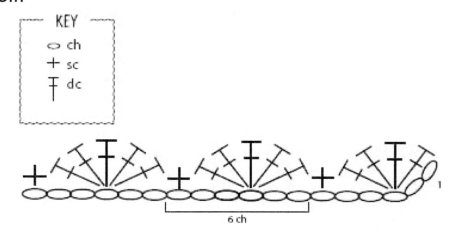

Simple Loop Edging

Make a foundation chain of a multiple of 5 ch plus an extra 3 ch.

Row 1 1 sc into 2nd ch from hook, 1 sc in next ch, * 5 ch, miss 3 ch, 1 sc in each of next 2 ch; rep from * to end.

Row 2 5 ch, * 1 sc in 3rd ch of next 5 ch sp in previous row, 3 ch, 1 sc in same place, 5ch; rep from * to end,

sl st into last sc.

Fasten off.

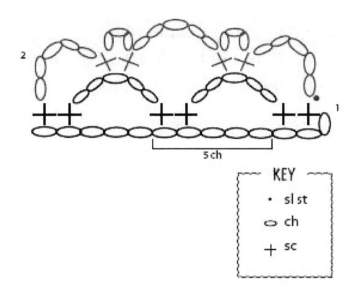

Picot Loop Edging

Make a foundation chain of a multiple of 5 ch plus an extra 2 ch.

Row 1 Sc into 2nd ch from hook, * 5 ch, miss 4 ch, 1 sc into next ch; rep from * to end.

Row 2 1 ch, (3 sc, 3 ch, sl st into 3rd ch from hook, 3 sc) into each 5 ch sp to end.

Fasten off.

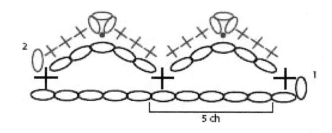

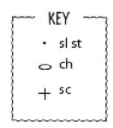

KEY
- sl st
- ch
+ sc

Gothic Flower Edging

Make a foundation chain of a multiple of 8 ch plus an extra 1 ch.

Row 1 1 sc into 2nd ch from hook, 1 sc into each ch to end.

Row 2 3 ch, miss 2 sc, (tr2tog, 4 ch, sl st, 4 ch, tr2tog) all into next sc, * 3 ch, miss 7 sc, (tr2tog, 4 ch, sl st, 4 ch, tr2tog) all into next sc; rep from * to last 3 sc, miss 2 sc, 1 dc into last sc.

Row 3 1 ch, 1 sc into dc, 5 ch, tr3tog into same sc as petals, * 5 ch, sc into each of next 3 ch, 5 ch, tr3tog into same sc as petals; rep from * to end, 5 ch, 1 sc into 3rd of 3 ch at beg of previous row.

Row 4 1 ch, 7 sc into 5 ch sp, 5 ch, 7 sc into next 5 ch sp, * miss 1 sc, sl st into next sc, miss 1 sc, 7 sc into 5 ch sp, 5 ch, 7 sc into next 5 ch sp; rep from * to end, sl st into last sc.

Row 5 1 ch, * miss sl st and 1 sc, 1 sc into each of next 5 sc, miss 1 sc, (3 sc, 3 ch, sl st into 3rd ch from hook, 3 sc) all into 5 ch sp, miss 1 sc, 1 sc into each of next 5 sc; rep from * to end.

Fasten off.

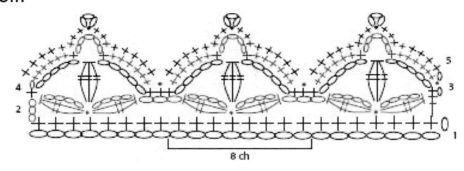

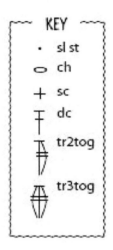

Clover Border

Make a foundation chain of 13 ch.

Foundation Row 1 dc into 4th ch from hook, 1 dc into next ch, 5 ch, miss 6 ch, (1 dc, 3 ch, 1 dc, 3 ch, 1 dc, 3 ch, 1 dc) all into last ch, turn.

Row 1 1 ch, (1 sc, 1 hdc, 3 dc, 1 hdc, 1 sc) all into each 3 ch sp, 5 ch, miss 4 ch, 1 dc into 5th ch, 1 dc into each of next 2 dc, 1 dc into 3rd of 3 ch at beg of previous row.

Row 2 3 ch (counts as 1 dc), 1 dc into each of next 3 dc, 1 dc into first ch, 5 ch, (1 dc, 3 ch, 1 dc, 3 ch, 1 dc, 3 ch, 1 dc) all into middle dc of 2nd petal.

Row 3 1 ch, (1 sc, 1 hdc, 3 dc, 1 hdc, 1 sc) all into each 3 ch sp, 5 ch, miss 4 ch, 1 dc into 5th ch, 1 dc into each of next 4 dc, 1 dc into 3rd of 3 ch at beg of previous row.

Row 4 3 ch (counts as 1 dc), 1 dc into each of next 5 dc, 1 dc into first ch, 5 ch, (1 dc, 3 ch, 1 dc, 3 ch, 1 dc, 3 ch, 1 dc) all into middle dc of 2nd petal.

Row 5 1 ch, (1 sc, 1 hdc, 3 dc, 1 hdc, 1 sc) all into each 3 ch sp, 5 ch, miss 4 ch, 1 dc into 5th ch, 1 dc into each of next 6 dc, 1 dc into 3rd of 3 ch at beg of previous row.

Row 6 3 ch (counts as 1 dc), 1 dc into each of next 2 dc, 5 ch, miss 4 dc, (1 dc, 3 ch, 1 dc, 3 ch, 1 dc, 3 ch, 1 dc) all into next dc.

Repeat these 6 rows.

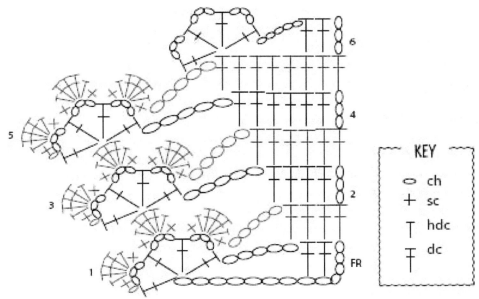

KEY

○ ch
+ sc
T hdc
╤ dc

Fringe

Make a foundation chain of 18 ch.

Foundation Row 1 dc into 5th ch from hook, 1 dc into next ch, 3 ch, miss 4 ch, (3 dc, 1 ch, 3 dc) all into next ch, 3 ch, miss 4 ch, 1 dc into next ch, 1 ch, miss 1 ch, 1 dc into next ch.

Row 1 4 ch (counts as 1 dc and 1 ch), miss ch sp, 1 dc into next dc, 3 ch, (3 dc, 1 ch, 3 dc) all into ch sp at centre of fan, 3 ch, 1 dc into each of next 2 dc, 1 dc into 4th of 4 ch.

Row 2 3 ch (counts as 1 dc), 1 dc into each of next 2 dc, 3 ch, (3 dc, 1 ch, 3 dc) all into ch sp at centre of fan, 3 ch, 1 dc into next dc, 1 ch, 1 dc into 3rd of 4 ch.

Rep rows 1 and 2, ending with row 2.

Fringe is worked into the row ends.

10 ch, sl st into space at end of row just worked, * 10 ch, sl st into top of dc at end of next row, 10 ch, sl st into next sp; rep from * to foundation ch, 10 ch, sl st into last sp.

Fasten off.

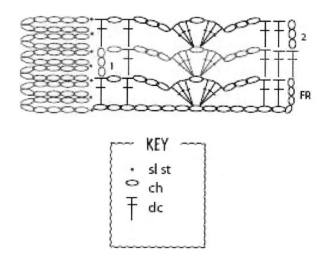

Picot Fringe

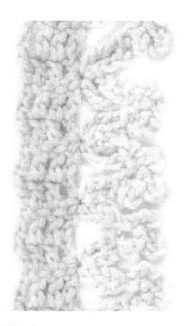

Make a foundation ch of 7 ch.

Foundation Row 1 dc into 5th ch from hook, 1 dc into each of next 2 ch.

Row 1 3 ch (counts as 1 dc), 1 dc into each of next 2 dc, 1 dc into top of tch.

Rep row 1 for length required.

Fasten off.

Edging is worked into row ends.

Rejoin yarn to base of first dc, (4 ch, 1 tr) all into same place, * (5 ch, sl st into top of tr) 3 times, (1 tr, 4 ch, sl st, 4 ch, 1 tr) all into base of dc in row above; rep from * to last row, (5 ch, sl st into top of tr) 3 times, (1 tr, 4 ch, sl st) into top of dc in last row.

Fasten off.

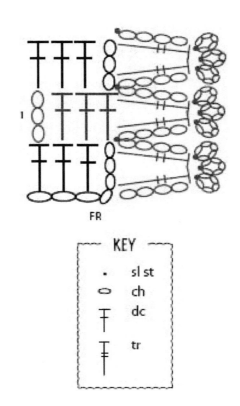

Picot Shell

Make a foundation ch of a multiple of 6 ch plus an extra 2 ch.

Row 1 1 sc into 2nd ch from hook, 1 sc into each ch to end.

Row 2 1 ch, 1 sc into first sc, miss 2 sc, 7 dc into next sc, miss 2 sc, * 1 sc into next sc, miss 2 sc, 7 dc into next sc, miss 2 sc, 1 sc into next sc; rep from * to end.

Row 3 1 ch, 1 sc into first sc, * miss first dc of fan, (1 sc into next dc, 3 ch, sl st into 3rd ch from hook, 1 sc into next dc) twice, 1 sc into next dc, 3 ch, sl st into first ch, miss last dc of fan, 1 sc into sc between fans; rep from * to end.

Fasten off.

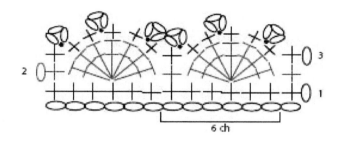

KEY
- · sl st
- ◯ ch
- + sc
- ⊤ dc

Fan and Double Crochet

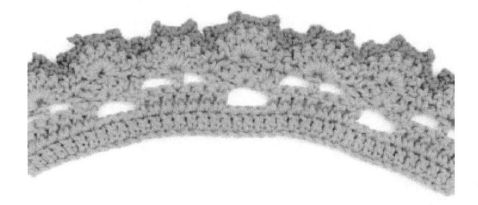

Make a foundation ch of a multiple of 11 ch plus an extra 9 ch.
Row 1 1 dc into 4th ch from hook, 1 dc into each ch to end.

Row 2 3 ch (counts as 1 dc), 1 dc into each of next 6 dc, * 4 ch, miss 4 dc, 1 dc into each of next 7 dc; rep from * to end, working last dc into 3rd of 3 ch.

Row 3 5 ch (counts as 1 dc and 2 ch), (miss next 2 dc, 1 dc into next dc, 2 ch, miss next 2 dc, 1 dc into next dc, * miss 1 ch, 5 dc into next ch, miss 2 dc, 1 dc into next dc, 2 ch, miss 2 dc, 1 dc into next dc, 2 ch, miss 2 dc, 1 dc into next dc; rep from * to end, working last dc into 3rd of 3 ch.

Row 4 3 ch (counts as 1 dc), miss 2 ch sp, 7 dc into next dc, miss 2 ch sp, * 1 sc into next dc, miss 2 dc, 7 dc into next dc, miss 2 dc, 1 sc into next dc, miss 2 ch sp, 7 dc into next dc, miss 2 ch sp; rep from * to end, 1 sc into 3rd of 5 ch.

Row 5 1 ch (counts as 1 sc), * 1 sc into first dc of fan, (1 sc into next dc, 3 ch, sl st into 1st ch, 1 sc into next dc) 3 times, miss sc between fans; rep from * to end, 1 sc into 3rd of 3 ch.

Fasten off.

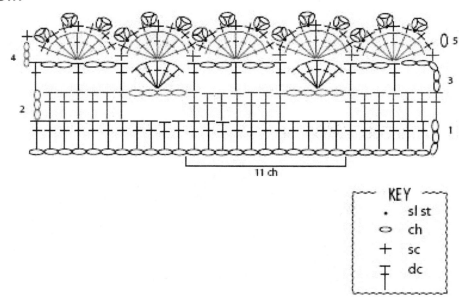

Sunrise Braid

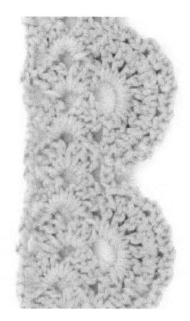

Make a foundation ch of 10 ch.

Foundation Row (3 dc, 3 ch, 3 dc) all into 7th ch from hook, miss 2 ch, 1 tr into last ch.

Row 1 4 ch (counts as 1 tr), (3 dc, 3 ch, 3 dc) all into 3 ch sp at centre of shell, 1 tr into top of tch.

Row 2 As row 1.

Row 3 4 ch (counts as 1 tr), (3 dc, 3 ch, 3 dc) all into 3 ch sp at centre of shell, 1 ch, (1 dc, 1 ch) 8 times into 4 ch sp at beg of previous row, miss 1 tr at end of first row below and sl st into 4th of 4 ch at beg of 2nd row below.

Row 4 3 ch, miss 1 ch and 1 dc, 1 sc into ch sp, (3 ch, 1 sc) all into next six ch sps, 4 ch, miss 1 dc and 1 ch, (3 dc, 3 ch, 3 dc) all into 3 ch sp at centre of shell, 1 tr into top of tch.

Rep these 4 rows.

Fasten off.

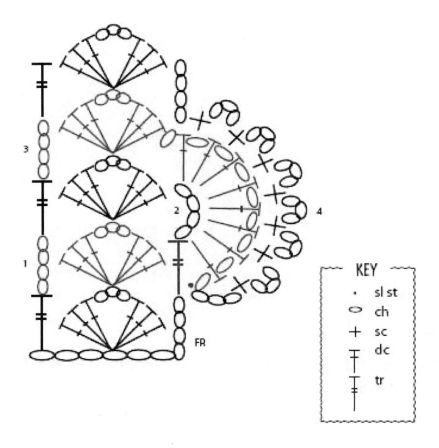

Arch Edging

Make a foundation ch of a multiple of 10 ch plus an extra 7 ch.
Row 1 1 sc into 2nd ch from hook, 1 sc into each ch to end.

Row 2 1 ch, 1 sc into first sc, * 5 ch, miss 4 sc, 1 sc into next sc; rep from * to end.

Row 3 6 ch (counts as 1 dc and 3 ch), 1 sc into first 5 ch sp, * 3 ch, (2 dc, 4 ch, 2 dc) all into next 5 ch sp, 3 ch, 1 sc into next 5 ch sp; rep from * to last sc, 3 ch, 1 dc into last sc.

Row 4 1 ch, 1 sc into dc, 4 ch, miss 3 ch sp and sc, * 1 sc into next 3 ch sp, 10 dc into 4 ch sp, 1 sc into next 3 ch sp, 4 ch; rep from * to tch, 1 sc in 3rd of 3 ch.

Fasten off.

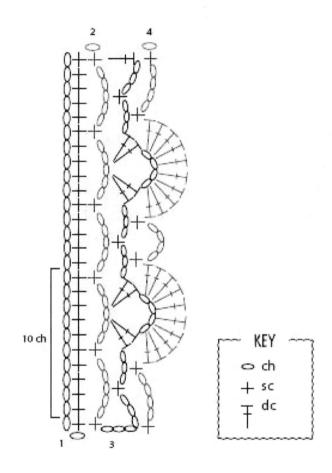

Large Fan Braid

Make 5 ch and join with sl st to form a ring.

Foundation Row 8 ch, (1 dtr, 1 ch) 6 times into ring, 1 dtr into ring, 9 ch, sl st into ring, turn.

Row 1 1 ch, into 9 ch sp work (2 sc, 4 ch, sl st in 4th ch from hook) 4 times, 2 sc into same sp, (1 sc into next tr, 1 sc into next ch sp) 3 times, 5 ch, miss 1 tr, (1 sc into next ch sp, 1 sc into next tr) 3 times, turn.

Row 2 8 ch, (1 dtr, 1 ch) 6 times into ring, 1 dtr into ring, 9 ch, sl st into ring, turn.

Rep rows 1 and 2.

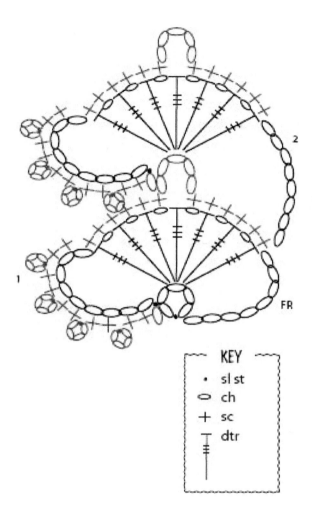

KEY
- sl st
○ ch
+ sc
┬ dtr

Blossom Braid

Make 9 ch.

Foundation Row 1 dc into 7th ch from hook, 1 dc into each of last 2 ch.

Row 1 6 ch, 6 dc into 6 ch sp.

Row 2 (3 ch, sl st into dc) into each of next 6 dc, 6 ch, 3 dc into 6 ch sp.

Rep rows 1 and 2.

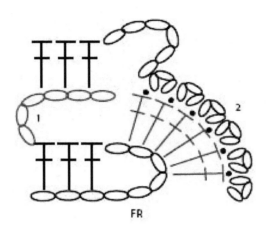

KEY
· sl st
o ch
┬ dc

Braid

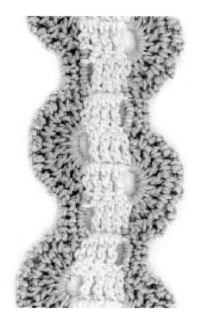

Make a foundation ch of 8 ch.

Foundation Row 1 tr into 5th ch from hook, 1 tr into each of next 3 ch to end.

Row 1 4 ch (counts as 1 tr), 1 tr into each of next 4 tr to end.

Rep row 1 for length required, making an even number of rows.

First Edging

Turn braid so row ends are horizontal and work from right to left.

Row 1 1 ch, miss tr at beg of first row, * (1 ch, 1 dc) 8 times into tch at beg of next row, 1 ch, miss tr of next row, 1 sc into top of tch of next row, 3 sc into tch, 1 sc into top of next tr, miss tr at beg of next row; rep from * to end, working last sc into foundation ch, turn.

Row 2 1 ch, miss sc at base of tch, * 1 sc into each of next 3 sc, * 1 ch, miss 1 sc and 1 ch and 1 dc, 1 sc into ch sp, (3 ch, 1 sc) all into next six ch sps, 1 ch, miss 1 dc and 1 ch and 1 sc; rep from * to end, ending with 1 sc into top of last tr.

Second Edging

Rejoin yarn to end of foundation ch and work rows 1 and 2.

Fasten off.

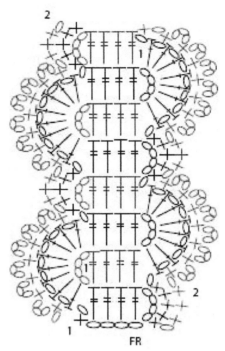

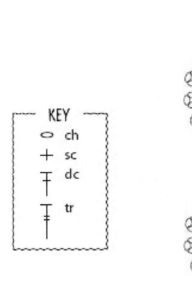

Teardrop Edging

Make a foundation ch of a multiple of 14 ch plus an extra 2 ch.

Row 1 1 sc into 2nd ch from hook, 1 sc into each ch to end.

Row 2 1 ch, 1 sc into first sc, * 1 ch, miss 1 sc, 1 sc into next sc; rep from * to end.

Row 3 5 ch (counts as 1 dc and 2 ch), miss 1 ch sp, 1 sc into next ch sp, 3 ch, miss next ch sp, 6 dc into next ch sp, 3 ch, miss 1 ch sp, 1 sc into next ch sp, * 5 ch, miss next 2 ch sps, 1 sc into next ch sp, 3 ch, miss next ch sp, 6 dc into next ch sp, 3 ch, miss 1 ch sp, 1 sc into next ch sp; rep from * to last ch sp, 2 ch, miss last ch sp, 1 dc into last sc.

Row 4 1 ch, 1 sc into dc, * 5 ch, 1 dc into each of next 3 dc, 5 ch, 1 dc into each of next 3 dc, 5 ch, 1 sc into next 5 ch sp; rep from * to end.

Row 5 3 ch (counts as 1 dc), 1 dc into first 5 ch sp, * 5 ch, into 5 ch sp between groups of dc work (2 dc, 5 ch, sl st into 5th ch from hook) 4 times, 2 dc into same sp, 5 ch, dc2tog working first leg into next 5 ch sp and second leg into next 5 ch sp; rep from * to end, working second leg of last dc2tog into last sc.

Fasten off.

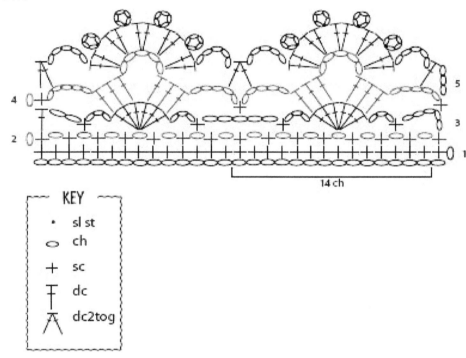

Fan and Filet Edging

Make a foundation ch of a multiple of 6 ch plus an extra 4 ch.

Row 1 1 dc into 4th ch from hook, * 2 ch, miss 2 ch, 1 dc into next ch; rep from * to end.

Row 2 3 ch (counts as 1 dc), 8 dc into same dc, miss 1 dc, 9 dc into next dc; rep from * to end.

Fasten off.

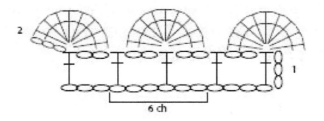

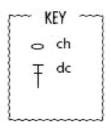

Filigree Arch

Make a foundation ch of a multiple of 10 ch plus an extra 4 ch.

Row 1 1 sc into 2nd ch from hook, 1 sc into each ch to end.

Row 2 1 ch, 1 sc into first sc, * 1 ch, miss 1 sc, 1 sc into next sc; rep from * to end.

Row 3 1 ch, 1 sc into each of first sc and ch sp, 1 ch, 1 sc into next ch sp, 6 ch, miss 2 ch sps, * (1 sc into next ch sp, 1 ch) twice, 1 sc into next ch sp, 6 ch, miss 2 ch sps; rep from * to last 2 ch sps, 1 sc into next ch sp, 1 ch, 1 sc into next ch sp, 1 sc into last sc.

Row 4 1 ch, 1 sc into first sc, 1 ch,

1 sc into next ch sp, * (4 sc, 3 ch, 4 sc) all into 6 ch sp, 1 sc into next ch sp,

1 ch, 1 sc into next ch sp; rep from * to end, working last sc into last sc.

Fasten off.

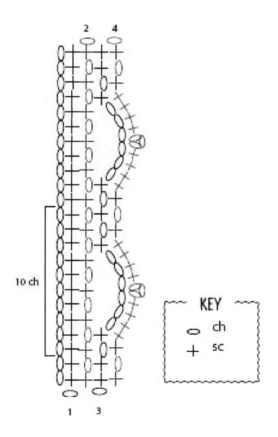

Daisy Chain

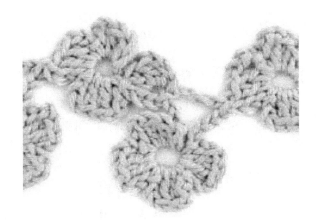

Make 4 ch.

Row 1 2 dc into 4th ch from hook, 4 ch, (2 dc, 3 ch, sl st, 3 ch, 2 dc) all into 4th ch from hook, * 9 ch, 2 dc into 4th ch from hook, 4 ch, (2 dc, 3 ch, sl st, 3 ch, 2 dc) all into 4th ch from hook; rep from * for number of daisies required, do not turn.

Row 2 (worked along the base of row 1 to complete the daisies) 3 ch, sl st into same place as other petals for first daisy, (3 ch, 2 dc, 3 ch, sl st) all into same place, 3 ch, sl st into top edge of last petal of this daisy, * 8 ch, (2 dc, 3 ch, sl st, 3 ch) 3 times all into 4th ch from hook, (2 dc, 3 ch, sl st) all into same place, 4 ch, sl st into top edge of first petal of next daisy, 3 ch, sl st into centre of this daisy, (3 ch, 2 dc, 3 ch, sl st) all into same place, 3 ch, sl st into top edge of last petal of this daisy; rep from * to end.

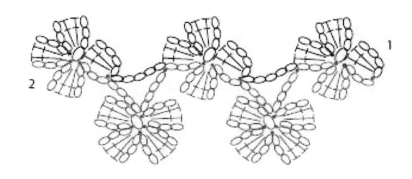

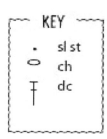

Picot Eyelet Edging

Make a foundation ch of a multiple of 6 ch plus an extra 4 ch.

Row 1 1 dc into 4th ch from hook, * 1 ch, miss 1 ch, 1 dc into next ch; rep from * to end.

Row 2 1 ch, 1 sc into first dc, * 1 ch, miss 1 ch and 1 dc, (2 dc, 2 ch, 2 dc) all into next ch, 1 ch, miss 1 dc and 1 ch, 1 sc into next dc; rep from * to end.

Row 3 3 ch, (1 dc, 5 ch, sl st into 3rd ch from hook, 2 ch, 1 dc) all into first sc, * 1 ch, 1 sc into 2 ch sp of fan below, 1 ch, (1 dc, 5 ch, sl st into 3rd ch from hook, 2 ch, 1 dc) all into next sc; rep from * to end.

Fasten off.

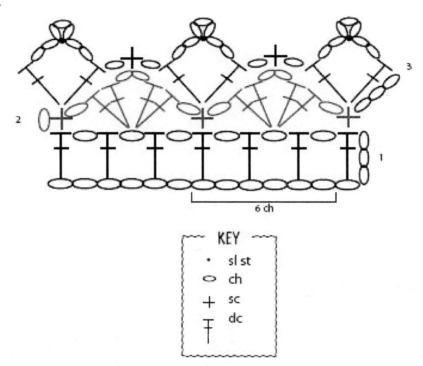

Trefoil Loops

Make a foundation ch of a multiple of 8 ch plus an extra 2 ch.

Row 1 1 sc into 2nd ch from hook, 1 sc into every

ch to end.

Row 2 1 ch, 1 sc into first sc, * 9 ch, miss 7 sc, 1 sc into next sc; rep from * to end.

Row 3 4 ch, 1 tr into first sc, 4 ch, 1 sc into first 9 ch sp,

* 9 ch, 1 sc into next 9 ch sp; rep from * to end, 4 ch, 1 tr into last sc.

Row 4 1 ch, 1 sc into first tr, * 7 ch, 1 sc into 3rd ch from hook, (3 ch, 1 sc into same place) twice, 4 ch, 1 sc into next 9 ch sp; rep from * to end, ending with last sc into last tr.

Fasten off.

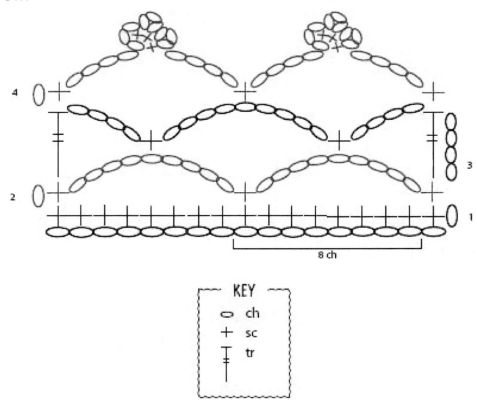

Sawtooth Edging

Make a foundation ch of a multiple of 5 ch plus an extra 1 ch.

Row 1 1 sc into 2nd ch from hook, 1 sc into every ch to end.

Row 2 4 ch, 1 tr into first sc, 1 dc into next sc, 1 hdc into next sc, 1 sc into next sc, sl st into next sc, * 4 ch, 1 tr into next sc, 1 dc into next sc, 1 hdc into next sc, 1 sc into next sc, sl st into next sc; rep from * to end.

Fasten off.

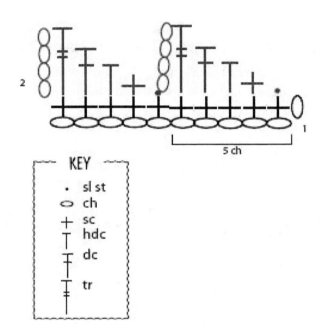

Mexican Edging

Make a foundation ch of a multiple of 18 ch plus an extra 14 ch.

Row 1 1 sc into 2nd ch from hook, 1 sc into every ch to end.

Row 2 1 ch, 1 sc into first sc, * 5 ch, miss 5 sc, 1 sc into next sc; rep from * to end.

Row 3 3 ch, 1 dc into first sc, 3 ch, 1 sc into first 5 ch sp, * 10 ch, 1 sc into next 5 ch sp, (5 ch, 1 sc into next 5 ch sp) twice; rep from * to last 5 ch sp, 10 ch, 1 sc into last 5 ch sp, 3 ch, 1 dc into last sc.

Row 4 (tr2tog, 5 ch) 7 times into each 10 ch sp to end, omitting last 5 ch, sl st into last dc.

Fasten off.

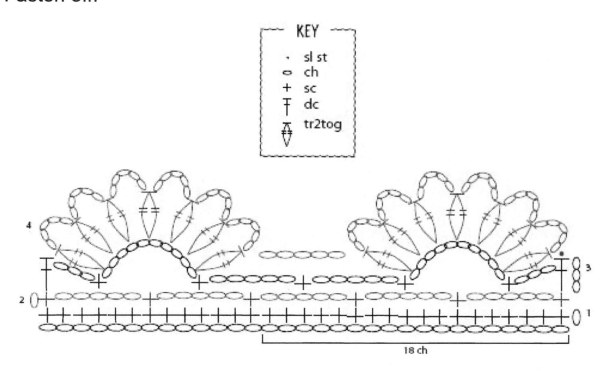

Hoop Edging

First Motif Make 8 ch, sl st into first ch to form a ring, 1 ch, into ring work 4 sc, 4 ch, 4 sc, 5 ch, sl st into last sc, 7 ch, sl st into same sc, 5 ch, sl st into same sc, 4 sc, 4 ch, 4 sc, sl st into first sc to close ring. Do not turn.

Second Motif * 18 ch, sl st into 8th ch from hook, 1 ch, into ring work 4 sc, 2 ch, sl st into 4 ch loop of previous motif, 2 ch, 4 sc, 5 ch, sl st into last sc, 7 ch, sl st into same sc, 5 ch, sl st into same sc, 4 sc, 4 ch, 4 sc, sl st into first sc to close ring; rep from * for required length, do not turn.

Top Edging 1 ch, 10 sc into each loop across the top. Fasten off.

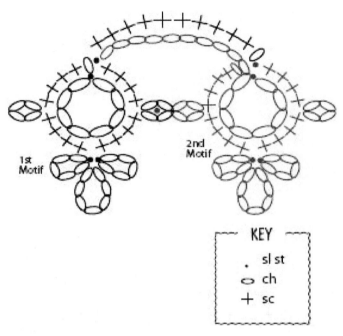

Large Eyelet Edging

Make 20 ch.

Foundation Row 1 tr into 5th ch from hook, 1 tr into next ch, 3 ch, miss 4 ch, (1 dc, 2 ch, 1 dc) all into next ch, 3 ch, miss 4 ch, (1 dc, 2 ch, 1 dc) all into next ch, 6 ch, sl st into last ch.

Row 1 1 ch, into 6 ch loop work (2 sc, 4 ch) 3 times and 2 sc, sl st into next dc, 5 ch (counts as 1 dc and 2 ch), (tr3tog, 2 ch, 1 dc) all into 2 ch sp, (1 dc, 2 ch, tr3tog, 2 ch, 1 dc) all into next 2 ch sp, 1 ch, 1 tr into each of next 2 tr, 1 dc into 4th of 4 ch.

Row 2 4 ch (counts as 1 tr), 1 tr into each of next 2 tr, 3 ch, (1 dc, 2 ch, 1 dc) all into top of tr cluster, 3 ch, (1 dc, 2 ch, 1 dc) all into top of next tr cluster, 6 ch, sl st into 3rd of 5 ch.

Rep rows 1 and 2.

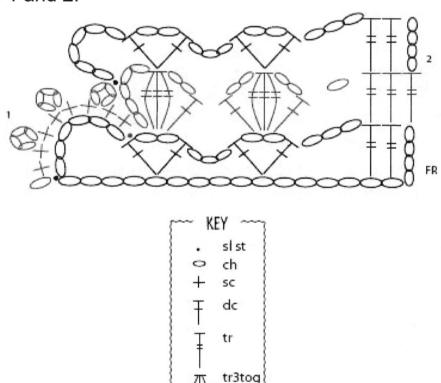

Lacy Fan Braid

Make 11 ch.

Foundation Row 1 dc into 4th ch from hook, 1 dc into each of next 3 ch, 2 ch, miss 2 ch, 1 dc into each of next 2 ch.

Row 1 3 ch (counts as 1 dc), 1 dc into next dc, 1 dc into each of next 2 ch, 4 ch, miss 4 dc, 1 dc into 3rd of 3 ch.

Row 2 5 ch, 1 dc into first dc, 1 dc into each of next 4 ch, 2 ch, miss 2 dc, 1 dc into next dc, 1 dc into 3rd of 3 ch.

Row 3 3 ch (counts as 1 dc), 1 dc into next dc, 1 dc into each of next 2 ch, 4 ch, miss 4 dc, 1 dc into last dc, (1 ch, 1 dc) 9 times into 5 ch loop, sl st to base of dc on row below.

Row 4 3 ch, miss 1 dc and 1 ch, (1 sc into next dc, 3 ch) 8 times, 1 dc into first dc, 1 dc into each of next 4 ch, 2 ch, miss 2 dc, 1 dc into next dc, 1 dc into 3rd of 3 ch.

Rep rows 1 to 4 for required length.

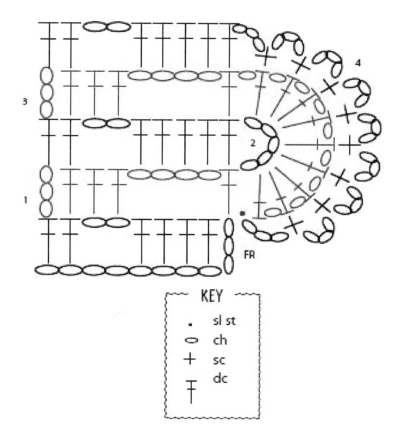

Up and Down Edging

Make a foundation ch of a multiple of 12 ch plus an extra 2 ch.

Row 1 1 sc into 2nd ch from hook, 1 sc into each ch to end.

Row 2 1 ch, 1 sc into first sc, * 2 ch, miss 1 sc, 1 hdc into next sc, 2 ch, miss 1 sc, 1 dc into next sc, 2 ch, miss 1 sc, 1 tr into next sc, 2 ch, miss 1 sc, 1 dc into next sc, 2 ch, miss 1 sc, 1 hdc into next sc, 2 ch, miss 1 sc, 1 sc into next sc; rep from * to end.

Row 3 * 5 ch, 1 sc into 2 ch sp; rep from * to end, 5ch, sl st into last sc.

Fasten off.

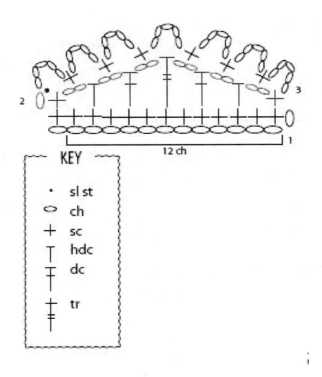

Picot Arch

Make a foundation ch of a multiple of 8 ch plus an extra 2 ch.

Row 1 1 sc into 2nd ch from hook, 1 sc into each ch to end.

Row 2 1 ch, 1 sc into first sc, * 10 ch, miss 7 sc, 1 sc into next sc; rep from * to end.

Row 3 1 ch, work 14 sc into each 10 ch sp to end.

Row 4 1 ch, * miss 2 sc, (1 sc into each of next 2 sc, 4 ch) 4 times, 1 sc into each of next 2 sc, miss last 2 sc; rep from * into each 14 sc arch to end, 1 ch, sl st into last sc.

Fasten off.

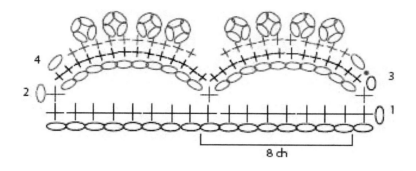

Flower Garland

Flower Row 5 ch, * tr2tog into 5th ch from hook, 4 ch, sl st into same ch at base of tr2tog, (4 ch, tr2tog, 4 ch, sl st into same ch) 3 times, 20 ch; rep from * for required length, omitting last 20 ch.

Row 2 1 ch, (10 sc, 3 ch, 10 sc) into each 15 ch loop.

Row 3 4 ch (counts as tr), miss sc at base of this ch and next 3 sc, 1 tr into next sc, * 7 ch, 1 sc into 3 ch loop, 7 ch, tr2tog working first leg into 6th sc from 3 ch loop and second leg into 5th sc on other side of flower; rep from * to end, ending with second leg of tr2tog into last sc.

Row 4 3 ch (counts as dc), * 6 dc into 7 ch sp, 1 dc into sc, 6 dc into 7 ch sp, 1 dc into top of tr2tog; rep from * to end.

Fasten off.

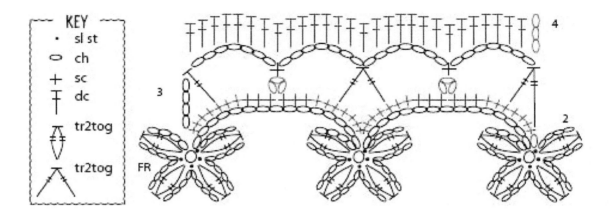

Diagonal Squares

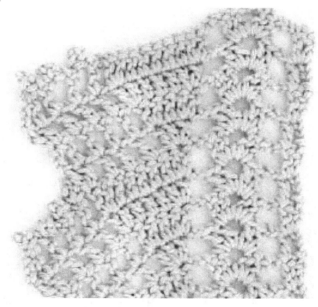

Make 19 ch.

Foundation Row 1 dc into 4 ch from hook, 2 ch, miss 2 ch, (2 dc, 2 ch, 2 dc) all into next ch, 2 ch, miss 3 ch, 3 dc into next ch, 1 ch, miss 1 ch, (1 dc into next ch, 1 ch, miss 1 ch) 3 times, 2 dc into last ch.

Row 1 3 ch (counts as 1 dc), (1 dc into next dc, 1 ch) 4 times, 2 dc into next dc, 1 dc into next dc, 2 dc into next dc, 2 ch, (2 dc, 2 ch, 2 dc) all into 2 ch sp in centre of shell, 2 ch, 1 dc into next dc, 1 dc into 3rd of 3 ch.

Row 2 3 ch (counts as 1 dc), 1 dc into next dc, 2 ch, (2 dc, 2 ch, 2 dc) all into 2 ch sp in centre of shell, 2 ch, 2 dc into next dc, 1 dc into each of next 3 dc, 2 dc into next dc, (1 ch, 1 dc into next dc) 4 times, 1 dc into 3rd of 3 ch.

Row 3 3 ch (counts as 1 dc), (1 dc into next dc, 4 ch, sl st into 4th ch from hook, 1 ch) 4 times, 2 dc into next dc, 1 dc into each of next 5 dc, 2 dc into next dc, 2 ch, (2 dc, 2 ch, 2 dc) all into 2 ch sp in centre of shell, 2 ch, 1 dc into next dc, 1 dc into 3rd of 3 ch.

Row 4 3 ch (counts as 1 dc), 1 dc into next dc, 2 ch, (2 dc, 2 ch, 2 dc) all into 2 ch sp in centre of shell, 2 ch, 3 dc into next dc, (1 ch, miss 1 dc, 1 dc into next dc) 3 times, 1 ch, miss 1 dc, 2 dc into next dc.

Rep rows 1 to 4 for required length.

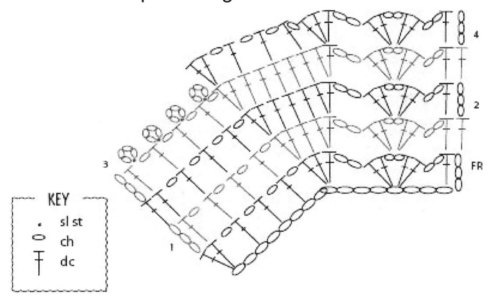

Bridge Edging

Make a foundation ch of a multiple of 6 ch plus an extra 4 ch.

Row 1 1 sc into 2nd ch from hook, 1 sc into each ch to end.

Row 2 4 ch (counts as 1 dc and 1 ch), miss sc at base of tch and next sc, 1 dc into next sc, * 1 ch, miss 1 sc, 1 dc into next sc; rep from * to end.

Row 3 3 ch (counts as 1 dc), 2 dc into first ch sp, * 5 ch, miss next 2 ch sp, 2 dc into next ch sp; rep from * to end, 1 dc into 3rd of 3 ch.

Row 4 1 ch, (1 sc, 1 hdc, 5 dc, 1 hdc, 1 sc) into each 5 ch sp to end, 1 ch, sl st into 3rd of 3 ch.

Fasten off.

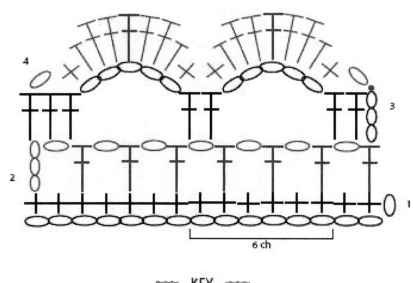

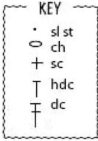

KEY
- • sl st
- ○ ch
- + sc
- T hdc
- ⊤ dc

Simple Loop Trim

Make a foundation ch of a multiple of 3 ch plus an extra 2 ch.

Row 1 1 sc into 2nd ch from hook, 1 sc into each ch to end.

Row 2 1 ch, 1 sc into first sc, * 5 ch, miss 2 sc, 1 sc into next sc; rep from * to end.

Row 3 1 ch, (3 sc, 3 ch, 3 sc) into each 5 ch sp to end.

Fasten off.

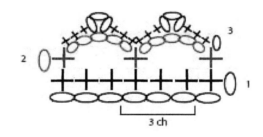

Treble Blocks

Make a foundation ch of a multiple of 10 ch plus an extra 3 ch.

Row 1 1 sc into 2nd ch from hook, 1 sc into each ch to end.

Row 2 3 ch (counts as 1 dc), 1 dc into each of next 2 sc, * 3 ch, miss 2 sc, 1 tr into each of next 3 sc, 3 ch, miss 2 sc, 1 dc into each of next 3 sc; rep from * to end, ending with last dc into ch.

Row 3 1 ch, 1 sc into first dc, (1 sc, 3 ch, 1 sc) all into next dc, 1 sc into next dc, * 3 sc into 3 ch sp, 1 sc into first tr, (1 sc, 3 ch, 1 sc) all into next tr, 1 sc into next tr, 3 sc into 3 ch sp, 1 sc into first dc, (1 sc, 3 ch, 1 sc) all into next dc, 1 sc into next dc; rep from * to end, ending with last sc into 3rd of 3 ch.

Fasten off.

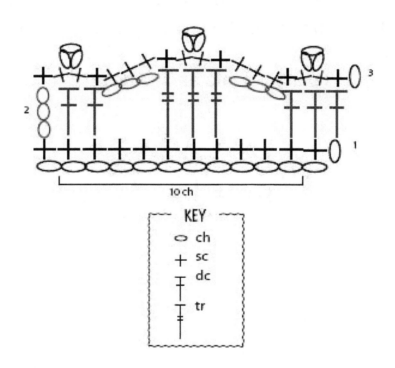

Small Eyelet Braid

Make 6 ch.

Row 1 1 sc into 4th ch from hook, 2 ch, 1 dc into last ch, * 5 ch, 1 sc into 4th ch from hook, 2 ch, 1 dc into top of last dc; rep from * for required length.

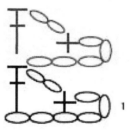

```
KEY
○ ch
+ sc
T dc
```

Cluster Lace Edging

Make a foundation ch of a multiple of 6 ch plus an extra 2 ch.

Row 1 1 sc into 2nd ch from hook, 1 sc into each ch to end.

Row 2 3 ch, (1 dc, 5 ch, tr3tog into top of dc, 1 dc) all into first sc, * 3 ch, miss 5 sc, (1 dc, 5 ch, tr3tog into top of dc, 1 dc) all into next sc; rep from * to end.

Fasten off.

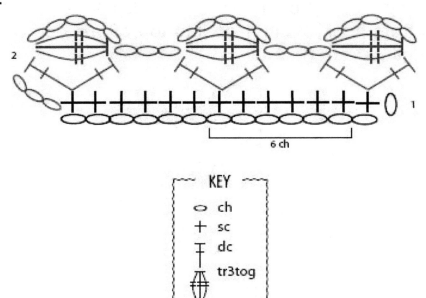

Three Loop Braid

Make 5 ch.

Row 1 1 dc into 5th ch from hook, * 4 ch, sl st into top of dc, 4 ch, 1 dc into same place, 1 tr into base of 1st dc made, 8 ch, dc into 5th ch from hook: rep from * for required length, omitting last 8 ch.

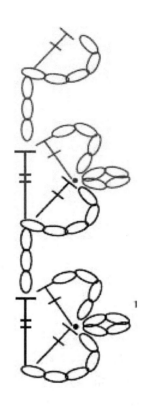

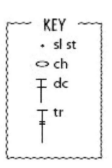

Quick Loops

Make a foundation ch of a multiple of 4 ch plus an extra 2 ch.
Row 1 1 sc into 2nd ch from hook, 1 sc into each ch to end.

Row 2 1 ch, 1 sc into first sc, * 4 ch, 1 sc into 3rd ch from hook, 2 ch, miss 3 sc, 1 sc into next sc; rep from * to end.

Fasten off.

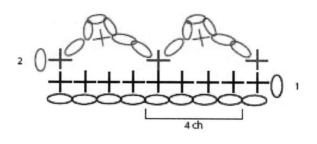

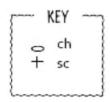

Clam Shell Edging

Make a foundation ch of a multiple of 3 ch.

Row 1 1 sc into 2nd ch from hook, 1 sc into each ch to end.

Row 2 1 ch, 1 sc into each of first 2 sc, * 11 ch, insert hook into 2nd ch from hook, yoh, draw a loop through, insert hook in each of next 9 ch and draw a loop through, yoh, draw a loop through all 11 loops on hook, 1 ch, miss 1 sc, 1 sc into each of next 2 sc; rep from * to end.

Fasten off.

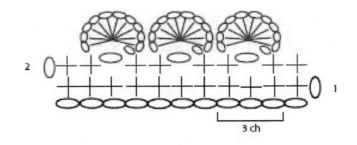

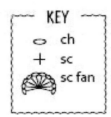

Scallop Edging

Make a foundation ch of a multiple of 11 ch plus an extra 4 ch.

Row 1 1 sc into 2nd ch from hook, 1 sc into each ch to end.

Row 2 1 ch, 1 sc into first sc, 1 ch, miss 1 sc, 1 sc into next sc, * 5 ch, 1 dc into top of sc just made, miss 2 sc, 1 dc into next sc, 5 ch, 1 dc into top of dc just made, miss 2 sc, 1 dc into next sc, 5 ch, 1 dc into top of dc just made, miss 2 sc, 1 sc into next sc, 1 ch, miss 1 sc, 1 sc into next sc; rep from * to end.

Fasten off.

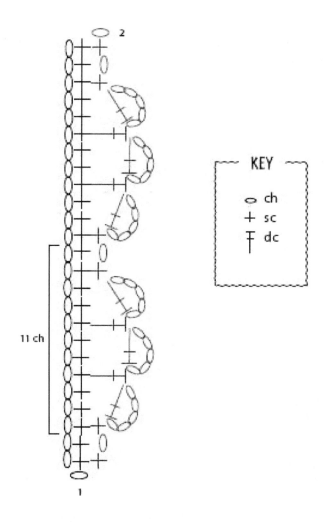

Picot Shells

Make a foundation ch of a multiple of 6 ch plus an extra 2 ch.

Row 1 1 sc into 2nd ch from hook, 1 sc into each of next 2 ch, * 5 ch, miss 1 ch, 1 sc into each of next 5 ch; rep from * to end, ending with 3 sc.

Row 2 1 ch, 1 sc into first sc, * (1 sc, 3 ch) 5 times into 5 ch sp, 1 sc into same 5 ch sp, miss 2 sc, 1 sc into next sc; rep from * to end.

Fasten off.

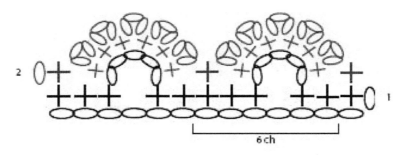

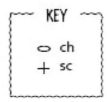

Flowers and Picots

Make a foundation ch of a multiple of 6 ch plus an extra 1 ch.

Row 1 1 sc into 2nd ch from hook, 1 sc into each ch to end.

Row 2 3 ch (counts as 1 dc), * miss 2 sc, into next sc work (tr2tog, 4 ch, 1 sc into 3rd ch from hook, 1 ch) twice, tr2tog, miss 2 sc, 1 dc into next sc; rep from * to end, ending with last dc into ch.

Fasten off.

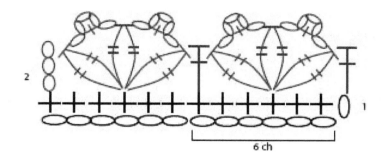

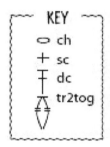

Butterfly Edging

Make a foundation ch of a multiple of 8 ch plus an extra 2 ch.

Row 1 1 sc into 2nd ch from hook, 1 sc into each ch to end.

Row 2 1 ch, 1 sc into first sc, * miss 3 sc, (2 tr, 4 ch, 1 sc, 4 ch, 2 tr) all into next sc, miss 3 sc, 1 sc into next sc; rep from * to end.

Row 3 1 ch, 1 sc into first sc, * 1 sc into each of first 2 tr, (1 sc, 3 ch, sl st into 3rd ch from hook, 1 sc, 3 ch, sl st into 3rd ch from hook, 1 sc) all into each of next two 4 ch sps, 1 sc into each of next 2 tr, 1 sc into sc between shells; rep from * to end.

Fasten off.

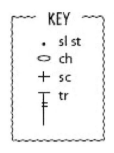
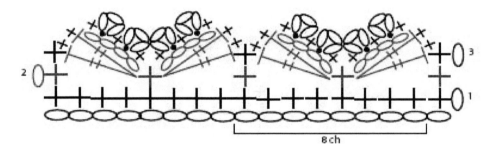

Ric Rac Braid

Foundation Row 5 ch, into 5th ch from hook work (1 dc, 1 ch) twice and 1 dc.

Row 1 1 ch, miss 1 dc and 1 ch and 1 dc, then into middle ch sp of the shell just made work (1 dc, 1 ch) 3 times and 1 dc.

Rep row 1 for required length.

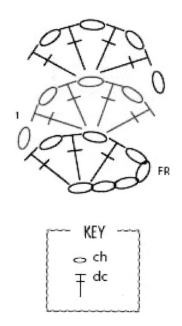

KEY
- ch
- dc

Simple Picot Edging

Make a foundation ch of an odd number of ch.

Row 1 1 sc into 2nd ch from hook, 1 sc into each ch to end.

Row 2 1 ch, 1 sc into each of next 2 sc, * 3 ch, sl st into 3rd ch from hook, 1 sc into each of next 2 sc; rep from * to end.

Fasten off.

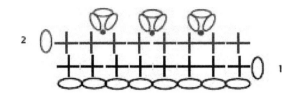

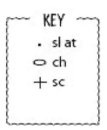

Crowns

Make a foundation ch of a multiple of 8 ch plus an extra 6 ch.

Row 1 1 sc into 2nd ch from hook, * 5 ch, miss 3 ch, 1 sc into next ch; rep from * to end.

Row 2 3 ch, into first 5 ch sp work (1 dc, 2 ch, 1 dc, 5 ch, sc into 4th ch from hook, 2 ch, 1 dc, 2 ch, 1 dc), * miss next 5 ch sp, into next 5 ch sp work (1 dc, 2 ch, 1 dc, 5 ch, sc into 4th ch from hook, 2 ch, 1 dc, 2 ch, 1 dc); rep from * to end, 1 dc into last sc.

Fasten off.

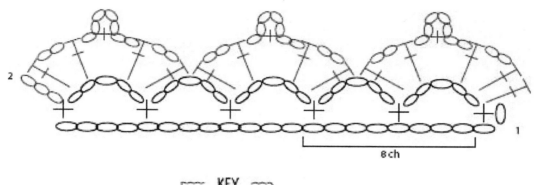

Shark's Tooth

Make 7 ch.

Foundation Row 1 sc into 2nd ch from hook, 1 hdc into next ch, 1 dc into next ch, 1 ch, miss 1 ch, 1 dc into each of last 2 ch.

Row 1 1 ch, 1 sc into each of first 2 dc, 1 sc into ch sp.

Row 2 4 ch, 1 sc into 2nd ch from hook, 1 hdc into next ch, 1 dc into next ch, 1 ch, miss 1 sc, 1 dc into of each last 2 sc.

Rep rows 1 and 2.

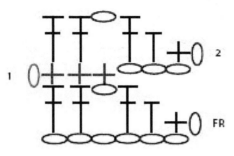

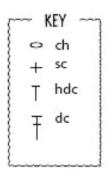

V Stitch Edging

Make a foundation ch of a multiple of 3 ch.

Row 1 1 sc into 2nd ch from hook,

1 sc into each ch to end.

Row 2 3 ch (counts as 1 dc), miss

1 sc, (1 dc, 1 ch, 1 dc) all into next sc, * miss 2 sc, (1 dc, 1 ch, 1 dc) all into next sc; rep from * to last 2 sc, miss

1 sc, 1 dc into last sc.

Row 3 1 ch, 1 sc into first dc, * into ch sp in middle of V st work (1 ch,

1 sc, 3 ch, sl st into 3rd ch from hook, 1 sc, 1ch), 1 sc into sp between V sts; rep from * to end, working last sc into 3rd of 3 ch. Fasten off.

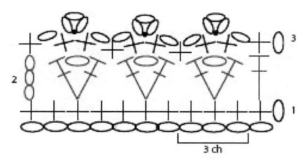

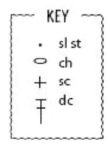

Simple Ric Rac Braid

Make a foundation ch of a multiple of 8 ch plus an extra 1 ch.

Row 1 Sc3tog working first leg into 2nd ch from hook, second leg into next ch and third leg into next ch,

3 sc into each of next 2 ch, * (sc3tog worked into next 3 ch) twice, 3 sc into each of next 2 ch; rep from

* to last 3 ch, sc3tog worked into

last 3 ch.

Fasten off.

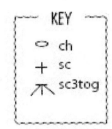

Clover Leaf Edging

Make a foundation ch of a multiple of 6 ch plus an extra 4 ch.

Row 1 1 sc into 2nd ch from hook,

1 sc into each ch to end.

Row 2 1 ch, 1 sc into first sc, 1 sc into each of next 2 sc, * miss 1 sc, (1 sc,

4 ch, 1 sc, 6 ch, 1 sc, 4 ch, 1 sc) all into next sc, miss 1 sc, 1 sc into each of next 3 sc; rep from * to end.

Fasten off.

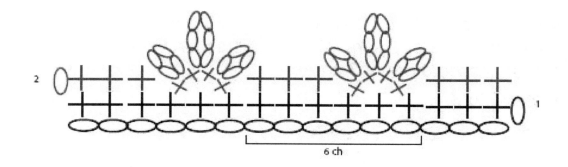

Spanish Edging

Make 22 ch.

Foundation Row 1 sc into 10th ch from hook, (5 ch, miss 3 ch, 1 sc into next ch) 3 times.

Row 1 5 ch (counts as 1 sc and 3 ch), 1 sc into first 5 ch sp, (5 ch, 1 sc into next 5 ch sp) twice.

Row 2 7 ch, 1 tr into first 5 ch sp, 3 ch, 1 tr into next 5 ch sp, 3 ch, 1 tr into 2nd of 5 ch.

Row 3 3 ch, 3 dc into first 3 ch sp, 3 dc into next 3 ch sp, 12 dc into 7 ch loop, sl st into 5 ch sp at beg of row below.

Row 4 (5 ch, miss 1 dc, 1 sc into next dc) 5 times, 5 ch, miss 2 dc, 1 sc between next 2 dc, 5 ch, miss 3 dc, 1 sc between next 2 dc, 5 ch, miss 3 dc, 1 sc into 3rd of 3 ch.

Rep rows 1 to 4.

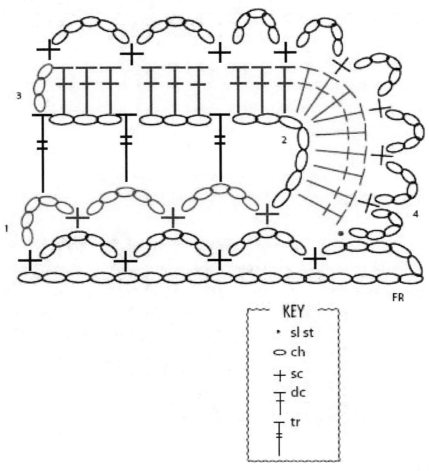

Chain Loop Ruffle

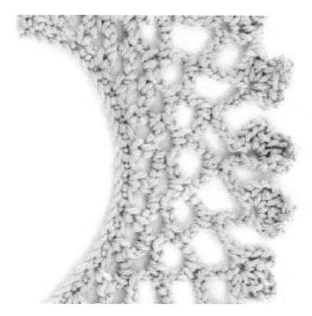

Make a foundation ch of a multiple of 4 ch.

Row 1 1 sc into 2nd ch from hook, 1 sc into each ch to end.

Row 2 1 ch, 1 sc into first sc, * 4 ch, miss 1 sc, 1 sc into next ch; rep from * to end.

Row 3 5 ch (counts as 1 dc and 2 ch), 1 sc into first 4 ch sp, * 4 ch, 1 sc into next 4 ch sp; rep from * to end, 2 ch, 1 dc into last sc.

Row 4 1 ch, 1 sc into dc, 6 ch, * 1 sc into next 4 ch sp, 6 ch; rep from * to tch, 1 sc into 3rd of 5 ch.

Row 5 6 ch (counts as 1 dc and 3 ch), 1 sc into first 6 ch sp, * 9 ch, 1 sc into 6th ch from hook, 6 ch, 1 sc into same ch, 5 ch, 1 sc into same ch, 3 ch, 1 sc into next 6 ch sp; rep from * to end, 3 ch, 1 dc into last sc.

Fasten off.

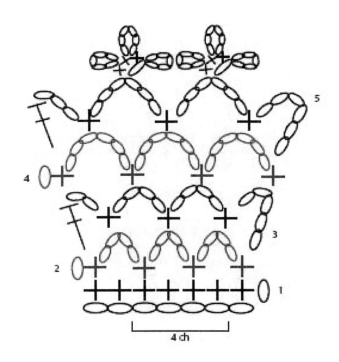

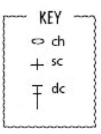

KEY
- ch
+ sc
dc

4 ch

Fabrics

Cushion panel

Choose any of the fabric stitches and work a foundation chain of a multiple of whole pattern repeats (plus any extra chain) that is long enough to cover one-third of the cushion. Work until the panel measures the same as the cushion and sew on. This design, worked in Fleurette, is made from wool worsted (DK) yarn using a size 7 (4.50mm) hook; the cushion measures 15in (38cm) square.

Crochet hook holder

This holder is covered in Zigzag Fabric, worked in three worsted (DK) yarns and a D3 (3.00mm) hook. Make a foundation chain in a multiple of whole pattern repeats long enough to fit up the side of the jar, then add an extra repeat to fold over to the inside (plus any extra chain at the end). Work until the stretched cover wraps around the jar, using a different colour for each row and carrying the yarns up the side of the work. Sew the two ends together, pull on to the jar, and fold the top to the inside.

Scarf

Make a patchwork scarf using a mix of fabric stitches. Choose your stitch, make a foundation chain of two or three pattern repeats, and work until the patch is as wide as you want the scarf. Make patches until you meet the required length, then sew or crochet together. This scarf is worked in two shades of tweed wool worsted (DK) using a G6 (4.00mm) hook. It is 3in wide and 59in long (7.5 by 150cm).

Curtain panel

Two vintage linens and a centre panel of crochet make a stylish curtain. This panel, in Star Lattice, is worked in mercerized cotton worsted (DK) using a G6 (4.00mm) hook; it is 8in wide and 22in long (20 by 55cm). Make a foundation chain of a multiple of pattern repeats (plus any extra chain) the width of the panel that you require. Work until the panel is the same length as the linens. Sew into place between the linens. To hang, add simple clasps to hook onto curtain rings, or sew on pieces of tape or brass rings to thread a pole through.

Lavender sachets

These colourful sachets are made from simple rectangles of fabric using Granny Fabric. They are worked in stripes of three shades of mercerized cotton worsted (DK) using an E4 (3.50mm) hook. Make a foundation chain of 44 ch and work until the sachet measures 5in (12.5cm), using a different colour for each row and carrying the yarns up the side of the work. Fold in half and work a row of sc around the base and side to join the back and front. Make a crochet chain for the drawstring or use some ribbon. Insert

a ready-made lavender pouch.

Filet Mesh

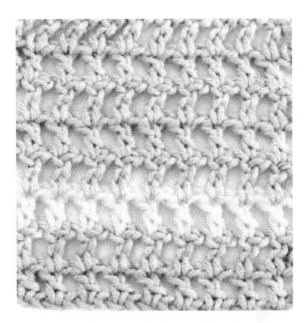

Make a foundation chain of a multiple of 2 ch plus an extra 1 ch.

Foundation Row 4 ch (counts as 1 dc and 1 ch), 1 dc into 6th ch from hook, * 1 ch, miss 1 ch, 1 dc into next ch; rep from * to end, turn.

Row 1 4 ch (counts as 1 dc and 1 ch), miss ch sp, * 1 dc into next dc, 1 ch; rep from * to end tch, 1 dc into 3rd of 4 ch at beg of previous row.

Rep row 1.

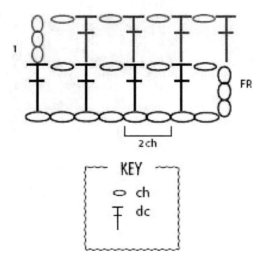

V Stitch Fabric

Make a foundation chain of a multiple of 3 ch plus an extra 1 ch.

Foundation Row 4 ch (counts as 1 dc and 1 ch), 1 dc into 4th ch from hook, * miss 2 ch, (1 dc, 1 ch, 1 dc) all into next ch; rep from * to end.

Row 1 4 ch (counts as 1 dc and 1 ch), 1 dc into ch sp between first 2 dc, * (1 dc, 1 ch, 1 dc) into ch sp between next 2 dc; rep from * to end.

Rep row 1.

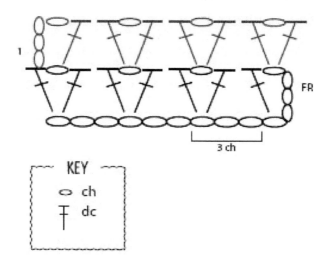

Shell Lace

Make a foundation chain of a multiple of 6 ch plus an extra 1 ch.

Foundation Row 4 ch (counts as 1 dc and 1ch), (1 dc, 1 ch, 1 dc, 1 ch) all into 4th ch from hook, * miss 5 ch, (1 dc, 1 ch) 6 times all into next ch; rep from * to last 6 ch, miss 5 ch, (1 dc, 1ch, 1 dc, 1 ch, 1 dc) all into last ch.

Row 1 4 ch (counts as 1 dc and 1 ch), (1 dc, 1 ch, 1 dc, 1 ch) all into dc at base of tch, * (1 dc, 1 ch) 6 times into centre ch sp of next shell; rep from * to last half shell, (1 dc, 1 ch, 1 dc, 1 ch, 1 dc) all into 3rd of 4 ch at beg of previous row.

Rep row 1.

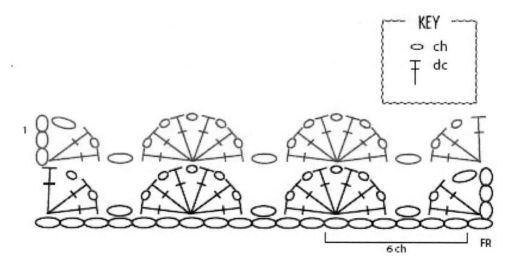

Large Daisy Fabric

Abbreviations

2 trnc – 2 tr not completed by (yoh twice, insert hook where indicated, yoh and draw loop through, yoh and draw through 2 loops on hook, yoh and draw through next 2 loops) twice (leaves 2 loops on hook).

3 trnc – 3 tr not completed by (yoh twice, insert hook where indicated, yoh and draw loop through, yoh and draw through 2 loops on hook, yoh and draw through next 2 loops) 3 times (leaves 3 loops on hook).

Make a foundation chain of a multiple of 8 ch plus an extra 1 ch.

Foundation Row 7 ch (counts as 1 tr and 1 dc), dc2tog into 3rd ch from hook, make a 3-petal-cluster as follows: 3 trnc into 4th ch from base of dc2tog, (miss 3 ch, 3 trnc into next ch) twice, yarn over hook and draw a loop through all 10 loops on hook to complete, * (3 ch, dc2tog into 3rd ch from hook) twice, 3-petal-cluster working the first petal into same ch as last petal of previous cluster; rep from * to end, 3 ch, dc2tog into 3rd ch from hook, 1 tr into same ch as last petal.

Row 1 4 ch (counts as tr), * (tr3tog, 3 ch, tr3tog, 3 ch, tr3tog) all into closing ch at centre of 3-petal-cluster; rep from * to end, 1 tr into closing loop of dc2tog in row below.

Row 2 4 ch (counts as 1 tr), 2 trnc into top of first petal, 3 trnc into top of middle petal, yarn over hook and draw a loop through all 6 loops on hook to complete, * (3 ch, dc2tog into 3rd ch from hook) twice, 3-petal-cluster working first petal into same place as last petal of previous cluster, middle petal into space between two petal-clusters, and last petal into top of middle petal of next petal-cluster: rep from * to last two petals, (3 ch, dc2tog in 3rd ch from hook) twice, 3 trnc into same place as last petal of previous petal-cluster, 3 trnc into top of tr, yarn over hook and draw a loop through all 6 loops on hook to complete.

Row 3 4 ch (counts as 1 tr), (tr2tog, 3 ch, tr3tog) all into closing ch at centre of petal-cluster, * (tr3tog, 3 ch, tr3tog, 3 ch, tr3tog) all into closing ch at centre of next petal-cluster; rep from * to last 2-petal-cluster, (tr3tog, 3 ch, tr3tog) all into closing ch at centre.

Row 4 7 ch (counts as 1 tr and 1 dc), dc2tog into 3rd ch from hook, 3-petal-cluster working first petal into top of petal at base of tch, middle petal into space between petal-clusters, and last petal into top of middle petal of next petal-cluster, * (3 ch, dc2tog in 3rd ch from hook) twice, 3-petal-cluster working first petal into same place as last petal of previous cluster, middle petal into space between two petal-clusters, and last petal into top of middle petal of next petal-cluster: rep from * to end, 3 ch, dc2tog into 3rd from hook, 1 tr into same place as last petal.

Rep these 4 rows.

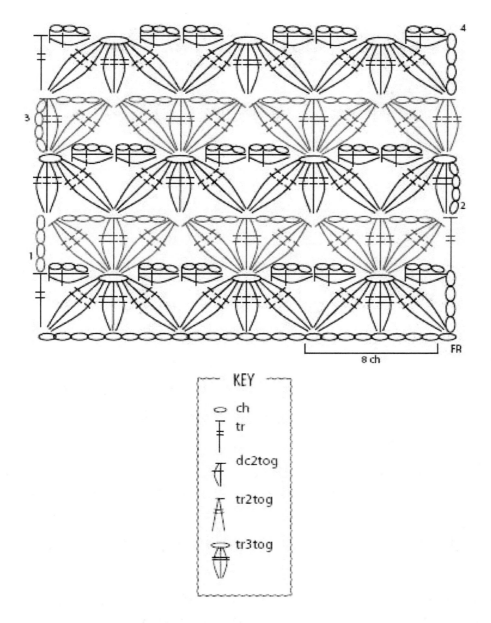

Large Hexagonal Eye

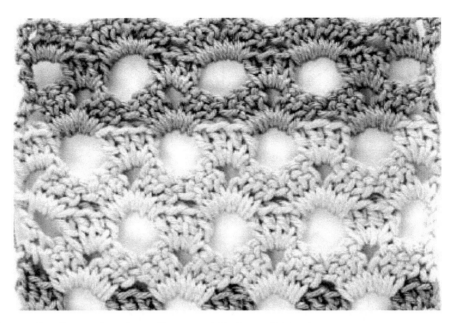

Make a foundation chain of a multiple of 6 ch.

Foundation Row 1 dc into 4th ch from hook, 1 dc into each of next 2 ch, * 2 ch, miss 2 ch, 1 dc into each of next 4 ch; rep from * to end.

Row 1 3 ch (counts as 1 dc), (3 dc, 2 ch, 3 dc) all into each 2 ch sp to end, 1 dc into 3rd of 3 ch.

Row 2 5 ch (counts as 1 dc and 2 ch), 4 dc into first 2 ch sp, * 2 ch, 4 dc into next 2 ch sp; rep from * to end, 2 ch, 1 dc into 3rd of 3 ch.

Row 3 5 ch (counts as 1 dc and 2 ch), 3 dc into first 2 ch sp, (3 dc, 2 ch, 3 dc) all into each 2 ch sp to end, (3 dc, 2 ch, 1 dc) all into last 5 ch sp.

Row 4 3 ch (counts as 1 dc), 3 dc into first 2 ch sp, * 2 ch, 4 dc into next 2 ch sp; rep from * to end, 4 dc into last 5 ch sp.

Rep rows 1 to 4.

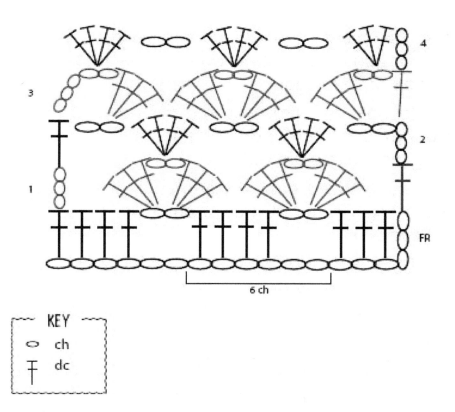

Cube Fabric

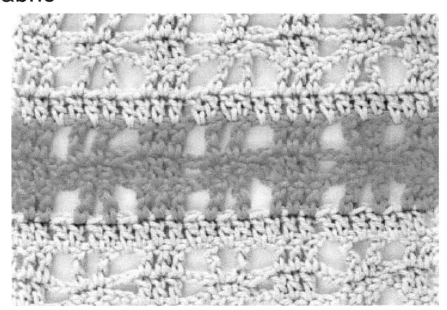

Make a foundation chain of a multiple of 8 ch plus an extra 5 ch.

Foundation Row 1 dc into 4th ch from hook, 1 dc into each ch to end.

Row 1 3 ch (counts as 1 dc), 1 dc into each of next 2 dc, * 3 ch, (miss 1 dc, 1 tr into next dc) twice, 3 ch, miss 1 dc, 1 dc into each of next 3 dc; rep from * to end.

Row 2 3 ch (counts as 1 dc), 1 dc into each of next 2 dc, * 3 ch, 1 sc into each of next 2 tr, 3 ch, 1 dc into each of next 3 dc; rep from * to end, working last dc into 3rd of 3 ch.

Row 3 3 ch (counts as 1 dc), 1 dc into each of next 2 dc, * 1 ch, 1 tr into first sc, 1 ch, 1 tr into next sc, 1 ch, 1 dc into each of next 3 dc; rep from * to end.

Row 4 3 ch (counts as 1 dc), 1 dc into each of next 2 dc, * (1 dc into next ch, 1 dc into next tr) twice, 1 dc into next ch, 1 dc into each of next 3 dc; rep from * to end, working last dc into 3rd of 3 ch.

Rep rows 1 to 4.

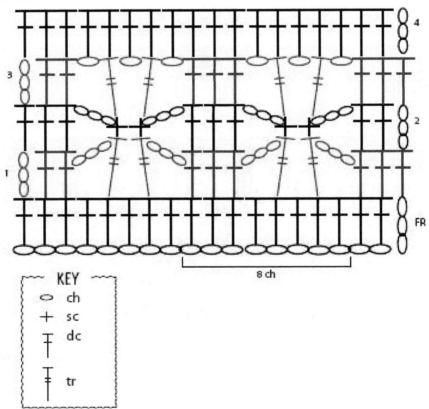

Diamond Lace

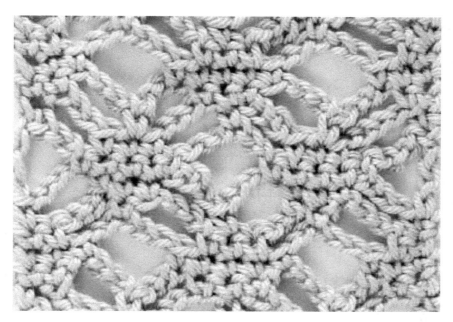

Make a foundation chain of a multiple of 10 ch plus an extra 2 ch.

Foundation Row 1 sc into 2nd ch from hook, 1 sc into each of next 2 ch, * 5 ch, miss 5 ch, 1 sc into each of next 5 ch; rep from * to end, ending with 3 sc.

Row 1 1 ch, 1 sc into first sc, 1 sc into next sc, * 4 ch, 1 sc into 3rd ch of 5 ch loop, 4 ch, miss 1 sc, 1 sc into each of next 3 sc; rep from * to end, ending with 2 sc.

Row 2 1 ch, 1 sc into first sc, * 4 ch, 1 sc into 4th ch of loop below, 1 sc into next sc, 1 sc into next ch, 4 ch, miss 1 sc, 1 sc into next sc; rep from * to end.

Row 3 6 ch (counts as 1 tr and 2 ch), * 1 sc into 4th ch of loop below, 1 sc into each of next 3 sc, 1 sc into next ch, 5 ch; rep from * to end, 2 ch, 1 tr into last sc.

Row 4 1 ch, 1 sc into top of tr, * 4 ch, miss 1 sc, 1 sc into each of next 3 sc, 4 ch, 1 sc into 3rd ch of 5 ch loop; rep from * to end, ending with last sc into 3rd ch of 6 ch.

Row 5 1 ch, 1 sc into first sc, 1 sc into next ch, * 4 ch, miss 1 sc, 1 sc into next sc, 4 ch, 1 sc into 4th ch of loop below, 1 sc into next sc, 1 sc into next ch; rep from * to end, ending with 2 sc.

Row 6 1 ch, 1 sc into first sc, 1 sc into next sc, * 1 sc into next ch, 5 ch, 1 sc into 4th ch of next 4 ch loop, 1 sc into each of next 3 sc; rep

from * to end, ending with 1 sc into each of last 2 sc.
Rep rows 1 to 6.

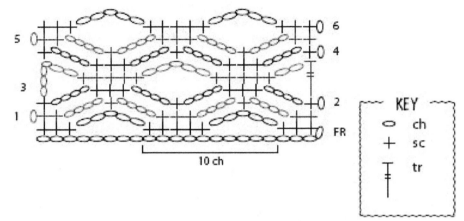

Crown Lace

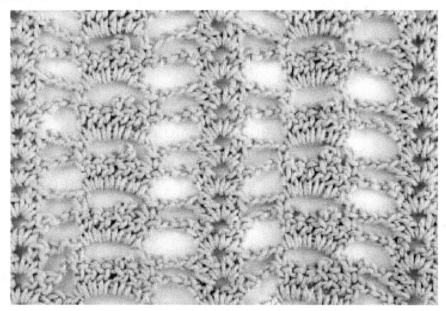

Make a foundation chain of a multiple of 16 ch plus an extra 9 ch.

Foundation Row 1 dc into 6th ch from hook, (1 dc, 2 ch, 2 dc) all into same ch, * 3 ch, miss 4 ch, 1 sc into next ch, 6 ch, miss 5 ch, 1 sc into next ch, 3 ch, miss 4 ch, (2 dc, 2 ch, 2 dc) all into next ch; rep from * to last 3 ch, miss 2 ch, 1 dc into last ch.

Row 1 3 ch (counts as 1 dc), (2 dc, 2 ch, 2 dc) all into 2 ch sp of cluster below, * 3 ch, (3 dc, 3 ch, sl st into 3rd ch from hook, 3 dc) all into 6 ch sp, 3 ch, (2 dc, 2 ch, 2 dc) all into 2 ch sp of cluster below; rep from * to end, 1 dc into top of tch.

Row 2 3 ch (counts as 1 dc), (2 dc, 2 ch, 2 dc) all into 2 ch sp of cluster below, * 3 ch, 1 sc into first dc, 6 ch, 1 sc into last dc, 3 ch, (2 dc, 2 ch, 2 dc) all into 2 ch sp of cluster below; rep from * to end, 1 dc into 3rd of 3 ch.

Rep rows 1 and 2.

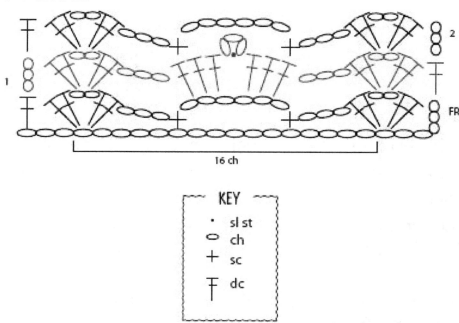

KEY
- • sl st
- ○ ch
- + sc
- ⊤ dc

Treble Fans

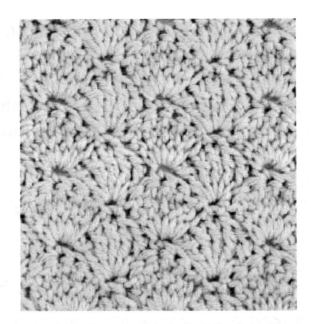

Make a foundation chain of a multiple of 6 ch plus an extra 2 ch.

Foundation Row 1 sc into 2nd ch from hook, * miss 2 ch, 5 tr into next ch, miss 2 ch, 1 sc into next ch; rep from * to end.

Row 1 4 ch (counts as 1 tr), 2 tr into first sc, * miss 2 tr, 1 sc into next tr, miss 2 tr, 5 tr into next sc; rep from * to end, ending with 3 tr into last sc.

Row 2 1 ch, 1 sc into first tr, * miss 2 tr, 5 tr into next sc, miss 2 tr, 1 sc into next tr; rep from * end.

Rep rows 1 and 2.

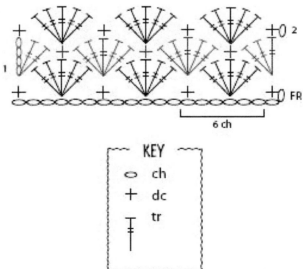

Double Crochet Fans

Make a foundation chain of a multiple of 8 ch plus an extra 2 ch.

Foundation Row 1 sc into 2nd ch from hook, * miss 3 ch, 7 dc into next ch, miss 3 ch, 1 sc into next ch; rep from * to end.

Row 1 3 ch (counts as 1 dc), 3 dc into first sc, * miss 3 dc, 1 sc into next dc, miss 3 dc, 7 dc into next sc; rep from * to end, ending with 4 dc into last sc.

Row 2 1 ch, 1 sc into first dc, * miss 3 dc, 7 dc into next sc, miss 3 dc, 1 sc into next dc; rep from * end.

Rep rows 1 and 2.

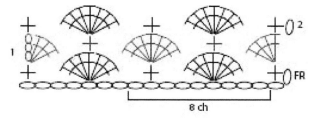

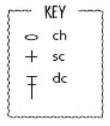

Hexagonal Eye

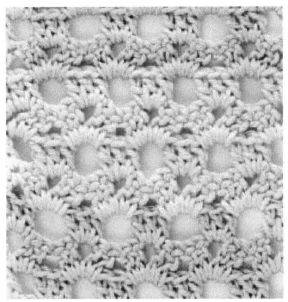

Make a foundation chain of a multiple of 5 ch.

Foundation Row 1 dc into 4th ch from hook, 1 dc into next ch, * 2 ch, miss 2 ch, 1 dc into each of next 3 ch; rep from * to end.

Row 1 3 ch (counts as 1 dc), (2 dc, 2 ch, 2 dc) all into each 2 ch sp to end, 1 dc into 3rd of 3 ch.

Row 2 5 ch (counts as 1 dc and 2 ch), 3 dc into first 2 ch sp, * 2 ch, 3 dc into next 2 ch sp; rep from * to end, 2 ch, 1 dc into 3rd of 3 ch.

Row 3 5 ch (counts as 1 dc and 2 ch), 2 dc into first 2 ch sp, (2 dc, 2 ch, 2 dc) all into each 2 ch sp to end, (2 dc, 2 ch, 1 dc) all into last 5 ch sp.

Row 4 3 ch (counts as 1 dc), 2 dc into first 2 ch sp, * 2 ch, 3 dc into next 2 ch sp; rep from * to end, 3 dc into last 5 ch sp.

Rep rows 1 to 4.

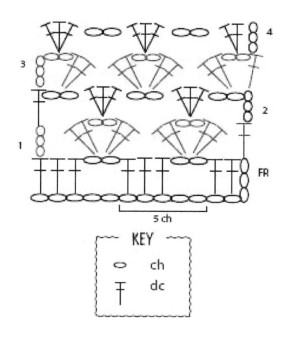

Spreading Fans

Make a foundation chain of a multiple of 12 ch plus an extra 7 ch.

Foundation Row 1 dc into 7th ch from hook, * 3 ch, miss 3 ch, 1 sc into each of next 5 ch, 3 ch, miss 3 ch, (1 dc, 3 ch, 1 dc) all into next ch; rep from * to end.

Row 1 4 ch (counts as 1 tr), 4 tr into first 3 ch sp, * 1 ch, miss 3 ch sp and 1 sc, 1 sc into each of next 3 sc, 1 ch, miss 1 sc and 3 ch sp, 9 tr into next 3 ch sp; rep from * to end, ending with 5 tr into first part of 6 ch sp.

Row 2 1 ch, 1 sc into each of first 3 tr, * 3 ch, miss 2 tr and 1 ch and 1 sc, (1 dc, 3 ch, 1 dc) all into next sc, 3 ch, miss 1 sc and 1 ch and 2 tr, 1 sc into each of next 5 tr; rep from * to end, ending with 1 sc into each of last 2 tr and 4th of 4 ch.

Row 3 1 ch, 1 sc into each of first 2 sc, * 1 ch, miss 1 sc and 3 ch sp, 9 tr into next 3 ch sp, 1 ch, miss 3 ch sp and 1 sc, 1 sc into each of next 3 sc; rep from * to end, ending with 1 sc into each of last 2 sc.

Row 4 6 ch (counts as 1 dc and 3 ch), 1 dc into first sc, * 3 ch, miss 1 sc and 1 ch and 2 tr, 1 sc into each of next 5 tr, 3 ch, miss 2 tr and 1 ch and 1 sc, (1 dc, 3 ch, 1 dc) all into next sc; rep from * to end.

Rep rows 1 to 4.

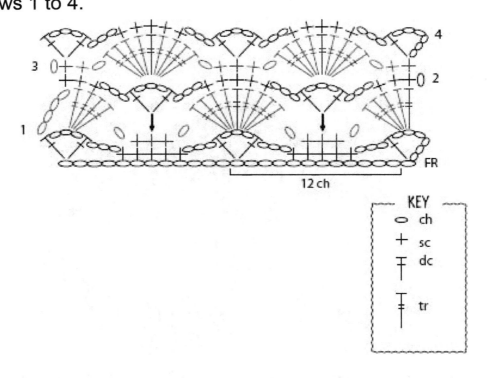

Shell and Net

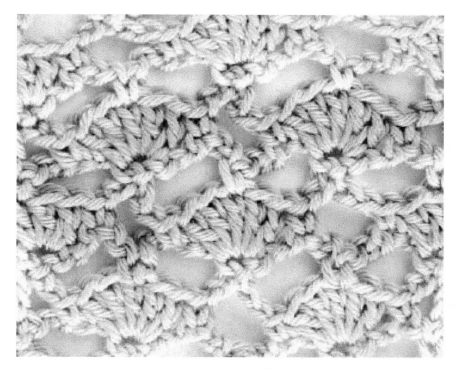

Make a foundation chain of a multiple of 12 ch plus an extra 5 ch.

Foundation Row 1 sc into 8th ch from hook, * miss 2 ch, 5 dc into next ch, miss 2 ch, 1 sc into next ch, 5 ch, miss 5 ch, 1 sc into next ch; rep from * to last 9 ch, miss 2 ch, 5 dc into next ch, miss 2 ch, 1 sc into next ch, 2 ch, 1 dc into last ch.

Row 1 1 ch, 1 sc into first dc, * 5 ch, 1 sc into 3rd dc of 5 dc fan, 5 ch, 1 sc into 3rd ch of next 5 ch sp below; rep from * to end, ending with 1 sc into 3rd ch of 7 ch loop.

Row 2 3 ch (counts as 1 dc), 2 dc into first sc, * 1 sc into 3rd ch of next 5 ch sp, 5 ch, 1 sc into 3rd ch of next 5 ch sp, 5 dc into next sc; rep from * to end, ending with 3 dc into last sc.

Row 3 1 ch, 1 sc into first dc, * 5 ch, 1 sc into 3rd ch of next 5 ch sp, 5 ch, 1 sc into 3rd dc of 5 dc fan; rep from * to end, ending with 1 sc into 3rd of 3 ch.

Row 4 5 ch (counts as 1 dc and 2 ch), * 1 sc into 3rd ch of next 5 ch sp, 5 dc into next sc, 1 sc into 3rd ch of next 5 ch sp, 5 ch; rep from * to end, ending with 2 ch, 1 dc into last sc.

Rep rows 1 to 4.

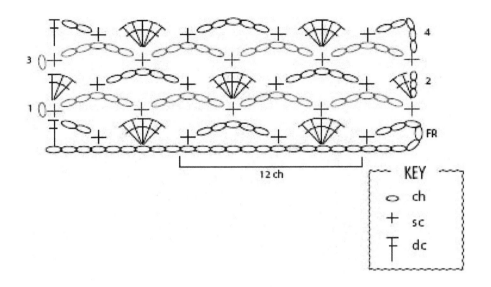

Seed Stitch

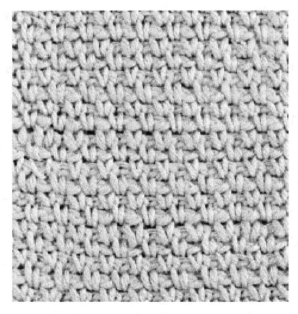

Make a foundation chain of a multiple of 2 ch.

Foundation Row 1 sc into 2nd ch from hook, * 1 ch, miss 1 ch, 1 sc into next ch; rep from * to end.

Row 1 1 ch, 1 sc into first sc, 1 sc into next ch sp, * 1 ch, 1 sc into next ch sp; rep from * to last sc, 1 sc into last sc.

Row 2 1 ch, 1 sc into first sc, * 1 ch,

1 sc into next ch sp; rep from * to last 2 sc, 1 ch, 1 sc into last sc.

Rep rows 1 and 2.

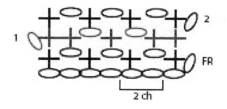

KEY
○ ch
+ sc

Fan Stripes

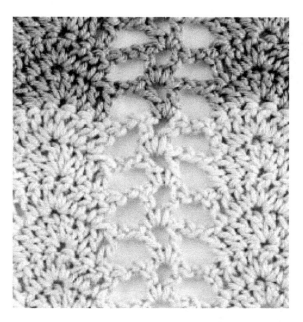

Make a foundation chain of a multiple of 16 ch plus an extra 5 ch.

Foundation Row 1 dc into 5th ch from hook, * 2 ch, miss 5 ch, 1 dc into each of next 2 ch, 4 dc into next ch, 1 dc into each of next 2 ch, 2 ch, miss 5 ch, (1 dc, 2 ch, 1 dc) all into next ch; rep from * to end, ending with (1 dc, 1 ch, 1 dc) all into last ch.

Row 1 4 ch (counts as 1 dc and 1 ch), 1 dc into same place, * 2 ch, miss 1 dc, 1 dc into each of next 2 dc, 4 dc into next dc, 1 dc into each of next

2 dc, 2 ch, miss 2 dc and 2 ch and 1 dc, (1 dc, 2 ch, 1 dc) all into next 2 ch sp; rep from * to end, ending with

(1 dc, 1 ch, 1 dc) all into last ch sp.
Rep row 1.

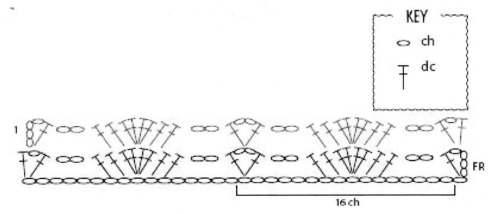

Star Lattice

Make a foundation chain of a multiple of 8 ch plus an extra 2 ch.

Foundation Row 1 sc into 2nd ch from hook, * 2 ch, miss 3 ch, (1 dc, 5 ch, 1 dc) all into next ch, 2 ch,

miss 3 ch, 1 sc into next ch; rep

from * to end.

Row 1 6 ch (counts as 1 tr and 2 ch), 1 dc into first sc, * 2 ch, 1 sc into next 5 ch sp, 2 ch, (1 dc, 5 ch, 1 dc) all into next sc; rep from * to end, ending with (1 dc, 2 ch, 1 tr) all into last sc.

Row 2 1 ch, 1 sc into first tr, * 2 ch, (1 dc, 5 ch, 1 dc) all into next sc, 2 ch, 1 sc into next 5 ch sp; rep from * to end, working last sc into 4th of 6 ch.

Rep rows 1 and 2.

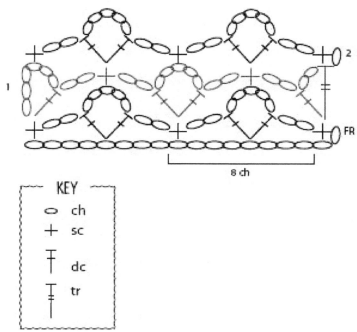

Large Clam Shell

Make a foundation chain of a multiple of 15 ch plus an extra 5 ch.

Foundation Row 2 dc into 5th ch from hook, * miss 6 ch, 4 tr into each of next 2 ch, miss 6 ch, (2 dc, 2 ch, 2 dc) all into next ch; rep from * to end, ending with (2 dc, 1 ch,

1 dc) all into last ch.

Row 1 4 ch (counts as 1 dc and 1 ch), 2 dc into same place, * 1 dc into each of next 8 tr, (2 dc, 2 ch, 2 dc) all into next 2 ch sp; rep from * to end, ending with (2 dc,

1 ch, 1 dc) all into last ch sp.

Row 2 4 ch, 3 tr into first ch sp, * miss 4 dc, (2 dc, 2 ch,

2 dc) all into next dc, 8 tr into next 2 ch sp; rep from

* to end, ending with 4 tr into last ch sp.

Row 3 3 ch (counts as 1 dc), 1 dc into each of next 3 tr, * (2 dc, 2 ch, 2 dc) all into next 2 ch sp, 1 dc into each of next 8 tr; rep from * to end, ending with 1 dc into each of last 3 tr and 4th of 4 ch.

Row 4 4 ch (counts as 1 dc and 1 ch), 2 dc into same place, * 8 tr into next 2 ch sp, miss 4 dc, (2 dc, 2 ch, 2 dc) all into next dc; rep from * to end, ending with (2 dc,

1 ch, 1 dc) all into 3rd of 3 ch.

Rep rows 1 to 4.

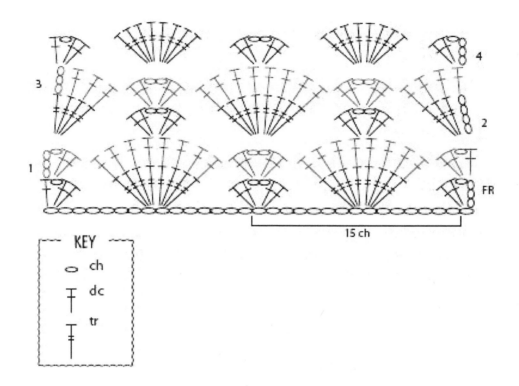

Clam Fabric

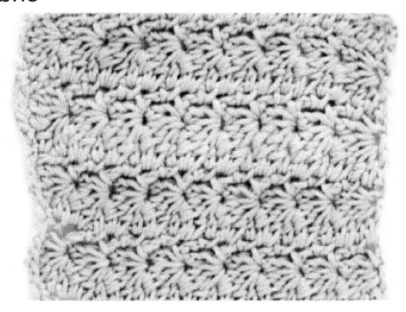

Make a foundation chain of a multiple of 4 ch plus an extra 3 ch.

Foundation Row Dc6tog working first leg into 3rd ch from hook and next 5 legs into next 5 ch, * 3 ch, dc6tog working first 3 legs around last dc of previous cluster, fourth leg into last ch used by previous cluster, and fifth and sixth legs worked into next 2 ch; rep from * to last ch, 1 dc into last ch.

Row 1 3 ch (counts as 1 sc and 1 ch), 1 sc into next 3 ch sp, * 1 ch, 1 sc into next 3 ch sp; rep from * to end, 1 sc into same ch as first leg of cluster below.

Row 2 5 ch, dc6tog working first leg into 3rd ch from hook, second and third legs into next 2 ch, fourth and fifth legs into next 2 sc and sixth leg into next ch, * 3 ch, dc6tog working first 3 legs around last dc of previous cluster, fourth leg into last ch used by previous cluster, fifth leg into next sc, and sixth leg into next ch; rep from * to end, ending with 1 dc into 2nd of 3 ch.

Rep rows 1 and 2.

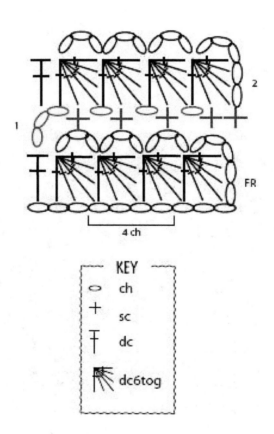

Simple Filet Crochet

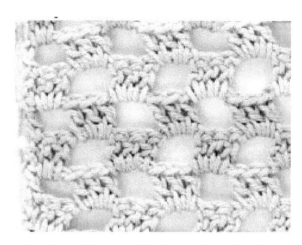

Make a foundation chain of a multiple of 6 ch plus an extra 1 ch.

Foundation Row 1 dc into 8th ch from hook, 1 dc into each of next 2 ch, * 3 ch, miss 3 ch, 1 dc into each of next 3 ch; rep from * to last 3 ch, 2 ch, miss 2 ch, 1 dc into last ch.

Row 1 3 ch (counts as 1 dc), 2 dc into next 2 ch sp, * 3 ch, miss 3 dc, 3 dc into next 3 ch sp; rep from * to last end, working last 3 dc nto last ch sp.

Row 2 5 ch (counts as 1 dc and 2 ch), 3 dc into next 3 ch sp, * 3 ch, miss 3 dc, 3 dc into next 3 ch sp; rep from * to last 2 dc and 3 ch, 2 ch, 1 dc into 3rd of 3 ch.

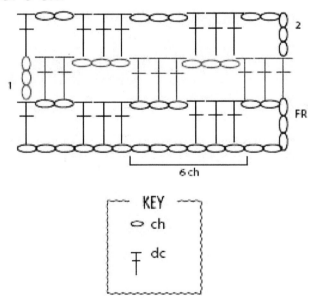

Small Filet Crochet

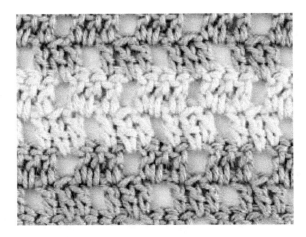

Make a foundation chain of a multiple of 4 ch plus an extra 2 ch.

Foundation Row 1 dc into 6th ch from hook, 1 dc into each of next 2 ch, * 1 ch, miss 1 ch, 1 dc into each of next 3 ch; rep from * to last 2 ch, 1 ch, miss 1 ch, 1 dc into last ch.

Row 1 3 ch (counts as 1 dc), 1 dc into next ch, 1 dc into next dc, * 1 ch, miss 1 dc, 1 dc into next dc, 1 dc into next ch sp, 1 dc into next dc; rep from * to end, working last 2 dc into last ch sp.

Row 2 4 ch (counts as 1 dc and 1 ch), miss 1 dc, * 1 dc into next dc, 1 dc into next ch sp, 1 dc into next dc, 1 ch, miss 1 dc; rep from * to end, 1 dc into 3rd of 3 ch.

Rep rows 1 and 2.

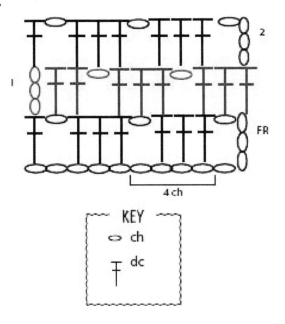

Buttonhole Fabric

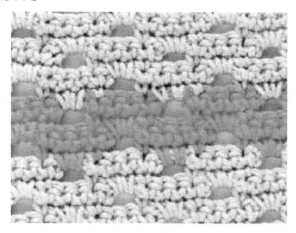

Make a foundation chain of a multiple of 6 ch plus an extra 5 ch.

Foundation Row 1 sc into 2nd ch from hook, 1 sc into each of next 3 ch, * 3 ch, miss 2 ch, 1 sc into each of next 4 ch; rep from * to end.

Row 1 1 ch, 1 sc into each of first 4 sc, * 3 ch, 1 sc into each of next 4 sc; rep from * to end.

Row 2 1 ch, 1 sc into first sc, * 3 ch, miss 2 sc, 1 sc into next sc, 2 sc into next sp working over two ch loops from previous two rows, 1 sc into next sc; rep from * to last 3 sc, 3 ch, miss 2 sc, 1 sc into last sc.

Row 3 1 ch, 1 sc into first sc, 3 ch, * 1 sc into each of next 4 sc, 3 ch; rep from * to last sc, 1 sc into last sc.

Row 4 1 ch, 1 sc into first sc, * 2 sc into next sp working over two ch loops from previous two rows, 1 sc into next sc, 3 ch, 1 sc into next sc; rep from * to last ch sp, 2 sc into next sp working over two ch loops from previous two rows, 1 sc into last sc.

Rep rows 1 to 4.

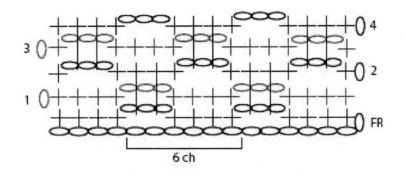

Square Stripes

Make a foundation chain of a multiple of 6 ch plus an extra 2 ch.

Foundation Row 1 sc into 2nd ch from hook, 1 sc into each ch to end.

Row 1 1 ch, 1 sc into each sc to end.

Row 2 3 ch (counts as 1 dc), * miss 2 sc, 1 dc into next sc, 3 ch, 3 dc worked around stem of dc just made, miss 2 sc, 1 dc into next sc;

rep from * to end.

Row 3 5 ch (counts as 1 dc and 2 ch), * 1 sc into 3rd of 3 ch at beg of square, 2 ch, 1 dc into dc between squares, 2 ch; rep from * to end, working last dc into 3rd of 3 ch.

Row 4 1 ch, 1 sc into first dc, * 2 sc into next 2 ch sp, 1 sc into next sc, 2 sc into next 2 ch sp, 1 sc into next dc; rep from * to end, ending with last sc into 3rd of 5 ch.

Rep rows 1 to 4.

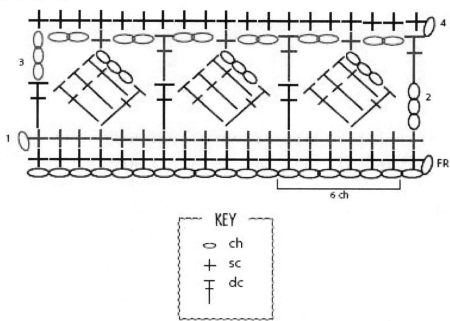

Squares

Make a foundation chain of a multiple of 6 ch plus an extra 4 ch.

Foundation Row 1 dc into 7th ch from hook, 3 ch, 3 dc worked around stem of dc just made, miss 2 ch, 1 dc into next ch, * miss 2 ch, 1 dc into next ch, 3 ch, 3 dc worked around stem of dc just made, miss 2 ch, 1 dc into next ch; rep from * to end.

Row 1 5 ch (counts as 1 dc and 2 ch), * 1 sc into 3rd of

3 ch at beg of square, 2 ch, 1 dc into dc between squares, 2 ch; rep from * to end, working last dc into 3rd of 3 ch.

Row 2 3 ch (counts as 1 dc), 1 dc into next sc, 3 ch, 3 dc worked around stem of dc just made, miss 2 ch, 1 dc into next dc, * miss 2 ch, 1 dc into next sc, 3 ch, 3 dc worked around stem of dc just made, miss 2 ch, 1 dc into next dc; rep from * to end.

Rep rows 1 and 2.

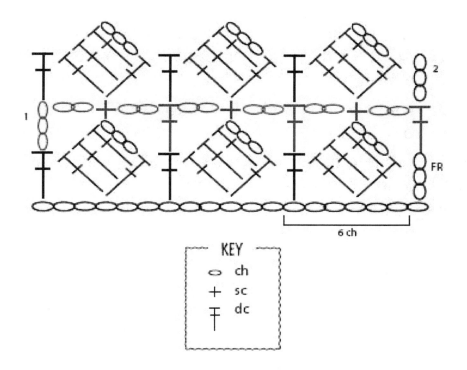

Sawtooth Fabric

Make a foundation chain of a multiple of 4 ch plus an extra 2 ch.

Foundation Row 1 sc into 2nd ch from hook, * 4 ch, 1 tr into next foundation ch, 1 dc into next ch, 1 hdc into next ch, 1 sc into next ch; rep from * to end.

Row 1 5 ch (counts as 1 dc and 2 ch), miss 1 hdc and 1 dc and 1 tr, 1 sc into 4th of 4 ch at beg of first triangle, * 3 ch, 1 sc into 4th of 4 ch at beg of next triangle; rep from * to last triangle, 2 ch, 1 dc into first sc.

Row 2 1 ch, 1 sc into first dc, 4 ch, (1 dc, 1 hdc) all into 2 ch sp, 1 sc into next sc, * 4 ch, (1 tr, 1 dc, 1 hdc) all into next 3 ch sp, 1 sc into next sc; rep from * to last ch sp, (1 hdc, 1 dc, 1 tr) all into last ch sp.

Row 3 1 ch, 1 sc into tr, * 3 ch, 1 sc into 4th of 4 ch at beg of next triangle; rep from * to end.

Row 4 1 ch, 1 sc into first sc, * 4 ch, (1 tr, 1 dc, 1 hdc) all into next 3 ch sp, 1 sc into next sc; rep from * to end.

Rep rows 1 to 4.

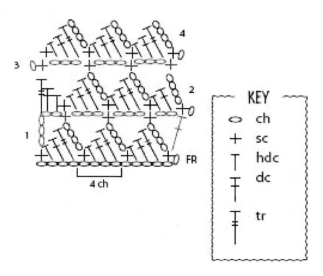

Fleurette

Make a foundation chain of a multiple of 10 ch plus an extra 6 ch.

Foundation Row (1 sc, 4 ch, 1 sc) all into 6th ch from hook, * 3 ch, miss 4 ch, (1 dc, 1 ch, 1 dc) all into next ch, 3 ch, miss 4 ch, (1 sc, 4 ch, 1 sc, 4 ch, 1 sc, 4 ch, 1 sc) all into next ch; rep from * to end, ending with (1 sc, 4 ch, 1 sc, 2 ch, 1 dc) into last ch.

Row 1 4 ch (counts as 1 dc and 1 ch), 1 dc into same place, * 3 ch, (1 sc, 4 ch, 1 sc, 4 ch, 1 sc, 4 ch, 1 sc) all into 1 ch sp at centre of next V st, 3 ch, (1 dc, 1 ch, 1 dc) all into centre 4 ch loop of next cluster; rep from * to end, working last V st into last 4 ch sp.

Row 2 5 ch, (1 sc, 4 ch, 1 sc) all into first 1 ch sp, * 3 ch, (1 dc, 1 ch, 1 dc) all into centre 4 ch loop of next cluster, 3 ch, (1 sc, 4 ch, 1 sc, 4 ch, 1 sc, 4 ch, 1 sc) all into 1 ch sp at centre of next V st; rep from * to end, ending with (1 sc, 4 ch, 1 sc, 2 ch, 1 dc) into last ch sp.

Rep rows 1 and 2.

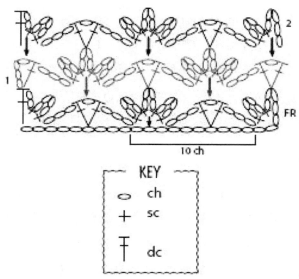

Bar and Arch

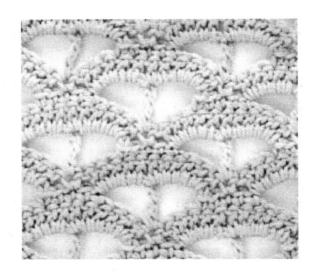

Make a foundation chain of a multiple of 14 ch plus an extra 4 ch.

Foundation Row 1 tr into 4th ch from hook, * 4 ch, miss 4 ch, 1 sc into each of next 5 ch, 4 ch, miss 4 ch, 1 tr into next ch; rep from * to end.

Row 1 3 ch (counts as 1 dc), * 5 dc into next 4 ch sp, miss 2 sc, 1 sc into next sc, miss 2 sc, 5 dc into next 4 ch sp, 1 dc into next tr; rep from * to end.

Row 2 1 ch, 1 sc into first dc, 1 sc into each of next 2 dc, * 4 ch, 1 tr into next sc, 4 ch, miss 3 dc, 1 sc into each of next 5 dc; rep from * to end, ending with 1 sc into each of last 2 sc, 1 sc into 3rd of 3 ch.

Row 3 1 ch, 1 sc into first sc, * 5 dc into next 4 ch sp, 1 dc into tr, 5 dc into next 4 ch sp, miss 2 sc, 1 sc into next sc; rep from * to end.

Row 4 4 ch, 1 tr into first sc, * 4 ch, miss 3 dc, 1 sc into each of next 5 dc, 4 ch, 1 tr into next sc; rep from * to end.

Rep rows 1 to 4.

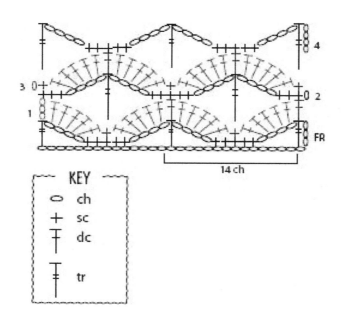

Small Bar and Arch

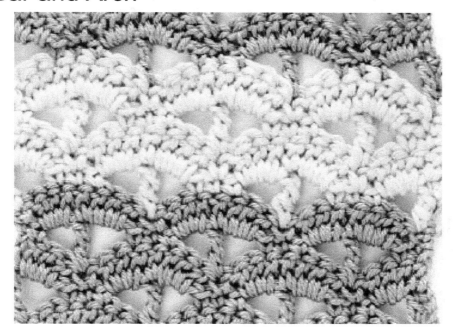

Make a foundation chain of a multiple of 8 ch plus an extra 4 ch.

Foundation Row 1 tr into 4th ch from hook, * 2 ch, miss 2 ch, 1 sc into each of next 3 ch, 2 ch, miss 2 ch, 1 tr into next ch; rep from * to end.

Row 1 3 ch (counts as 1 dc), * 3 dc into next 2 ch sp, miss 1 sc, 1 sc into next sc, miss 1 sc, 3 dc into next 2 ch sp, 1 dc into next tr; rep from * to end.

Row 2 1 ch, 1 sc into first dc, 1 sc into next dc, * 2 ch, 1 tr into next sc, 2 ch, miss 2 dc, 1 sc into each of next 3 dc; rep from * to end, ending with 1 sc into last 1 dc, 1 sc into 3rd of 3 ch.

Row 3 1 ch, 1 sc into first sc, * 3 dc into next 2 ch sp, 1 dc into tr, 3 dc into next 2 ch sp, miss 1 sc, 1 sc into next sc; rep from * to end.

Row 4 4 ch, 1 tr into first sc, * 2 ch, miss 2 dc, 1 sc into each of next 3 dc, 2 ch, 1 tr into next sc; rep from * to end.

Rep rows 1 to 4.

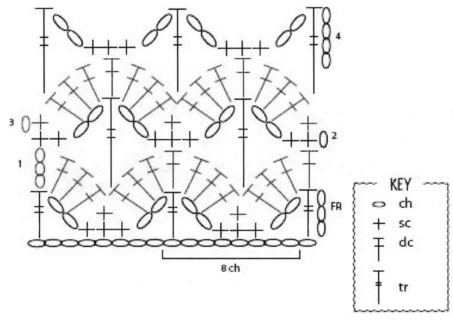

Small Spreading Fans

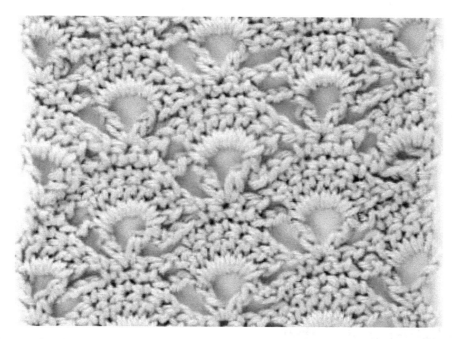

Make a foundation chain of a multiple of 12 ch plus an extra 7 ch.

Foundation Row 1 dc into 7th ch from hook, * 3 ch, miss 3 ch, 1 sc into each of next 5 ch, 3 ch, miss 3 ch, (1 dc, 3 ch, 1 dc) all into next ch; rep from * to end.

Row 1 3 ch (counts as 1 dc), 3 dc into first 3 ch sp, * 1 ch, miss 3 ch sp and 1 sc, 1 sc into each of next 3 sc, 1 ch, miss 1 sc and 3 ch, 7 dc into next 3 ch sp; rep from * to end, ending with 4 dc into first part of 6 ch sp.

Row 2 1 ch, 1 sc into each of first 3 dc, * 3 ch, miss 1 dc and 1 ch and 1 sc, (1 dc, 3 ch, 1 dc) all into next sc, 3 ch, miss 1 sc and 1 ch and 1 dc, 1 sc into each of next 5 dc; rep from * to end, ending with 1 sc into each of last 2 dc and 3rd of 3 ch.

Row 3 1 ch, 1 sc into each of first 2 sc, * 1 ch, miss 1 sc and 3 ch sp, 7 dc into next 3 ch sp, 1 ch, miss 3 ch sp and 1 sc, 1 sc into each of next 3 sc; rep from * to end, ending with 1 sc into each of last 2 sc.

Row 4 6 ch (counts as 1 dc and 3 ch), 1 dc into first sc, * 3 ch, miss 1 sc and 1 ch and 1 dc, 1 sc into each of next 5 dc, 3 ch, miss 1 dc and 1 ch and 1 sc, (1 dc, 3 ch, 1 dc) all into next sc; rep from * to end.

Rep rows 1 to 4.

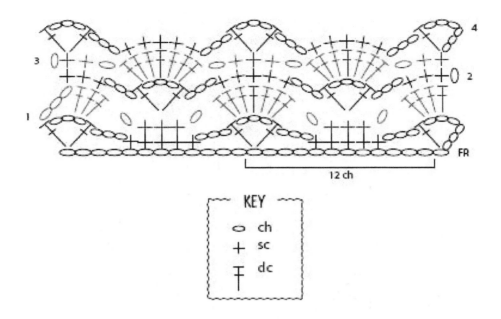

Four-Petal Floral Fabric

Make a foundation chain of a multiple of 11 ch plus an extra 4 ch.

Foundation Row 1 dc into 4th ch from hook, * miss 4 ch, (dc3tog, 5 ch, dc3tog) all into next ch, 5 ch, (dc3tog, 5 ch, dc3tog) all into next ch, miss 4 ch, 1 dc into next ch; rep from * to end.

Row 1 4 ch (counts as 1 dc and 1 ch), * 1 sc into next 5 ch sp, 3 ch; rep from * to end, 1 ch, 1 dc into last dc.

Row 2 3 ch (counts as 1 dc), miss 1 ch, * miss 1 sc and 3 ch sp, (dc3tog, 5 ch, dc3tog, 5 ch, dc3tog, 5 ch, dc3tog) all into next sc, miss 3 ch sp and 1 sc, 1 dc into next 3 ch sp; rep from * to end, ending with last dc into 3rd of 4 ch.

Rep rows 1 and 2.

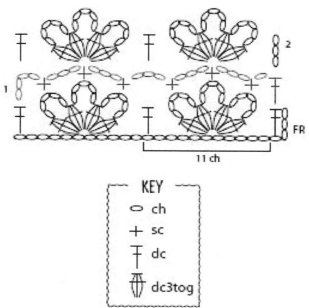

Filet Stripes

Make a foundation chain of a multiple of 2 ch plus an extra 6 ch.

Foundation Row 1 dc into 6th ch from hook, * 1 ch, miss 1 ch, 1 dc into next ch; rep from * to end.

Row 1 3 ch (counts as 1 dc), miss 1 ch sp, work 2 dc into each dc to end, miss 1 ch of tch, 2 dc into next ch.

Row 2 4 ch (counts as 1 dc and 1 ch), miss 1 dc, 1 dc into next dc, * 1 ch, miss 1 dc, 1 dc into next dc; rep from * to end, ending with 1 dc into 3rd of 3 ch.

Rep rows 1 and 2.

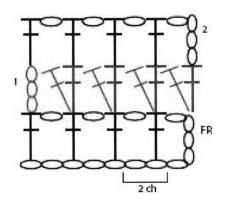

Open Boxes

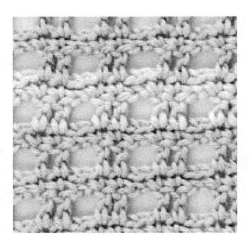

Make a foundation chain of a multiple of 4 ch plus an extra 3 ch.

Foundation Row 1 sc into 2nd ch from hook, 1 sc into next ch, * 2 ch, miss 2 ch, 1 sc into each of next 2 ch; rep from * to end.

Row 1 3 ch (counts as 1 dc), 1 dc into next sc, * 2 ch, 1 dc into each of next 2 sc; rep from * to end.

Row 2 1 ch, 1 sc into each of first 2 dc, * 2 ch, 1 sc into each of next 2 dc; rep from * to end, ending with last sc into 3rd of 3 ch.

Rep rows 1 and 2.

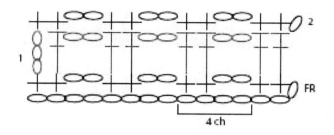

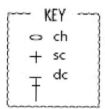

Large Squares

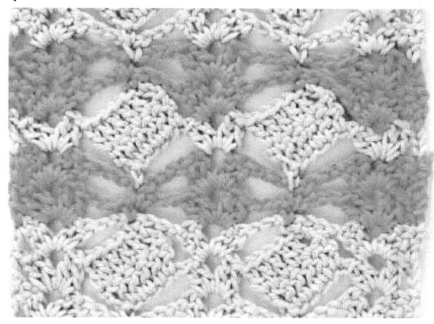

Make a foundation chain of a multiple of 10 ch plus an extra 9 ch.

Foundation Row (2 dc, 2 ch, 2 dc) all into 6th ch from hook, * 3 ch, miss 4 ch, 1 sc into next ch, 3 ch, miss 4 ch, (2 dc, 2 ch, 2 dc) all into next ch; rep from * to last 3 ch, miss 2 ch, 1 dc into last ch.

Row 1 3 ch (counts as 1 dc), (2 dc, 2 ch, 2 dc) all into 2 ch sp of V st, * 3 ch, 1 sc into next sc, 3 ch, (2 dc, 2 ch, 2 dc) all into 2 ch sp at centre of V st; rep from * to end, 1 dc into top of tch.

Row 2 3 ch (counts as 1 dc), (2 dc, 2 ch, 2 dc) all into 2 ch sp of V st, * 5 ch, 1 sc into next sc, turn work, 3 ch, 1 dc into each ch of 5 ch loop, turn work, 3 ch (counts as 1 dc), 1 dc into each of next 4 dc, 1 dc into 3rd of 3 ch, (2 dc, 2 ch, 2 dc) all into 2 ch sp of next V st; rep from * to end, 1 dc into 3rd of 3 ch.

Row 3 3 ch (counts as 1 dc), (2 dc, 2 ch, 2 dc) all into 2 ch sp of next V st, * 3 ch, 1 sc into 3rd of 3 ch at corner of square, 3 ch, (2 dc, 2 ch, 2 dc) all into 2 ch sp of next V st; rep from * to end, 1 dc into 3rd of 3 ch.

Row 4 As row 1.

Rep rows 1 to 4.

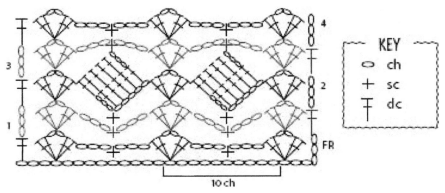

Seafoam Fabric

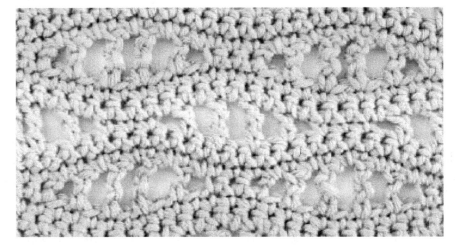

Make a foundation chain of a multiple of 12 ch plus an extra 2 ch.

Foundation Row 1 sc into 2nd ch from hook, 1 sc into each ch to end.

Row 1 1 ch, 1 sc into each of first 2 sc, * 1 ch, miss 1 sc, 1 hdc into next sc, (1 ch, miss 1 sc, 1 dc into next sc) twice, 1 ch, miss 1 sc, 1 hdc into next sc, 1 ch, miss 1 sc, 1 sc into each of next 3 sc; rep from * to end, ending with 2 sc.

Row 2 1 ch, 1 sc into each of first 2 sc, * 1 sc into next ch sp, 1 sc into hdc, (1 sc into next ch sp, 1 sc into next dc) twice, 1 sc into next ch sp, 1 sc into next hdc, 1 sc into next ch sp, 1 sc into each of next 3 sc; rep from * to end, ending with 2 sc.

Row 3 1 ch, 1 sc into each sc to end.

Row 4 3 ch (counts as 1 dc), * 1 dc into next sc, 1 ch, miss 1 sc, 1 hdc into next sc, 1 ch, miss 1 sc, 1 sc into each of next 3 sc, 1 ch, miss 1 sc, 1 hdc into next sc, 1 ch, miss 1 sc, 1 dc into next sc, 1 ch, miss 1 sc; rep from * to end, replacing last ch with 1 dc into last sc.

Row 5 1 ch, 1 sc into each of first 2 dc, * 1 sc into next ch sp, 1 sc into hdc, 1 sc into next ch sp, 1 sc into each of next 3 sc, 1 sc into next ch sp, 1 sc into hdc, (1 sc into next ch sp, 1 sc into dc) twice; rep from * to end, ending with 1 sc into 3rd of 3 ch.

Row 6 As row 3.

Rep rows 1 to 6.

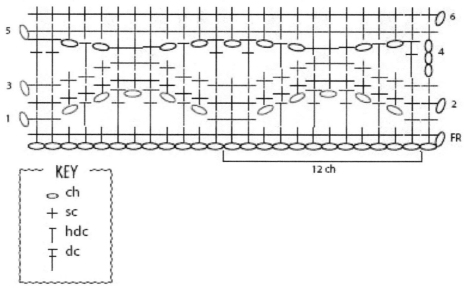

Simple Lace

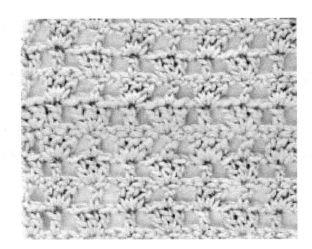

Make a foundation chain of a multiple of 6 ch plus an extra 4 ch.

Foundation Row 1 dc into 4th ch from hook, * 1 ch, miss 2 ch, 1 dc into next ch, 1 ch, miss 2 ch, 3 dc into next ch; rep from * to end, ending with 2 dc into last ch.

Row 1 4 ch (counts as 1 dc and 1 ch), miss 1 dc and 1 ch sp, 3 dc into next dc, * 1 ch, miss 1 ch sp and 1 dc, 1 dc into centre dc of fan, 1 ch, miss 1 dc and 1 ch sp, 3 dc into next dc; rep from * to end, 1 ch, 1 dc into 3rd of 3 ch.

Row 2 3 ch (counts as 1 dc), 1 dc into same place, * 1 ch, miss 1 ch sp and 1 dc, 1 dc into centre dc of fan, 1 ch, miss 1 dc and 1 ch sp, 3 dc into next dc; rep from * to end, ending with 2 dc into 3rd of 4 ch.

Rep rows 1 and 2.

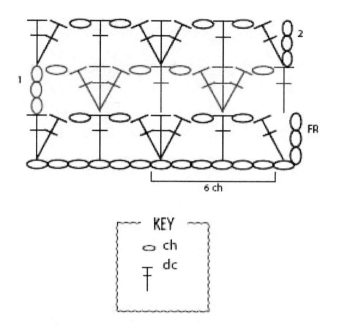

Vertical Fan Stripes

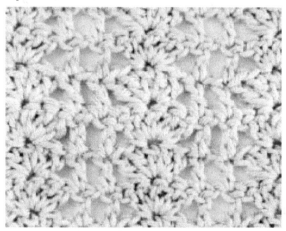

Make a foundation chain of a multiple of 8 ch plus an extra 6 ch.

Foundation Row 1 dc into 6th ch from hook, * miss 2 ch, 5 dc into next ch, miss 2 ch, 1 dc into next ch, 1 ch, miss 1 ch, 1 dc into next ch; rep from * to end.

Row 1 4 ch (counts as 1 dc and 1 ch), miss 1 ch sp, 1 dc into next dc, * miss first 2 dc of fan, 5 dc into next dc, miss last 2 dc of fan, 1 dc into next dc, 1 ch, 1 dc into next dc; rep from * to end, ending with last dc into top of tch.

Rep row 1.

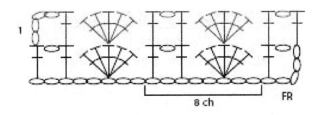

Bias Fans

Make a foundation chain of a multiple of 4 ch plus an extra 3 ch.

Foundation Row 1 sc into 2nd ch from hook, * 3 ch, 4 dc into side of sc just made, miss 3 foundation ch, 1 sc into next foundation ch; rep from * to last ch, 3 ch, 1 tr into last ch.

Row 1 1 ch, 1 sc into tr, 3 ch, 4 dc into side of sc just made, * 1 sc into 3rd of 3 ch at top of next triangle, 3 ch, 4 dc into side of sc just made; rep from * to last triangle, 1 sc into 3rd of 3 ch at top of last triangle, 3 ch, 1 tr into last sc in row below.

Rep row 1.

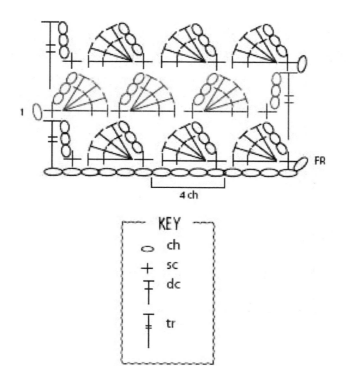

Building Blocks

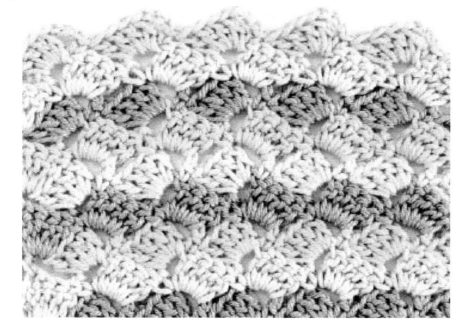

Make a foundation chain of a multiple of 4 ch plus an extra 3 ch.

Foundation Row 1 sc into 2nd ch from hook, * 3 ch, 4 dc into side of sc just made, miss 3 foundation ch, 1 sc into next foundation ch; rep from * to last ch, 3 ch, 1 tr into last ch.

Row 1 1 ch, 1 sc into tr, 3 ch, 4 dc into 3 ch sp below, * 1 sc into 3rd of 3 ch at top of next block, 3 ch, 4 dc into 3 ch sp down side of block below; rep from * to last block, 1 sc into 3rd of 3 ch at top of block, 3 ch, 1 tr into last sc in row below.

Rep row 1.

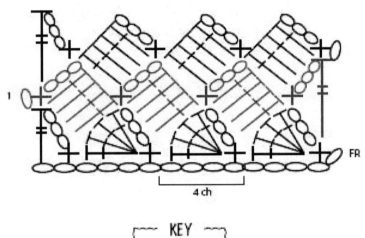

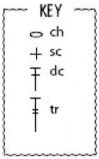

Small Fan Lace

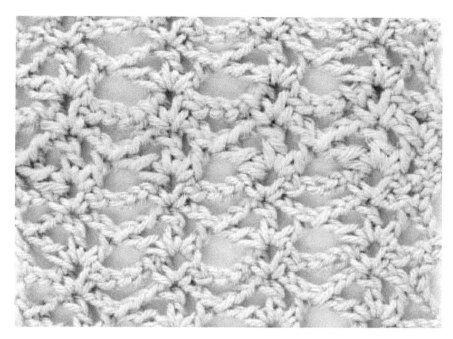

Make a foundation chain of a multiple of 5 ch plus an extra 4 ch.

Foundation Row (1 dc, 2 ch, 1 dc, 2 ch, 1 dc) all worked into 6th ch from hook, * miss 4 ch, (1 dc, 2 ch, 1 dc, 2 ch, 1 dc) all worked into next ch; rep from * to last 3 ch, miss 2 ch, 1 dc into last ch.

Row 1 5 ch (counts as 1 dc and 2 ch), miss 1 dc and 2 ch sp, (1 sc, 3 ch, 1 sc) all worked into centre dc of fan, * 4 ch, miss 1 dc and 2 ch sp of next fan, (1 sc, 3 ch, 1 sc) all worked into centre dc of fan; rep from * to end, 2 ch, 1 dc into top of tch.

Row 2 3 ch (counts as 1 dc), (1 dc, 2 ch, 1 dc, 2 ch, 1 dc) all worked into each 3 ch loop to end, 1 dc into 3rd of 5 ch.

Rep rows 1 and 2.

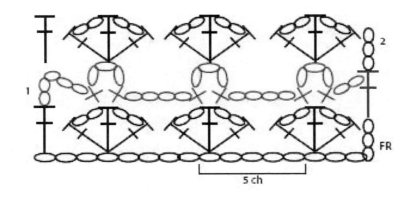

Small Shell Stripes

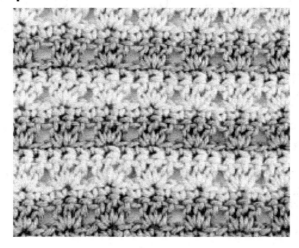

Make a foundation chain of a multiple of 3 ch plus an extra 2 ch.

Foundation Row 1 sc into 2nd ch from hook, 1 sc into each ch to end.

Row 1 3 ch (counts as 1 dc), 1 dc into same place, * miss 2 sc, 3 dc into next sc; rep from * to end, ending with 2 dc into last sc.

Row 2 1 ch, 1 sc into each dc to end, 1 sc into 3rd of 3 ch.

Rep rows 1 and 2.

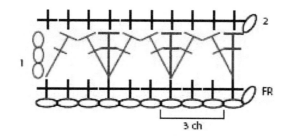

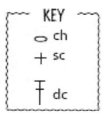

Buttonhole Stripes

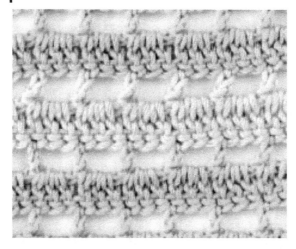

Make a foundation chain of a multiple of 3 ch.

Foundation Row 1 dc into 4th ch from hook, 1 dc into each ch to end.

Row 1 5 ch (counts as 1 dc and

2 ch), miss 2 dc, 1 dc into next dc,

* 2 ch, miss 2 dc, 1 dc into next dc; rep from * to end, ending with last dc into 3rd of 3 ch.

Row 2 3 ch (counts as 1 dc), * 2 dc into next 2 ch sp, 1 dc into next dc; rep from * to end, ending with last dc into 3rd of 3 ch.

Rep rows 1 and 2.

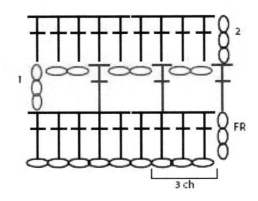

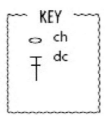

Granny Fabric

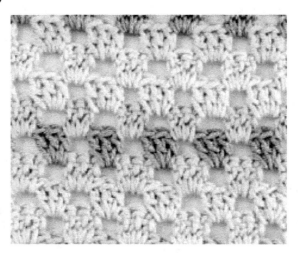

Make a foundation chain of a multiple of 4 ch.

Foundation Row 1 dc into 4th ch from hook, * 1 ch, miss 3 ch, 3 dc into next ch; rep from * to end, ending with 2 dc into last ch.

Row 1 3 ch (counts as 1 dc), 3 dc into next ch sp, * 1 ch, 3 dc into next ch sp; rep from * to end, 1 dc into 3rd of 3 ch.

Row 2 3 ch (counts as 1 dc), 1 dc into same place, * 1 ch, 3 dc into next ch sp; rep from * to end, 1 ch, 2 dc into 3rd of 3 ch.

Rep rows 1 and 2.

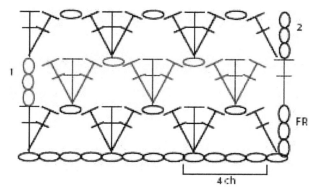

Large Shell and Net

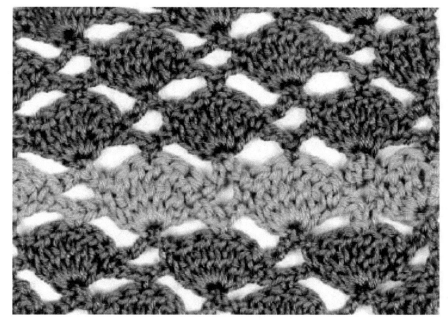

Make a foundation chain of a multiple of 12 ch plus an extra 5 ch.

Foundation Row 1 sc into 8th ch from hook, * miss 2 ch, 5 tr into next ch, miss 2 ch, 1 sc into next ch, 5 ch, miss 5 ch, 1 sc into next ch; rep from * to last 9 ch, miss 2 ch, 5 tr into next ch, miss 2 ch, 1 sc into next ch, 2 ch, 1 tr into last ch.

Row 1 1 ch, 1 sc into first tr, * 5 ch, 1 sc into 3rd tr of 5 tr fan, 5 ch, 1 sc into 3rd ch of next 5 ch sp below; rep from * to end, ending with 1 sc into 3rd ch of 7 ch loop.

Row 2 4 ch (counts as 1 tr), 2 tr into first sc, * 1 sc into 3rd ch of next 5 ch sp, 5 ch, 1 sc into 3rd ch of next 5 ch sp, 5 tr into next sc; rep from * to end, ending with 3 tr into last sc.

Row 3 1 ch, 1 sc into first tr, * 5 ch, 1 sc into 3rd ch of next 5 ch sp, 5 ch, 1 sc into 3rd tr of 5 tr fan; rep from * to end, ending with 1 sc into 4th of 4 ch.

Row 4 6 ch (counts as 1 tr and 2 ch), * 1 sc into 3rd ch of next 5 ch sp, 5 tr into next sc, 1 sc into 3rd ch of next 5 ch sp, 5 ch; rep from * to end, ending with 2 ch, 1 tr into last sc.

Rep rows 1 to 4.

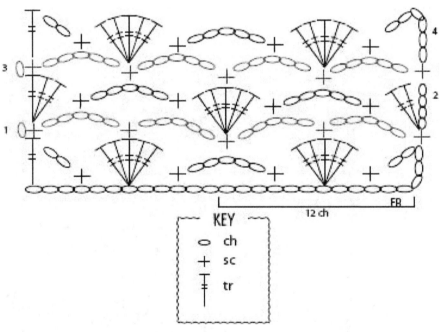

KEY
o ch
+ sc
┼ tr

Zig Zag Stripes

Make a foundation chain of a multiple of 6 ch plus an extra 2 ch.

Foundation Row 1 sc into 2nd ch from hook, 1 sc into each ch to end.

Row 1 1 ch, 1 sc into first sc, * 1 hdc into next sc, 1 dc into next sc, 3 tr into next sc, 1 dc into next sc, 1 hdc into next sc, 1 sc into next sc; rep from * to end.

Row 2 1 ch, sc2tog worked into first sc and hdc, * 1 sc into each of next dc and tr, 3 sc into next tr, 1 sc into each of next tr and dc, sc3tog worked over next hdc and sc and hdc; rep from * to end, ending with sc2tog worked over last hdc and sc.

Row 3 1 ch, sc2tog worked over first sc2tog and next sc, * 1 sc into each of next 2 sc, 3 sc into next sc, 1 sc into each of next 2 sc, sc3tog worked over next sc and sc3tog and sc; rep from * to end, ending with sc2tog worked over last sc and sc2tog.

Row 4 4 ch, tr2tog worked over first sc2tog and next sc, * 1 dc into next sc, 1 hdc into next sc, 1 sc into next sc, 1 hdc into next sc, 1 dc into next sc, tr3tog worked over next sc and sc3tog and sc; rep from * to end, ending with tr2tog worked over last sc and sc2tog.

Rep rows 1 to 4.

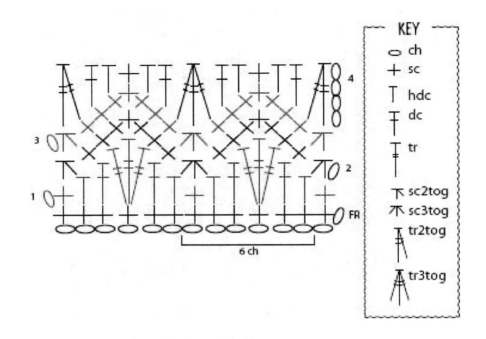

Fan and V Stitch

Make a foundation chain of a multiple of 8 ch plus an extra 7 ch.

Foundation Row (2 dc, 1 ch, 2 dc) all into 5th ch from hook, * miss 3 ch, (1 dc, 1 ch, 1 dc) all into next ch, miss 3 ch, (2 dc, 1 ch, 2 dc) all into next ch; rep from * to last 2 ch, miss 1 ch, 1 dc into last ch.

Row 1 3 ch (counts as 1 dc), * (2 dc, 1 ch, 2 dc) all into ch sp of fan, (1 dc, 1 ch, 1 dc) all into ch sp of V st; rep from * to last fan, (2 dc, 1 ch, 2 dc) all into ch sp of fan, 1 dc into top of tch.

Rep row 1.

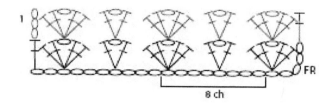

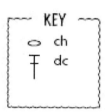

Zig Zag Fabric

Make a foundation chain of a multiple of 11 ch plus an extra 3 ch.

Foundation Row 3 dc into 4th ch from hook, * miss 1 ch, 1 dc into next ch, miss 1 ch, dc2tog working first leg into next ch then miss 1 ch then work second leg into next ch, miss 1 ch, 1 dc into next ch, miss 1 ch, 4 dc into each of next 2 ch; rep from * to end, omitting last set of 4 dc.

Row 1 3 ch (counts as 1 dc), 3 dc into same place, * miss 1 dc, 1 dc into next dc, miss 1 dc, dc2tog working first leg into next dc then miss dc2tog then work second leg into next dc, miss 1 dc, 1 dc into next dc, miss 1 dc, 4 dc into each of next 2 dc; rep from * to end, omitting last set of 4 dc.

Rep row 1.

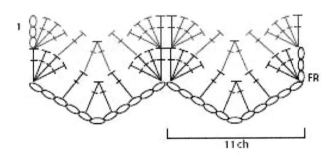

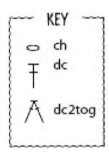

V Stitch Lattice

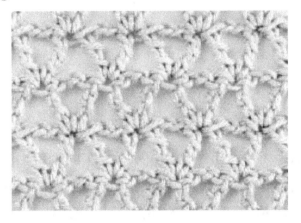

Make a foundation chain of a multiple of 3 ch plus an extra 2 ch.

Foundation Row (tr, 2 ch, tr) all into 6th ch from hook, * miss 2 ch, (tr, 2 ch, tr) all into next ch; rep from * to last 2 ch, miss 1 ch, 1 tr into last ch.

Row 1 6 ch (counts as 1 tr and 2 ch), tr into same place, * miss 1 tr and 2 ch, (tr, 2 ch, tr) all into next tr; rep from * to last V st, miss last V st, (tr, 2 ch, tr) all into top of tch.

Row 2 4 ch (counts as 1 tr), miss 2 ch, (tr, 2 ch, tr) all into next tr, miss 1 tr and 2 ch, * (1 tr, 2 ch, 1 tr) all into next tr, miss 1 tr and 2 ch; rep from * to end, 1 tr into 4th of 6 ch.

Rep rows 1 and 2.

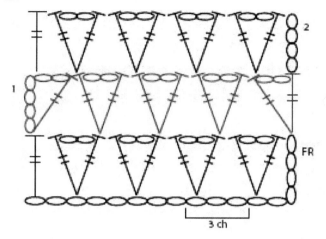

Large Lace Fan

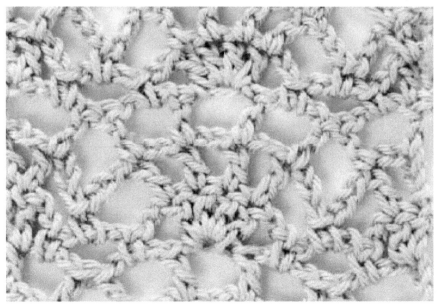

Make a foundation chain of a multiple of 9 ch plus an extra 4 ch.

Foundation Row 2 dc into 4th ch from hook, * 2 ch, miss 2 ch, 1 sc into next ch, 3 ch, miss 2 ch, 1 sc into next ch, 2 ch, miss 2 ch, 4 dc into next ch; rep from * to end, ending with only 3 dc into last ch.

Row 1 4 ch (counts as 1 dc and 1 ch), 1 dc into next dc, 2 ch, 1 dc into next dc, 3 ch, 1 sc into 3 ch sp, 3 ch, * (1 dc into next dc, 2 ch) 3 times, 1 dc into next dc, 3 ch, 1 sc into next 3 ch sp, 3 ch; rep from * to last 2 dc and tch, 1 dc into next dc, 2 ch, 1 dc into next dc, 1 ch, 1 dc into 3rd of 3 ch.

Row 2 5 ch (counts as 1 dc and 2 ch), 1 dc into next dc, 3 ch, 1 dc into next dc, * (1 dc into next dc, 3 ch) 3 times, 1 dc into next dc; rep from * to last half fan, 1 dc into first dc of half fan, 3 ch, 1 dc into next dc, 2 ch, 1 dc into 3rd of 4 ch.

Row 3 3 ch (counts as 1 dc), 2 dc into same place, * 2 ch, 1 sc into next 3 ch sp, 3 ch, 1 sc into next 3 ch sp, 2 ch, 4 dc into 2nd ch of next 3 ch sp; rep from * to end, ending with only 2 dc into 4th of 5 ch, 1 dc into next ch.

Rep rows 1 to 3.

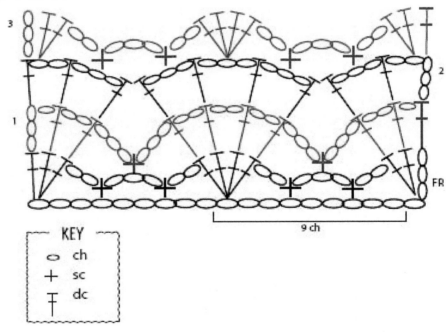

Fan Lattice

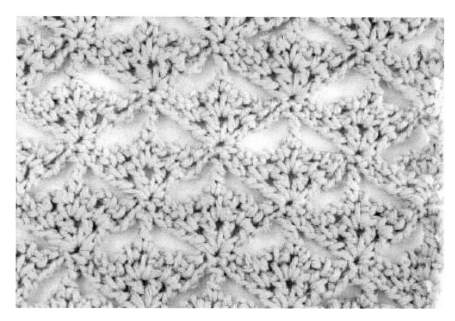

Make a foundation chain of a multiple of 10 ch plus an extra 5ch.

Foundation Row 1 tr into 5th ch from hook, * 3 ch, miss 4 ch, (1 dc, 1 ch, 1 dc, 1 ch, 1 dc, 1 ch, 1 dc) all into next ch, 3 ch, miss 4 ch, 1 tr into next ch; rep from * to end.

Row 1 1 ch, 1 sc into first tr, * 3 ch, 1 sc into first ch sp of next fan, 3 ch, (1 sc, 3 ch, 1 sc) all into next ch sp, 3 ch, 1 sc into last ch sp of fan, 3 ch, 1 sc into next tr; rep from * to end.

Row 2 4 ch (counts as 1 dc and 1 ch), (1 dc, 1 ch, 1 dc) all into first sc, * 3 ch, 1 tr into centre 3 ch loop of next fan, 3 ch, (1 dc, 1 ch, 1 dc, 1 ch, 1 dc, 1 ch, 1 dc) all into sc between fans; rep from * to end, ending with (1 dc, 1 ch, 1 dc, 1 ch, 1 dc) all into last sc.

Row 3 1 ch, (1 sc, 3 ch, 1 sc) all into first ch sp of fan, * 3 ch, 1 sc into last ch sp of fan, 3 ch, 1 sc into next tr, 3 ch, 1 sc into first ch cp of next fan, 3 ch, (1 sc, 3 ch, 1 sc) all into next ch sp; rep from * to end.

Row 4 4 ch, 1 tr into first 3 ch sp, * 3 ch, (1 dc, 1 ch, 1 dc, 1 ch, 1 dc, 1 ch, 1 dc) all into sc between fans, 3 ch, 1 tr into into centre 3 ch loop of next fan: rep from * to end, ending with last tr into last 3 ch sp.

Rep rows 1 to 4.

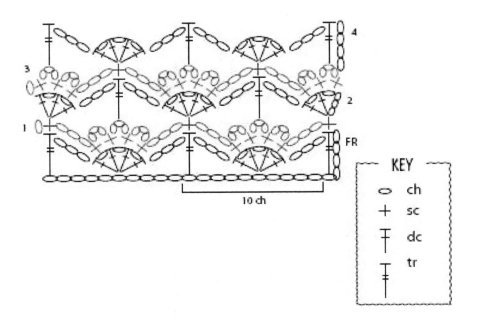

Clover Fan

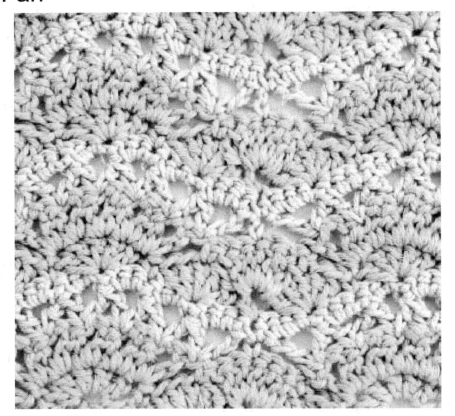

Make a foundation chain of a multiple of 18 ch plus an extra 2 ch.

Foundation Row 1 sc into 2nd ch from hook, * miss 2 ch, 5 dc into next ch, miss 2 ch, 1 sc into next ch; rep from * to end.

Row 1 3 ch (counts as 1 dc), 2 dc into sc at base of tch, * 1 sc into middle dc of fan, 1 ch, (1 dc, 2 ch) into first dc of next fan, dc2tog working first leg into same place as last dc and second leg into next dc (2 ch, dc2tog working first leg into same place as previous dc2tog and second leg into next dc) 3 times, 2 ch, 1 dc into same place as previous dc2tog, 1 ch, 1 sc into middle dc of next fan, 5 dc into sc between fans; rep from * to end, ending with 3 dc into last sc.

Row 2 1 ch, 1 sc into dc at base of tch, * miss 2 dc and 1 sc, 1 dc into next dc below, 2 ch, dc2tog working first leg into same place as last dc and second leg into top of next dc2tog below, (2 ch, dc2tog working first leg into same place as last dc2tog and second leg into top of next dc2tog) 4 times, 2 ch, 1 dc into same place as last leg of previous dc2tog, 1 sc into centre dc of fan; rep from * to end, ending with 1 sc into 3rd of 3 ch at beg of previous row.

Row 3 1 ch, 1 sc into first sc, * 1 sc into next dc, (2 sc into 2 ch sp, 1 sc into top of next dc2tog) 5 times, 2 sc into 2 ch sp, 1 sc into next dc, 1 sc into next sc; rep from * to end.

Row 4 1 ch, 1 sc into first sc, * miss 3 sc, 5 dc into next sc, miss 2 sc, 1 sc into next sc, miss 2 sc, 5 dc into next sc, miss 2 sc, 1 sc into next sc, miss 2 sc, 5 dc into next sc, miss 3 sc, 1 sc into next sc; rep from * to end.

Rep these 4 rows.

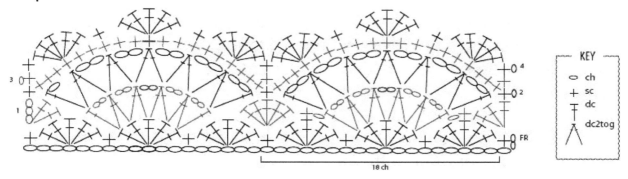

Old Shale

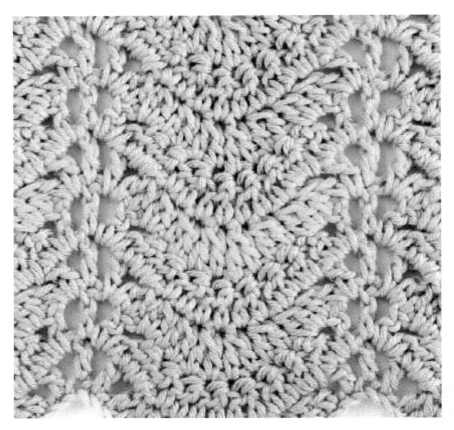

Make a foundation chain of a multiple of 19 ch plus an extra 2 ch.

Foundation Row 1 dc into 4th ch from hook, (dc2tog worked into next 2 ch) 3 times, * (2 ch, 1 dc into next ch) 3 times, 2 ch, (dc2tog worked into next 2 ch) 8 times; rep from * to end, ending with (dc2tog worked into next 2 ch) 4 times.

Row 1 3 ch (counts as 1 dc), miss first dc2tog, 1 dc into next dc2tog, dc2tog worked into next two dc2tog, * dc2tog worked into next 2 ch sp, dc2tog worked into next dc and next 2 ch sp, 2 ch, 1 dc into same 2 ch sp, 2 ch, 1 dc into next dc, 2 ch, 1 dc into next 2 ch sp, 2 ch, dc2tog worked into same 2 ch sp and next dc, dc2tog worked into next 2 ch sp, (dc2tog worked into next two dc2tog) 4 times; rep from * to end, ending with (dc2tog worked into next two dc2tog) twice.

Rep row 1.

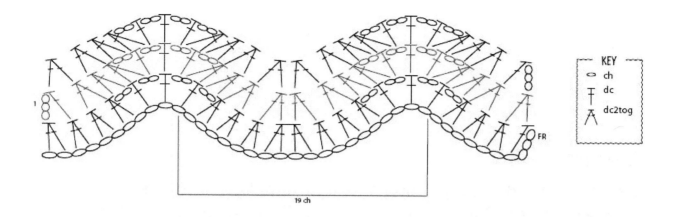

Motifs

Decorations

Several of the lacy motifs would make fabulous snowflake decorations for Christmas. These are Snowflakes worked in cream mercerized cotton. You can make different sizes by altering the size of the hook. The large one uses a G6 (4.00mm); the medium a D3 (3.00mm); the small one a B1 (2.00mm). Thread a ribbon through the centre picot at the top to finish.

Tote bag

Brighten up a bag by appliquéing several motifs to the front and back. We used the Frilly Circle motif, but you could work any of the motifs to co-ordinate with the fabric. Mercerized cotton worked with a

C2 (2.50mm) hook makes robust motifs to withstand daily use. Randomly sew the motifs onto the bag.

Necklace

This is made from Picot Hoops worked in mercerized cotton using a D3 (3.00mm) hook. They are linked together as they are worked. Link on the third row by working the picot as follows: 2 ch, insert hook through any picot on the previous motif, 3 ch. Repeat for the next picot so two picots are linked. Link another motif in the same way. To wear, work a crochet chain the required length on each side or tie on cotton waxed cord.

Skirt pocket

Add a decorative pocket to a plain skirt by working three hexagon motifs and joining together. These are Six-Petal Hexagons worked in two shades of denim cotton worsted (DK) using a G6 (4.00mm) hook. Sew or crochet them together. Sew the pocket onto your skirt, stitching around the edge but leaving the two top edges of each of the top motifs open.

Collar

Nine Simple Cluster Circles are worked in wool worsted (DK) and an E4 (3.50mm) hook. Each is joined to the previous one by linking the 5 ch loops together. Make one motif, make a second up to row 1. On row 2, work 2 ch of the 5 ch loop, put the hook into any 5 ch loop of the first motif and make 3 ch, work dc3tog into the next 2 ch sp and link to the next loop in the same way. Link another loop the same way so three loops are joined. Link the next motif so there are two empty loops along the top edge and four along the bottom. This curves the collar to fit round the neck.

Small Rounded Square

Make 4 ch and join with sl st to form a ring.

Rnd 1 5 ch (counts as 1 dc and 2 ch), (1 dc into ring, 2 ch) 7 times, sl st into 3rd of 5 ch at beg of rnd.

Rnd 2 Sl st into 2 ch sp, 4 ch (counts as 1 dc and 1 ch), (1 dc, 1 ch) 3 times all into same 2 ch sp, 1 sc into next 2 ch sp, * 1 ch, (1 dc, 1 ch) 4 times all into next 2 ch sp, 1 sc into next 2 ch sp; rep from * twice more, 1 ch, sl st into 3rd of 4 ch at beg of rnd.

Fasten off.

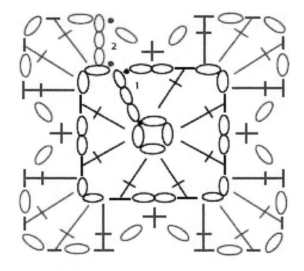

```
   KEY
 •  sl st
 ⌒  ch
 +  sc
 ┬  dc
```

Small Sunflower Square

Make 4 ch and join with sl st to form a ring.

Rnd 1 1 ch, 8 sc into ring, sl st to first dc at beg of rnd.

Rnd 2 3 ch, dc2tog into same place (counts as dc3tog), (3ch, dc3tog into next sc) 7 times, 3 ch, sl st into top of first dc3tog.

Rnd 3 Sl st into 3 ch sp, 1 ch, 1 sc into 3 ch sp, 3 ch, * (1 dc, 3 ch, 1 dc) all into next 3 ch sp, 3 ch, 1 sc into next 3 ch sp, 3 ch; rep from * twice more, (1 dc, 3 ch, 1 dc) all into next 3 ch sp, 3 ch, sl st into top of first sc.

Fasten off.

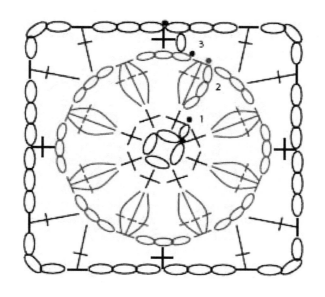

KEY
- sl st
- ch
- sc
- dc

Small Eight-Spoke Square

Make 4 ch and join with sl st to form a ring.

Rnd 1 6 ch (counts as 1 dc and 3 ch), 1 dc into ring, (1 ch, 1 dc, 3 ch, 1 dc into ring) 3 times, 1 ch, sl st into 3rd of 3 ch at beg of rnd.

Rnd 2 Sl st into 3 ch sp, 3 ch (counts as 1 dc), (2 dc, 3 ch, 3 dc) all into 3 ch sp, * 1 ch, dc3tog into 1 ch sp, 1 ch, (3 dc, 3 ch, 3 dc) into next 3 ch sp; rep from * twice more, 1 ch, dc3tog into 1 ch sp, 1 ch, sl st into 3rd of 3 ch at beg of rnd.

Fasten off.

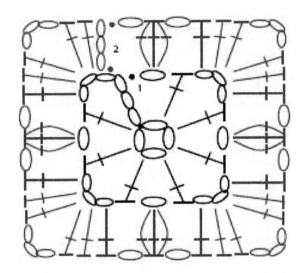

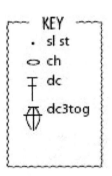

KEY
- sl st
- ch
- dc
- dc3tog

Moorish Square

Make 6 ch and join with sl st to form a ring.

Rnd 1 1 ch, 2 sc into ring, (7 ch, 4 sc into ring) 3 times, 7 ch, 2 sc into ring, sl st into top of first dc.

Rnd 2 * (1 sc, 8 dc, 1 sc) all into 7 ch loop, sl st into 2nd of 4 sc between loops: rep from * 3 times more.

Rnd 3 Sl st into 1 sc and 2 dc of loop, 1 ch, 1 sc into same place, 2 ch, miss 1 dc, (1 dc, 3 ch, 1 dc) all into next dc, 2 ch, miss 1 dc, 1 sc into next dc, 5 ch, * miss 1 sc and 1 dc of next loop, 1 sc into second dc, 2 ch, miss 1 dc, (1 dc, 3 ch, 1 dc) all into next dc, 2 ch, miss 1 dc, 1 sc into next dc, 5 ch; rep from * twice more, sl st into top of first sc.

Rnd 4 1 ch, * 1 sc into sc, 2 sc into 2 ch sp, 1 sc into dc, (2 sc, 3 ch, 2 sc) into 3 ch sp at corner, 1 sc into dc, 2 sc in 2 ch sp, 1 sc into sc, 5 sc into 5 ch sp; rep from * 3 times more, sl st into top of first sc.

Rnd 5 1 ch, * 1 sc into each of next 6 sc, (2 sc, 3 ch, 2 sc) into 3 ch sp at corner, 1 sc into each of next 11 sc; rep from * 3 times more, sl st into top of first sc.

Fasten off.

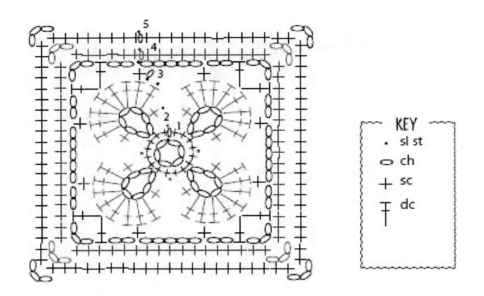

Large Sunflower Square

Make 6 ch and join with sl st to form a ring.

Rnd 1 1 ch, 12 sc into ring, sl st into top of first sc.

Rnd 2 5 ch (counts as 1 dc and 2 ch), (1 dc into next sc, 2 ch) 11 times, sl st into 3rd of 5 ch at beg of rnd.

Rnd 3 Sl st into first 2 ch sp, 3 ch, dc4tog into 2 ch sp (counts as dc5tog), (3 ch, dc5tog into next 2 ch sp) 11 times, 3 ch, sl st into top of first dc5tog.

Rnd 4 Sl st into first 3 ch sp, 1 ch, 1 sc into same space, 3 ch, (3 dc, 2 ch, 3 tr) all into next 3 ch sp, * (3 ch, 1 sc into next 3 ch sp) twice, 3 ch, (3 dc, 2 ch, 3 dc) all into next 3 ch sp; rep from * twice more, 3 ch, 1 sc into next 3 ch sp, 3 ch, sl st into sc at beg of rnd.

Rnd 5 Sl st into first 3 ch sp, 3 ch (counts as 1 dc), 2 dc into same sp, 1 ch, (3 dc, 2 ch, 3 dc) all into 2 ch sp at corner, * (1 ch, 3 dc into next 3 ch sp) 3 times, 1 ch, (3 dc, 2 ch, 3 dc) all into 2 ch sp at corner; rep from * twice more, (1 ch, 3 dc into next 3 ch sp) twice, 1 ch, sl st into 3rd of 3 ch at beg of rnd.

Fasten off.

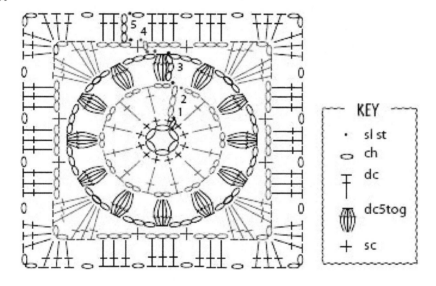

Granny Square

Make 4 ch and join with sl st to form a ring.

Rnd 1 5 ch (counts as 1 dc and 2 ch), (3 dc into ring, 2 ch) 3 times, 2 dc into ring, sl st into 3rd of 3 ch, sl st into first 2 ch sp.

Rnd 2 5 ch (counts as 1 dc and 2 ch), 3 dc into same 2 ch sp, * 1 ch, (3 dc, 2 ch, 3 dc) all into next 2 ch sp; rep from * twice more, 1 ch, 2 dc into same 2 ch sp as 5 ch at beg of rnd, sl st into 3rd of 5 ch, sl st into first 2 ch sp.

Rnd 3 5 ch (counts as 1 dc and 2 ch), 3 dc into same 2 ch sp, * 1 ch, 3 dc into next ch sp, 1 ch, (3 dc, 2 ch, 3 dc) all into corner 2 ch sp; rep from * twice more, 1 ch, 3 dc into next ch sp, 1 ch, 2 dc into same 2 ch sp as 5 ch at beg of rnd, sl st into 3rd of 5 ch.

Fasten off.

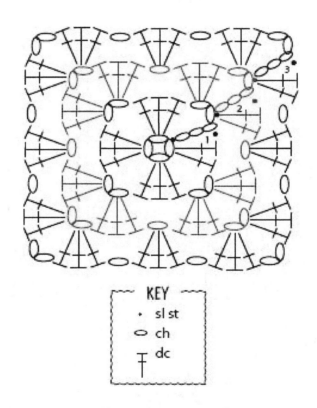

KEY
- sl st
- ch
- dc

Cluster Hexagon

Make 6 ch and join with sl st to form a ring.

Rnd 1 3 ch, dc2tog into ring (counts as dc3tog), 4 ch, (dc3tog into ring, 4 ch) 5 times, sl st into top of first dc3tog, sl st into first 4 ch sp.

Rnd 2 (3 ch, dc2tog, 3 ch, dc3tog) all into first 4 ch sp, (3 ch, dc3tog, 3 ch, dc3tog) all into each of next five 4 ch sps, 3 ch, sl st to top of first dc2tog, sl st into first 3 ch sp.

Rnd 3 (3 ch, dc2tog, 3 ch, dc3tog) all into first 3 ch sp, * 1 ch, dc3tog into next 3 ch sp, 1 ch, (dc3tog, 3 ch, dc3tog) all into next 3 ch sp; rep from * 4 times more, 1 ch, dc3tog into last 3 ch sp, 1 ch, sl st into top of first dc2tog.

Fasten off.

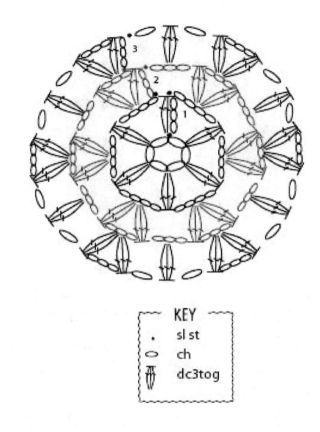

KEY
. sl st
○ ch
⫟ dc3tog

Cartwheel Hexagon

Make 6 ch and join with sl st to form a ring.

Rnd 1 6 ch (counts as 1 tr and 2 ch), (1 tr into ring, 2 ch) 11 times, sl st into 4th of 6 ch.

Rnd 2 3 ch (counts as 1 dc), (1 dc, 2 ch, 2 dc) all into first 2 ch sp, * 3 dc into next 2 ch sp, (2 dc, 2 ch, 2 dc) all into next 2 ch sp; rep from * 4 times more, 3 dc into last 2 ch sp, sl st into 3rd of 3 ch.

Fasten off.

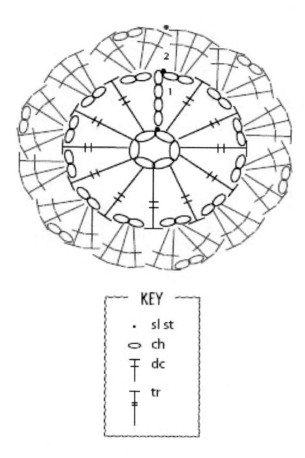

KEY
- • sl st
- ◯ ch
- ┬ dc
- ╪ tr

Hexagon and Circle

Make 6 ch and join with sl st to form a ring.

Rnd 1 3 ch, 17 dc into ring, sl st into 3rd of 3 ch.

Rnd 2 1 ch, 1 sc into same place, 5 ch, miss 2 dc, (1 sc into next tr, 5 ch, miss 2 dc) 5 times, sl st into first sc.

Rnd 3 3 ch (counts as 1 dc), (3 dc, 3 ch, 3 dc) all into each of next five 5 ch sps, (3 dc, 3 ch, 2 dc) all into last 5 ch sp, sl st to 3rd of 3 ch.

Fasten off.

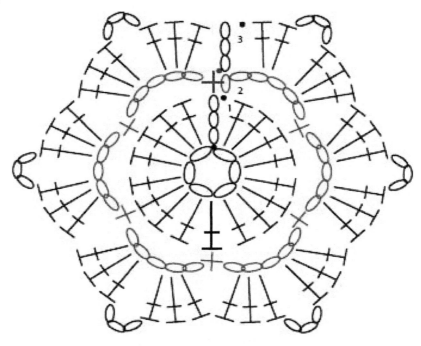

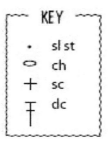

KEY
- • sl st
- ◯ ch
- + sc
- ⊤ dc

Small Open Hexagon

Make 4 ch and join with sl st to form a ring.

Rnd 1 6 ch (counts as 1 dc and 3 ch), (1 dc into ring, 3 ch) 5 times, sl st into 3rd of 6 ch.

Rnd 2 3 ch (counts as 1 dc), 4 dc into 3 ch sp, 2 ch, (5 dc into next 3 ch sp, 2 ch) 5 times, sl st into 3rd of 3 ch.

Fasten off.

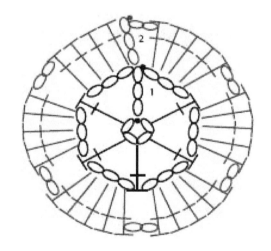

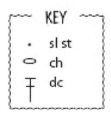

Solid Hexagon

Make 5 ch and join with sl st to form a ring.

Rnd 1 3 ch (counts as 1 dc), 11 dc into ring, sl st into 3rd of 3 ch.

Rnd 2 3 ch (counts as 1 dc), 1 dc into same place, 2 dc into next dc, 1 ch, (2 dc into each of next 2 dc, 1 ch) 5 times, sl st into 3rd of 3 ch.

Rnd 3 3 ch (counts as 1 dc), 1 dc into same place, 1 dc into each of next 2 dc, 2 dc into next dc, 2 ch, (2 dc into next dc, 1 dc into each of next 2 dc, 2 dc into next dc, 2 ch) 5 times, sl st into 3rd of 3 ch.

Fasten off.

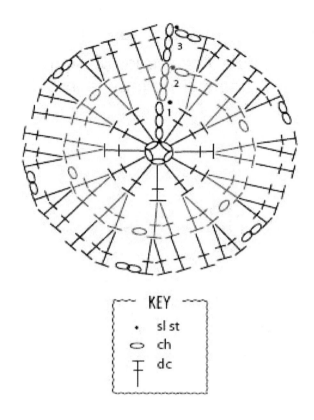

Popcorn Hexagon

Special abbreviation: Popcorn

Work 5 tr into same place, remove hook from last loop, insert into top of first tr and then through last loop again, yoh, pull a loop through 2 loops on hook.

Make 6 ch and join with sl st to form a ring.

Rnd 1 3 ch (counts as 1 dc), 17 dc into ring, sl st into 3rd of 3 ch.

Rnd 2 3 ch, popcorn into same place, (2 dc into each of next 2 dc, popcorn into next dc) 5 times, 2 dc into each of last 2 dc, sl st to top of first popcorn.

Fasten off.

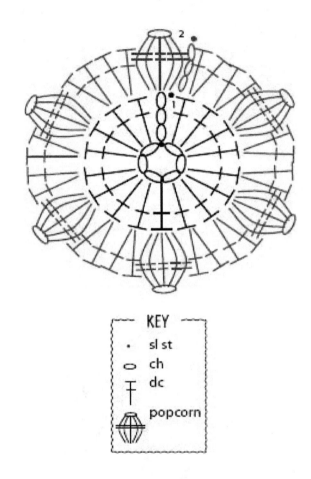

KEY
- sl st
- ch
- dc
- popcorn

Picot Hexagon

Make 6 ch and join with sl st to form a ring.

Rnd 1 1 ch (counts as 1 sc), 17 sc into ring, sl st into first sc.

Rnd 2 9 ch (counts as 1 dc and 6 ch), (1 dc into each of next 3 sc, 6 ch) 5 times, 1 dc into each of last 2 sc, sl st into 3rd of 9 ch.

Rnd 3 7 ch (counts as 1 dc and 4 ch), (1 dc into next dc, 2 dc into next dc, 1 dc into next dc, 4 ch) 5 times, 1 dc into next dc, 2 dc into last dc, sl st into 3rd of 7 ch.

Rnd 4 1 ch, 1 sc into same place, (3 ch, 1 sc worked into the two loops of previous two rnds, 3 ch, 1 sc into each of next 4 dc) 5 times, 3 ch, 1 sc worked into the two loops of previous two rnds, 3 ch, 1 sc into each of last 3 dc, sl st into first sc.

Fasten off.

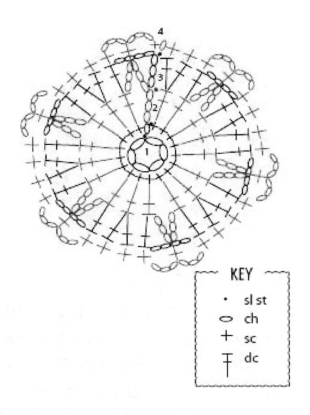

KEY
- • sl st
- ○ ch
- + sc
- ┼ dc

Fan Hexagon

Make 6 ch and join with sl st to form a ring.

Rnd 1 3 ch (counts as 1 dc), 2 dc into ring, 1 ch, (3 dc into ring, 1 ch) 5 times, sl st into 3rd of 3 ch.

Rnd 2 6 ch (counts as 1 dc and 3 ch), miss 2 dc, (3 dc into next ch sp, 3 ch) 5 times, miss 3 dc, 2 dc into last ch sp, sl st into 3rd of 6 ch.

Rnd 3 3 ch (counts as 1 dc), 1 dc into same place, 5 ch, (2 dc into next dc, 1 dc into next dc, 2 dc into next dc, 5 ch) 5 times, 2 dc into next dc, 1 dc into last dc, sl st into 3rd of 3 ch.

Fasten off.

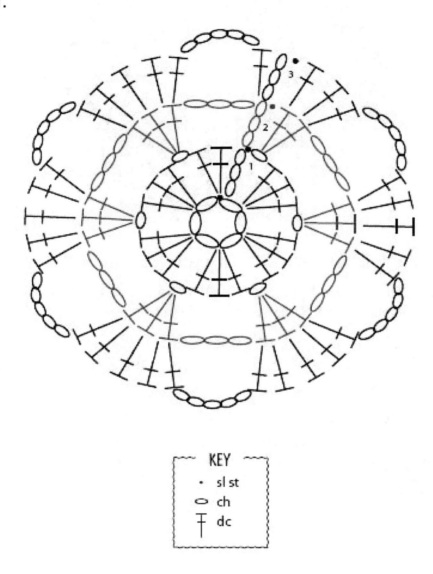

KEY
- sl st
- ch
- dc

Flower Hexagon

Make 6 ch and join with sl st to form a ring.

Rnd 1 3 ch (counts as 1 dc), 2 dc into ring, 3 ch, (3 dc into ring, 3 ch) 5 times, sl st into 3rd of 3 ch at beg of rnd.

Rnd 2 4 ch (counts as 1 tr), miss 2 dc, (3 tr, 2 ch, 3 tr) all into each of next five 3 ch sps, (3 tr, 2 ch, 2 tr) all into last 2 ch sp, sl st into 4th of 4 ch.

Rnd 3 3 ch (counts as 1 dc), 1 dc into each of next 3 tr, * (2 dc, 2 ch, 2 dc) all into 2 ch sp, 1 dc into each of next 6 tr; rep from * 4 times more, (2 dc, 2 ch, 2 dc) into last 2 ch sp, 1 dc into each of last 2 tr, sl st into 3rd of 3 ch.

Fasten off.

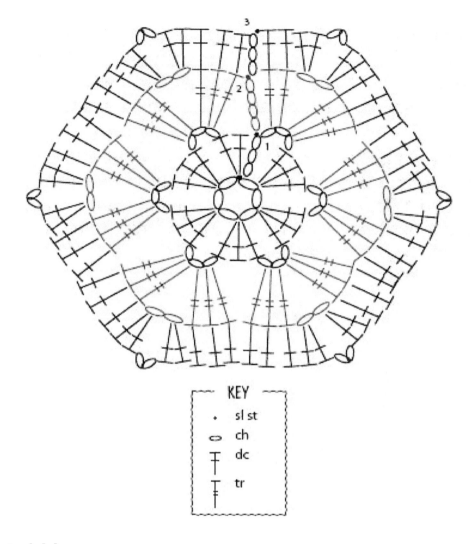

KEY
- sl st
- ch
- dc
- tr

Six-Petal Hexagon

Make 8 ch and join with sl st to form a ring.

Rnd 1 3 ch (counts as 1 dc), 17 dc into ring, sl st into 3rd of 3 ch.

Rnd 2 3 ch (counts as 1 dc), 2 dc into same place, 3 ch, * 1 sc into each of next 2 dc, (3 ch, 3 dc, 3 ch) all into next dc; rep from * 4 times more, 1 sc into each of last 2 dc, 3 ch, sl st into 3rd of 3 ch at beg of rnd.

Rnd 3 3 ch (counts as 1 dc), (1 dc, 2 ch, 2 dc) all into same place, 1 ch, miss 1 dc and 3 ch, 3 tr between 2 sc on previous rnd, * 1 ch, miss 3 ch and 1 dc, (2 dc, 2 ch, 2 dc) all into next dc, 1 ch, miss 1 dc and 3 ch, 3 tr between 2 sc on previous rnd; rep from * 4 times more, 1 ch, sl st into 3rd of 3 ch at beg of rnd.

Fasten off.

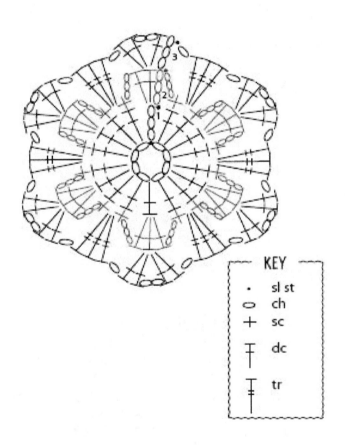

Star Hexagon

Make 4 ch and join with sl st to form a ring.

Rnd 1 6 ch (counts as 1 dc and 3 ch), (1 dc into ring, 3 ch) 5 times, sl st into 3rd of 6 ch, sl st into first 3 ch sp.

Rnd 2 3 ch, dc3tog into first 3 ch sp (counts as dc4tog), (5 ch, dc4tog into next 3 ch sp) 5 times, 5 ch, sl st into top of first dc4tog.

Rnd 3 3 ch (counts as 1 dc), (2 dc, 3 ch, 3 dc) all into first 3 ch sp, (3 dc, 3 ch, 3 dc) all into each of next five 3 ch sps, sl st into 3rd of 3 ch.

Fasten off.

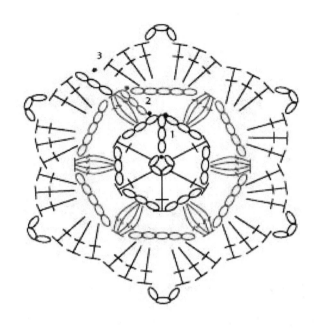

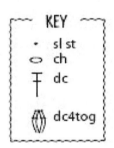

KEY
- sl st
- ch
- dc
- dc4tog

Starfish

Make 6 ch and join with sl st to form a ring.
Rnd 1 1 ch, 12 sc into ring, sl st into first sc.

Rnd 2 3 ch, dc4tog into same place (counts as dc5tog), (5 ch, miss 1 sc, dc5tog into next sc) 5 times, 5 ch, sl st into top of first dc5tog.

Rnd 3 1 ch, (5 sc into next 5 ch sp, 3 ch) 6 times, sl st into first sc.

Rnd 4 1 ch, * 1 sc into each of next 5 sc, (2 sc, 1 ch, 2 sc) all into 3 ch sp; rep from * 5 times more, sl st into first sc.

Fasten off.

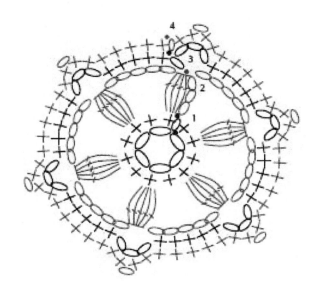

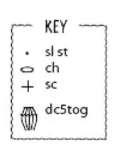

KEY
- • sl st
- ◦ ch
- + sc
- 🞄 dc5tog

English Rose Hexagon

Make 4 ch and join with sl st to form a ring.

Rnd 1 6 ch (counts as 1 dc and 3 ch), (1 dc into ring, 3 ch) 5 times, sl st to 3rd of 6 ch.

Rnd 2 1 ch, 1 sc into same place, 5 ch, (1 sc into next dc, 5 ch) 5 times, sl st to first sc, sl st into first 5 ch sp.

Rnd 3 1 ch, (1 sc, 2 hdc, 1 dc, 2 hdc, 1 sc) all into each 5 ch sp, sl st to first sc.

Fasten off.

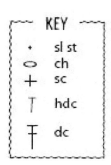

Daisy Hexagon

Make 4 ch and join with sl st to form a ring.

Rnd 1 3 ch, dc2tog into ring (counts as dc3tog), (3 ch, dc3tog into ring) 5 times, 1 ch, 1 hdc into top of first dc3tog.

Rnd 2 3 ch, dc2tog into sp made by hdc (counts as dc3tog), 5 ch, (dc3tog into next 3 ch sp, 5 ch) 5 times, sl st into top of first dc3tog.

Rnd 3 1 ch, 1 sc into same place, * (3 sc, 1 ch, 3 sc) into 5 ch sp, 1 sc into top of next dc3tog; rep from * 4 times more, (3 sc, 1 ch, 3 sc) into last 5 ch sp, sl st into first sc.

Fasten off.

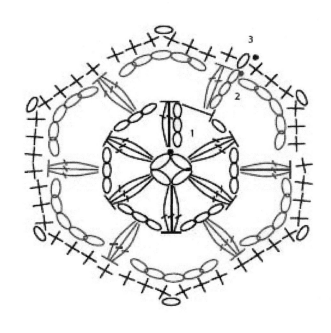

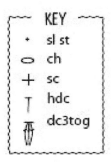

Small Daisy Hexagon

Make 4 ch and join with sl st to form a ring.

Rnd 1 1 ch, 6 sc into ring, sl st to first sc.

Rnd 2 3 ch (counts as 1 dc), 1 dc into same place, 3 ch, * 2 dc into next sc, 3 ch; rep from * 4 times more, sl st into 3rd of 3 ch, sl st into next dc.

Rnd 3 1 ch, 5 sc into each 3 ch sp, sl st to first sc.

Fasten off.

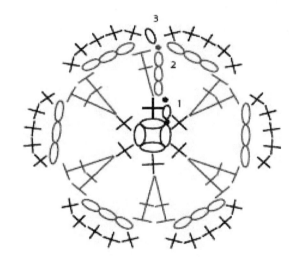

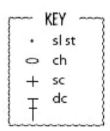

KEY
- • sl st
- ○ ch
- + sc
- ┬ dc

Four-Petal Square

Make 6 ch and join with sl st to form a ring.

Rnd 1 1 ch, (1 sc into ring, 2 ch, 4 dc into ring, 2 ch) 4 times, sl st into first sc.

Rnd 2 1 ch, 1 sc into same place, (5 ch, miss petal, 1 sc into next sc) 3 times, 5 ch, miss petal, sl st into first sc.

Rnd 3 3 ch (counts as 1 dc), (3 dc, 3 ch, 4 dc, 2 ch) all into first 5 ch sp, (4 dc, 3 ch, 4 dc, 2 ch) all into each of next three 5 ch sps, sl st into 3rd of 3 ch.

Fasten off.

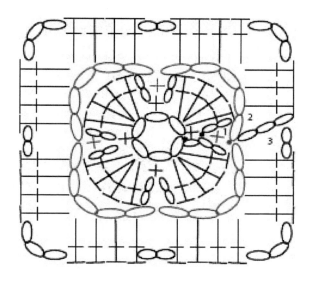

```
┌── KEY ──┐
│ •   sl st │
│ ○   ch   │
│ +   sc   │
│ ┬   dc   │
└──────────┘
```

Squared Wheel

Make 6 ch and join with sl st to form a ring.

Rnd 1 1 ch, 12 sc into ring, sl st into first sc.

Rnd 2 7 ch (counts as 1 tr and 3 ch), (1 tr into next sc, 3 ch) 11 times, sl st into 4th of 7 ch, sl st into each of next 2 ch.

Rnd 3 1 ch, 1 sc into 3 ch sp, 5 ch, (1 sc into next 3 ch sp, 5 ch) 11 times, sl st into first sc.

Rnd 4 3 ch (counts as 1 dc), 4 dc into first 5 ch sp, (7 dc into next 5 ch sp, 5 dc into each of next two 5 ch sp) 3 times, 7 dc into next 5 ch sp, 5 dc into last 5 ch sp, sl st into 3rd of 3 ch.

Fasten off.

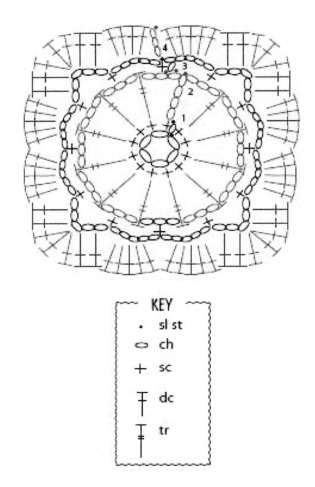

KEY
- · sl st
- ◯ ch
- + sc
- ⊤ dc
- ⊤ tr

Lace Rose Square

Make 6 ch and join with sl st to form a ring.

Rnd 1 1 ch, 16 sc into ring, sl st into first sc.

Rnd 2 7 ch (counts as 1 dc and 4 ch), (miss 1 sc, 1 dc into next sc, 4 ch) 7 times, sl st into 3rd of 7 ch.

Rnd 3 1 ch, (1 sc, 1 dc, 2 tr, 1 dc, 1 sc) all into each 4 ch sp, sl st into first sc.

Rnd 4 9 ch (counts as 1 tr and 5 ch), sl st between 2 tr of first petal, 5 ch, sl st between 2 tr of next petal, * 5 ch, miss 1 tr and 1 dc and 1 sc of this petal, work 1 tr between 2 sc, 5 ch, sl st between 2 tr of next petal, 5 ch, sl st between 2 tr of next petal; rep from * twice more, 5 ch, sl st into 4th of 9 ch.

Fasten off.

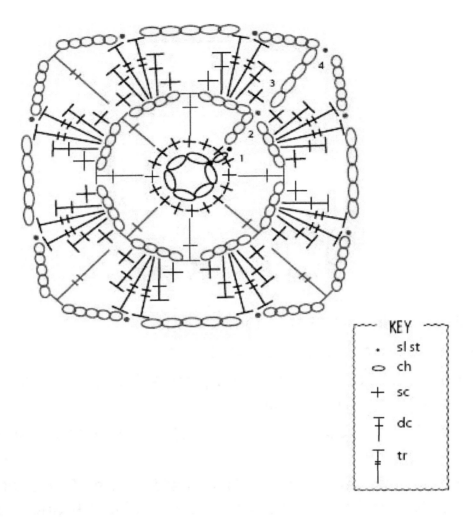

Lacy Flower Square

Make 6 ch and join with sl st to form a ring.

Rnd 1 5 ch (counts as 1 dc and 2 ch), (1 dc into ring, 2 ch) 7 times, sl st into 3rd of 5 ch.

Rnd 2 7 ch (counts as 1 dc and 4 ch), dc2tog into 4th ch from hook, (1 dc into next dc, 4 ch, dc2tog into 4th ch from hook) 7 times, sl st into base of first dc2tog.

Rnd 3 1 ch, 1 sc into same place, * 3 ch, miss 1 dc2tog, (tr3tog, 4 ch, tr3tog, 4 ch, tr3tog) all into next dc, 3 ch, miss 1 dc2tog, 1 sc into next dc; rep from * 3 times more, omitting last sc of last rep, sl st into first sc.

Rnd 4 1 ch, (3 sc into 3 ch sp, 4 sc into each of next three 4 ch sp, 3 sc into next 3 ch sp) 4 times, sl st into first sc.

Fasten off.

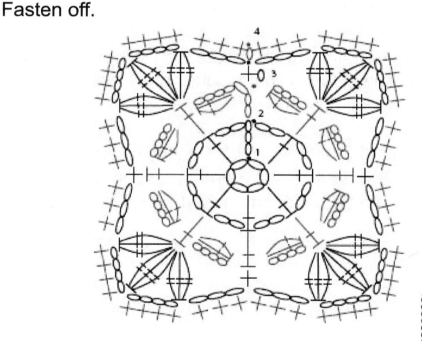

KEY
- · sl st
- ◦ ch
- + sc
- ⊤ dc
- ⊓ dc2tog
- ⊕ tr3tog

Eight-Petal Square

Make 6 ch and join with sl st to form a ring.

Rnd 1 1 ch, (1 sc into ring, 6 ch, 1 sc into 3rd ch from hook, 1 sc into next ch, 1 hdc into each of next 2 ch) 8 times, sl st into first sc. Fasten off.

Rnd 2 Rejoin yarn to top of petal, * 4 ch, (1 dc, 2 ch, 1 dc) all into top of next petal, 4 ch, sl st into top of next petal; rep from * 3 times more.

Rnd 3 1 ch, 1 sc into same place, 4 sc into first 4 ch sp, (1 sc into next dc, 2 sc into 2 ch sp, 1 sc into next dc, 4 sc into next 4 ch sp, 1 sc into next sl st, 4 sc into next 4 ch sp) 3 times, 1 sc into next dc, 2 sc into 2 ch sp, 1 sc into next dc, 4 sc into last 4 ch sp, sl st into first sc.

Fasten off.

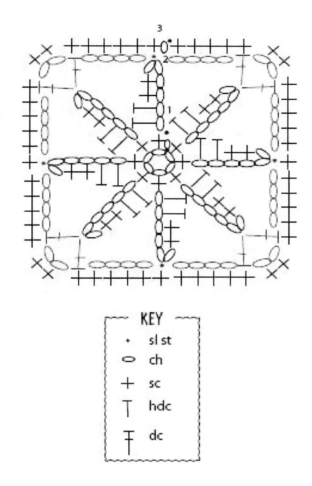

```
┌─── KEY ───┐
  •    sl st
  ○    ch
  +    sc
  T    hdc
  ╤    dc
└───────────┘
```

Large Loop Square

Make 6 ch and join with sl st to form a ring.
Rnd 1 1 ch, 12 sc into ring, sl st into first sc.

Rnd 2 7 ch (counts as 1 tr and 3 ch), 1 tr into same place, * 10 ch, miss 2 sc, (1 tr, 3 ch, 1 tr) all into next sc; rep from * twice more, 10 ch, sl st into 4th of 7 ch.

Rnd 3 3 ch (counts as 1 dc), into each 10 ch sp work (5 dc, 4 ch, sl st into 4th ch from hook, 4 dc, 4 ch, sl st into 4th ch from hook, 5 dc), omitting last dc on last rep, sl st into 3rd of 3 ch.

Fasten off.

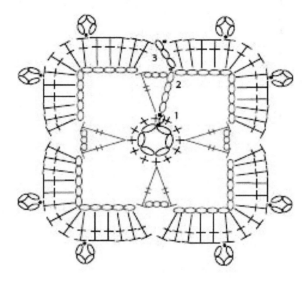

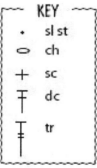

Maltese Square

Make 8 ch and join with sl st to form a ring.

Rnd 1 1 ch, 16 sc into ring, sl st into first sc.

Rnd 2 4 ch (counts as 1 tr), 2 tr into same place, 3 tr into next sc, (7 ch, miss 2 sc, 3 tr into each of next 2 sc) 3 times, 7 ch, sl st into 4th of 4 ch.

Rnd 3 1 ch, (1 sc into first tr of cluster, 1 hdc into next tr, 2 dc into each of next 2 tr, 1 hdc into next tr, 1 sc into next tr, 8 sc into 7 ch sp) 4 times, sl st into first sc.

Fasten off.

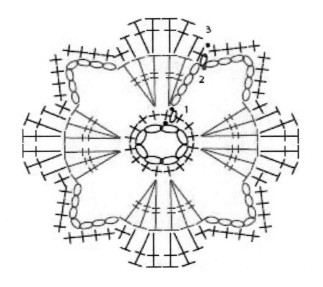

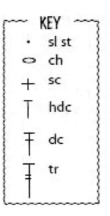

Snowflake

Make 4 ch and join with sl st to form a ring.

Rnd 1 1 ch, 8 sc into ring, sl st into first sc.

Rnd 2 1 ch, 1 sc into first sc, (8 ch, 1 sc into next sc) 7 times, 8 ch, sl st into first sc, 1 sl st into each of first 4 ch of first 8 ch loop.

Rnd 3 1 ch, 1 sc into 8 ch loop, * 4 ch, 1 sc into next 8 ch loop, 4 ch, (1 sc, 5 ch, 1 sc) all into next 8 ch loop; rep from * twice more, 4 ch, 1 sc into next 8 ch loop, 4 ch, 1 sc into next 8 ch loop, 5 ch, sl st into first sc, sl st into each of next 2 ch of first 4 ch sp.

Rnd 4 1 ch, *1 sc into 4 ch sp, 5 ch, 1 sc into next 4 ch sp, 6 ch, sl st into 4th ch from hook, 2 ch, 1 sc into 5 ch loop in rnd below, 4 ch, sl st into 4th ch from hook, 5 ch, sl st into 5th ch from hook, 4 ch, sl st into 4th ch from hook, 6 ch, sl st into 4th ch from hook, 2 ch; rep from * 3 times more, sl st into first sc.

Fasten off.

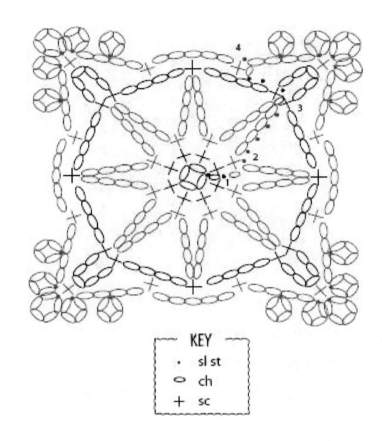

KEY
- sl st
○ ch
+ sc

Patchwork Square

Make 6 ch and join with sl st to form a ring.

Rnd 1 3 ch (counts as 1 dc), 15 dc into ring, sl st into 3rd of 3 ch.

Rnd 2 1 ch, 1 sc into same place, (miss 1 dc, 5 hdc into next dc, miss 1 dc, 1 sc into next dc) three times, miss 1 dc, 5 hdc into next dc, miss 1 dc, sl st into first sc.

Rnd 3 3 ch (counts as 1 dc), 6 dc into same place, (miss 2 hdc, 1 sc into next hdc, miss 2 hdc, 7 dc into next sc) 3 times, miss 2 hdc, 1 sc into next hdc, miss 2 hdc, sl st into 3rd of 3 ch, sl st into each of next 3 dc.

Rnd 4 1 ch, 1 sc into same place, (miss 3 dc, 9 tr into next sc, miss 3 dc, 1 sc into next dc) three times, miss 3 dc, 9 tr into next sc, miss 3 dc, sl st into first sc.

Fasten off.

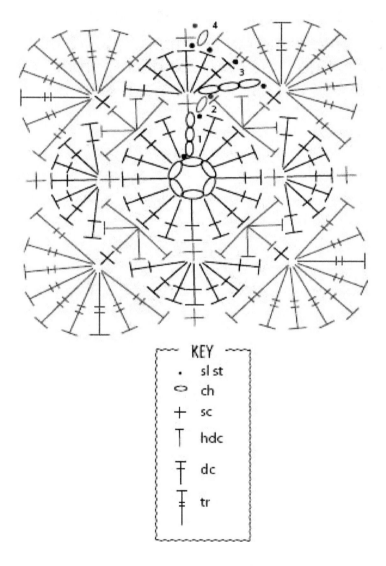

KEY
- · sl st
- ○ ch
- + sc
- T hdc
- ┬ dc
- ╪ tr

Small Patchwork Square

Make 6 ch and join with sl st to form a ring.

Rnd 1 3 ch (counts as 1 dc), 15 dc into ring, sl st into 3rd of 3 ch.

Rnd 2 1 ch, 1 sc into same place, * miss 1 dc, (2 hdc, 1 dc, 2 hdc) all into next dc, miss 1 dc, 1 sc into next dc; rep from * twice more, miss 1 dc, (2 hdc, 1 dc, 2 hdc) all into next dc, miss 1 dc, sl st into first sc.

Fasten off.

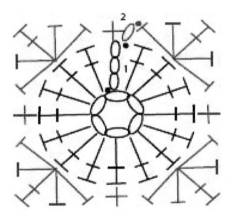

```
KEY
·  sl st
○  ch
+  sc
T  hdc
T  dc
```

Baltic Square

Special instruction

Popcorn = 5 dc popcorn

Make 8 ch and join with sl st to form a ring.

Rnd 1 3 ch, (popcorn into ring, 1 ch, popcorn into ring, 4 ch) 4 times, sl st to top of first popcorn.

Rnd 2 5 ch (counts as 1 dc and 2 ch), 1 dc into top of next popcorn, 2 ch, * (popcorn, 4 ch, popcorn) all into 4 ch sp at corner, 2 ch, 1 dc into top of next popcorn, 2 ch, 1 dc into top of next popcorn, 2 ch; rep from * twice more, (popcorn, 4 ch, popcorn) all into last 4 ch sp at corner, 2 ch, sl st into 3rd of 5 ch.

Fasten off.

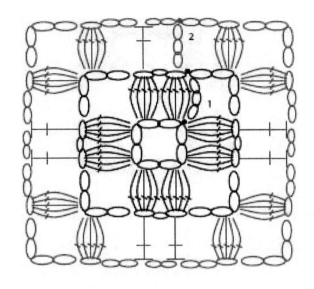

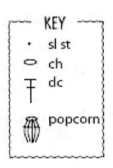

KEY
- sl st
- ch
- dc
- popcorn

Four-Petal Square

Make 6 ch and join with sl st to form a ring.

Rnd 1 3 ch and dc3tog into ring (count as dc4tog), (6 ch, dc4tog into ring) 3 times, 6 ch, sl st into top of first dc4tog, sl st into first 6 ch sp.

Rnd 2 3 ch (counts as 1 dc), (2 dc, 4 ch, 3 dc) all into first 6 ch sp, (3 dc, 4 ch, 3 dc) all into each of next three 6 ch sps, sl st into 3rd of 3

ch.
Fasten off.

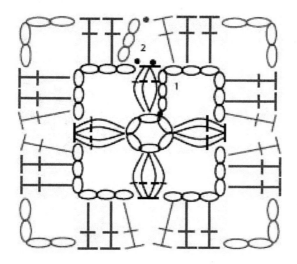

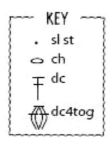

Diamond Square

Centre ring

(Make 4 ch, tr2tog into 4th ch from hook) 4 times, sl st into end of first cluster to form a ring.

Rnd 1 1 ch, 1 sc between last and first tr2tog clusters, 9 ch, 1 sc between first and second clusters, 9 ch, 1 sc between second and third clusters, 9 ch, 1 sc between third and fourth clusters, 9 ch, sl st into first sc.

Rnd 2 3 ch (counts as 1 dc), * (6 dc, 3 ch, 6 dc) all into 9 ch sp, 1 dc into next sc; rep from * 3 times more, omitting last dc, sl st into 3rd of 3 ch.

Fasten off.

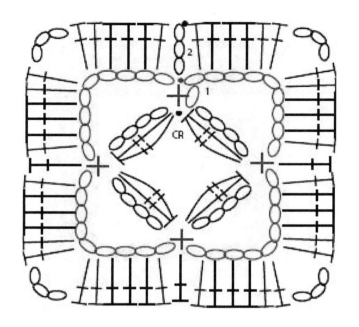

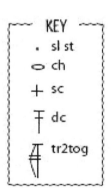

Filet Square

Make 12 ch and join with sl st to form a ring.

Rnd 1 5 ch (counts as 1 dc and 2 ch), * miss 2 ch of ring, (1 dc, 5ch, 1 dc) all into next ch, 2 ch; rep from * twice more, miss 2 ch of ring, 1 dc into ch at base of 5 ch at beg of rnd, 5 ch, sl st into 3rd of 5 ch at beg of rnd.

Rnd 2 3 ch (counts as 1 dc), 2 dc into 2 ch sp, 1 dc into next dc, * (3 dc, 5 ch, 3 dc) all into 5 ch sp at corner, 1 dc into next dc, 2 dc into 2 ch sp, 1 dc into next dc; rep from * twice more, (3 dc, 5 ch, 3 dc) all into 5 ch sp at corner, sl st to 3rd of 3 ch at beg of rnd.

Fasten off.

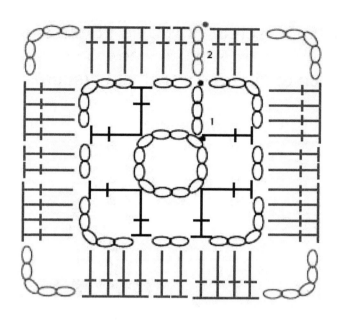

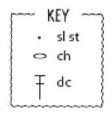

KEY
- sl st
- ch
- dc

Picot Hoop

Make 18 ch and join with sl st to form a ring.

Rnd 1 1 ch, 36 sc into ring, sl st into first sc.

Rnd 2 1 ch, 1 sc into each sc to end, sl st into first sc.

Rnd 3 1 ch, 1 sc into each of next 3 sc, (5 ch, sl st into 5th ch from hook, 1 sc into each of next 6 sc) 5 times, 5 ch, sl st into 5th ch from hook, 1 sc into each of next 3 sc, sl st into first sc.

Fasten off.

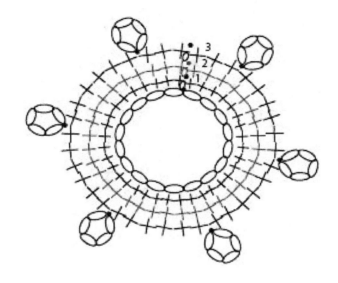

```
KEY
·  sl st
o  ch
+  sc
```

Cartwheel

Make 8 ch and join with sl st to form a ring.

Rnd 1 3 ch (counts as 1 dc), 15 dc into ring, sl st into 3rd of 3 ch.

Rnd 2 5 ch (counts as 1 dc and 2 ch), (1 dc into next dc, 2 ch) 15 times, sl st into 3rd of 5 ch.

Rnd 3 1 ch, 1 sc into same place, * 2 sc into next 2 ch sp, 1 sc into next dc; rep from * to end, omitting last sc, sl st into first sc.

Fasten off.

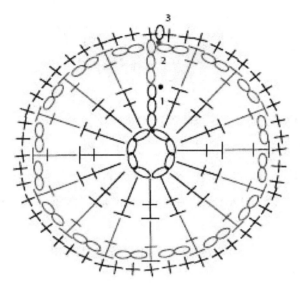

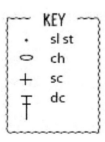

KEY
- . sl st
- ○ ch
- + sc
- ┬ dc

Rose Circle

Make 8 ch and join with sl st to form a ring.

Rnd 1 1 ch, 18 sc into ring, sl st into first sc.

Rnd 2 6 ch (counts as 1 hdc and 4 ch), miss sc at base of ch and next 2 sc, (1 hdc into next sc, 4 ch, miss next 2 sc) 5 times, sl st into 2nd of 6 ch.

Rnd 3 1 ch, (1 sc, 1 hdc, 2 dc, 1 hdc, 1 sc) all into each 4 ch sp, sl st into first sc. Fasten off.

Rnd 4 Rejoin yarn between 2 dc at top of petal, 1 ch, 1 sc into same place, 7 ch, (1 sc between 2 dc of next petal, 7 ch) 5 times, sl st into first sc.

Rnd 5 1 ch, 1 sc into same place, (7 sc into next 7 ch sp, 1 sc into next sc) 6 times omitting last sc of last rep, sl st into first sc.

Rnd 6 1 ch, 1 sc into each sc to end, sl st into first sc.

Fasten off.

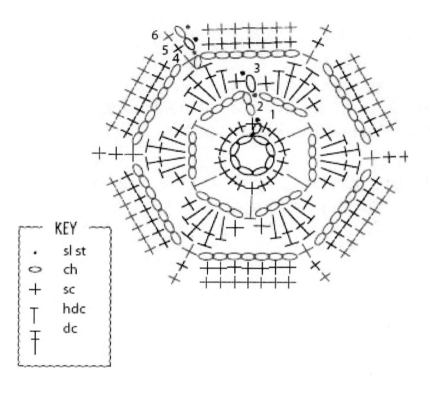

KEY
- · sl st
- ○ ch
- + sc
- T hdc
- ╤ dc

Frozen Star

Make 12 ch and join with sl st to form a ring.

Rnd 1 1 ch, 24 sc into ring, sl st into first sc.

Rnd 2 4 ch, tr3tog working the 3 legs into next 3 sc (counts as tr4tog), (7 ch, tr4tog working first leg into same sc as previous cluster and next 3 legs into next 3 sc) 7 times, 7 ch, sl st into top of first tr4tog.

Rnd 3 1 ch, 1 sc into same place, * (3 ch, miss 1 ch, 1 sc into next ch) 3 times, 3 ch, 1 sc into top of next tr4tog; rep from * 7 times more, omitting last sc from last rep, sl st into first sc, sl st into first 3 ch sp.

Rnd 4 1 ch, 1 sc into first 3 ch sp, 3 ch, * 1 sc into next 3 ch sp, 3 ch; rep from * to end, sl st into first sc.

Fasten off.

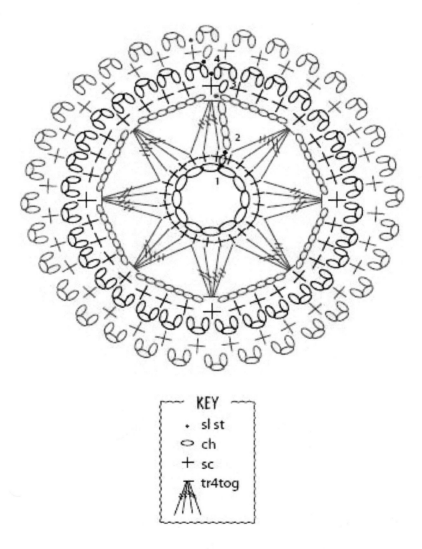

KEY
- sl st
- ch
- sc
- tr4tog

Celtic Circle

Make 6 ch and join with sl st to form a ring.

Rnd 1 (3 ch, 2 dc into ring, 3 ch, sl st into ring) 4 times.

Rnd 2 6 ch (counts as 1 dc and 3 ch), 1 dc into same place, 3 ch, miss first petal, * (1 dc, 3 ch, 1 dc) into sl st between petals, 3 ch, miss next petal; rep from * twice more, sl st into 3rd of 6 ch.

Rnd 3 3 ch (counts as 1 dc), 4 dc into first 3 ch sp, 2 ch, (5 dc into next 3 ch sp, 2 ch) 7 times, sl st into 3rd of 3 ch.

Rnd 4 1 ch, 1 sc into same place, 1 sc into each of next 4 dc, (1 sc, 3 ch, sl st into 3rd ch from hook, 1 sc) all into 2 ch sp, * 1 sc into each of next 5 dc, (1 sc, 3 ch, sl st into 3rd ch from hook, 1 sc) all into 2 ch sp; rep from * 6 times more, sl st into first sc.

Fasten off.

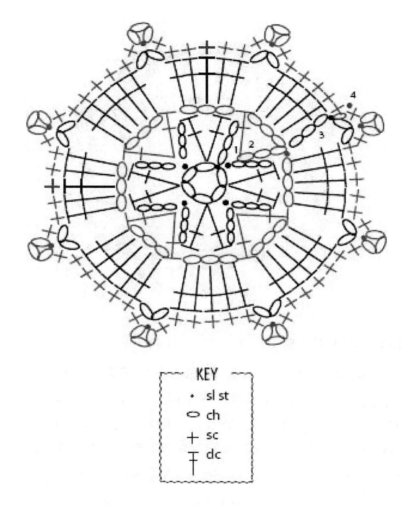

KEY
· sl st
○ ch
+ sc
⊤ dc

Lace Wheel

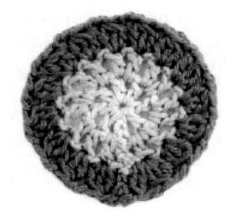

Make 4 ch and join with sl st to form a ring.

Rnd 1 4 ch (counts as 1 dc and 1 ch), (1 dc into ring, 1 ch) 7 times, sl st into 3rd of 4 ch.

Rnd 2 4 ch (counts as 1 dc and 1 ch), 1 dc into ch sp, 1 ch, (1 dc into next dc, 1 ch, 1 dc into next ch sp, 1 ch) 7 times, sl st into 3rd of 4 ch.

Rnd 3 3 ch, dc2tog into same place (count as dc3tog), 2 ch, (dc3tog into next dc, 2 ch) 15 times, sl st into 3rd of 3 ch.

Fasten off.

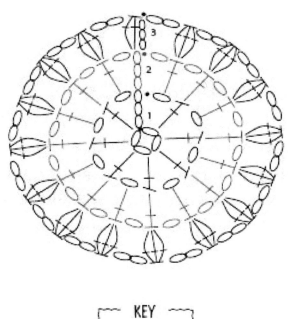

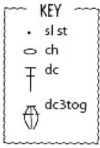

KEY
- sl st
- ch
- dc
- dc3tog

Dozen Cluster Circle

Make 10 ch and join with sl st to form a ring.

Rnd 1 4 ch and 1 tr into ring (count as tr2tog), 2 ch, (tr2tog into ring, 2 ch) 11 times, sl st into top of first tr2tog, sl st into first 2 ch sp.

Rnd 2 3 ch and dc2tog into first 2 ch sp (count as dc3tog), 3 ch, (dc3tog into next 2 ch sp, 3 ch) 11 times, sl st into top of first dc3tog.

Fasten off.

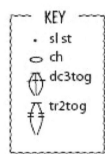

Star Circle

Make 4 ch and join with sl st to form a ring.

Rnd 1 1 ch, (1 sc into ring, 9 ch) 8 times, sl st into first sc. Fasten off.

Rnd 2 Rejoin yarn to 5th of 9 ch petal, 4 ch (counts as 1 dc and 1 ch), 1 dc into same place, 5 ch, * (1 dc, 1 ch, 1 dc) all into 5th ch of next petal, 5ch; rep from * 6 times, sl st into 3rd of 4 ch.

Rnd 3 3 ch (counts as 1 dc), 1 dc into 1 ch sp, 1 dc into next dc, * 5 dc into 5 ch sp, 1 dc into next dc, 1 dc into ch sp, 1 dc into next dc; rep from * 6 times more, 5 dc into 5 ch sp, sl st into 3rd of 3 ch.

Fasten off.

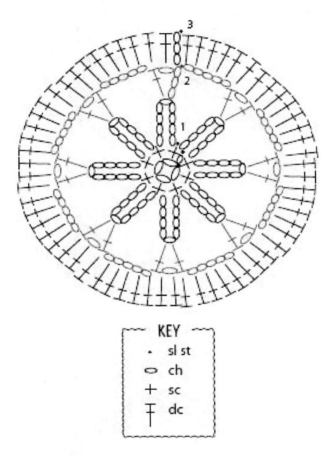

KEY
- • sl st
- ○ ch
- + sc
- ╤ dc

Two-Layer Cartwheel

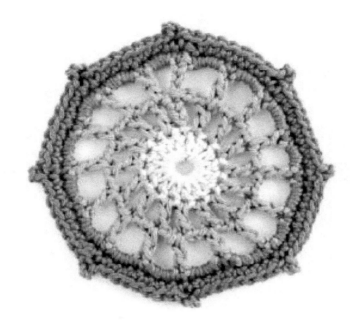

Make 6 ch and join with sl st to form a ring.

Rnd 1 3 ch (counts as 1 dc), 15 dc into ring, sl st into 3rd of 3 ch.

Rnd 2 5 ch (counts as 1 dc and 3 ch), (1 dc into next dc, 2 ch) 15 times, sl st into 3rd of 3 ch.

Rnd 3 6 ch (counts as 1 dc and 3 ch), (1 dc into next dc, 3 ch) 15 times, sl st into 3rd of 3 ch.

Rnd 4 1 ch, 1 sc into same place, 3 sc into first 3 ch sp, (1 sc into next dc, 3 sc into next 3 ch sp) 15 times, sl st into first sc.

Rnd 5 1 ch, 1 sc into first sc, (3 ch, sl st into 3rd ch from hook, 1 sc into each of next 8 sc) 8 times, omitting last sc on last rep, sl st into first sc.

Fasten off.

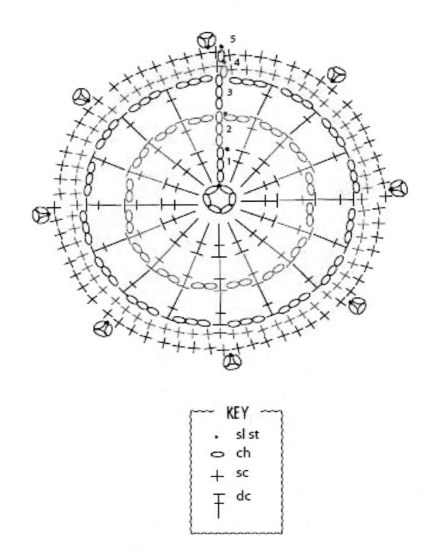

Double Crochet Circle

Make 6 ch and join with sl st to form a ring.

Rnd 1 6 ch (counts as 1 dc and 3 ch), (1 dc into ring, 3 ch) 9 times, sl st into 3rd of 3 ch, sl st into first 3 ch sp.

Rnd 2 3 ch (counts as 1 dc), 2 dc into first 3 ch sp, (2 ch, 3 dc into next 3 ch sp) 9 times, 2 ch, sl st into 3rd of 3 ch.

Rnd 3 6 ch (counts as 1 dc and 3 ch), (3 dc into next 2 ch sp, 3 ch) 9 times, 2 dc into last 2 ch sp, sl st to 3rd of 6 ch.

Fasten off.

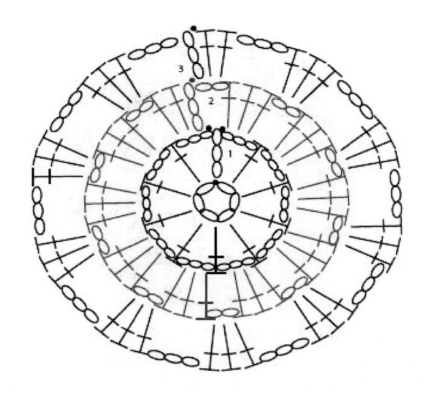

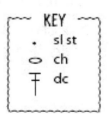

Picot Circle

Make 6 ch and join with sl st to form a ring.

Rnd 1 3 ch (counts as 1 dc), 1 dc into ring, (3 ch, sl st into 3rd ch from hook, 3 dc into ring) 7 times, 3 ch, sl st into 3rd ch from hook, 1 dc into ring, sl st into 3rd of 3 ch at beg of rnd. 24 dc.

Rnd 2 3 ch (counts as 1 dc), 2 dc into same place, (3 ch, miss 1 dc and picot and 1 dc, 3 dc into next dc) 7 times, 3 ch, sl st into 3rd of 3 ch.

Rnd 3 1 ch, 1 sc into same place, 1 sc into each of next 2 dc, (3 ch, 1 sc into next 3 ch sp, 3 ch, 1 sc into each of next 3 dc 7 times, 3 ch, 1 sc into next 3 ch sp, 3 ch, sl st into first sc.

Fasten off.

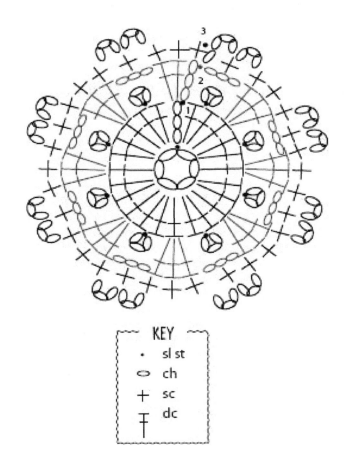

KEY
- · sl st
- ⌒ ch
- + sc
- ┬ dc

Frilly Circle

Make 6 ch and join with sl st to form a ring.

Rnd 1 1 ch, 16 sc into ring, sl st into first sc.

Rnd 2 3 ch (counts as 1 dc), 1 dc into each of next 15 sc, sl st into 3rd of 3 ch.

Rnd 3 1 ch, 1 sc into same place, (3 ch, sl st into 3rd ch from hook, 1 sc into next dc) 15 times, 3 ch, sl st into 3rd ch from hook, sl st into first sc.

Fasten off.

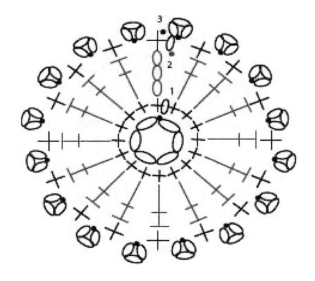

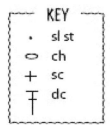

Simple Cluster Circle

Make 4 ch and join with sl st to form a ring.

Rnd 1 4 ch (counts as 1 tr), 1 tr into ring, (2 ch, 2 tr into ring) 11 times, 2 ch, sl st to 4th of 4 ch, sl st into next tr, sl st into first 2 ch sp.

Rnd 2 3 ch and dc2tog into 2 ch sp (count as dc3tog), (5 ch, dc3tog into next 2 ch sp) 11 times, 5 ch, sl st into top of first dc3tog.

Fasten off.

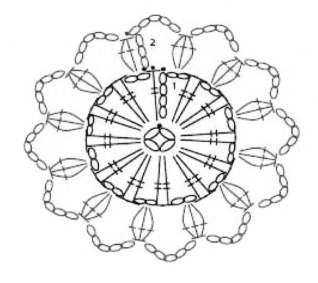

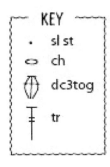

KEY
- sl st
- ch
- dc3tog
- tr

Very Lacy Circle

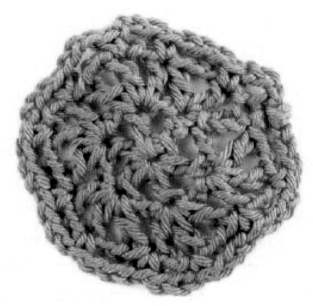

Make 4 ch and join with sl st to form a ring.

Rnd 1 5 ch (counts as 1 dc and 2 ch), (1 dc into ring, 2 ch) 5 times, sl st into 3rd of 5 ch.

Rnd 2 5 ch (counts as 1 dc and 2 ch), (1 dc, 2 ch, 1 dc) all into same ch at base of tch, * miss 2 ch, (1 dc, 2 ch, 1 dc, 2 ch, 1 dc) all into next dc; rep from * 4 times more, sl st into 3rd of 5 ch.

Rnd 3 1 ch, 1 sc into same place, (3 ch, 1 sc into next dc, 3 ch, 1 sc between next 2 dc) 5 times, 3 ch, 1 sc into next dc, 3 ch, sl st into first sc.

Fasten off.

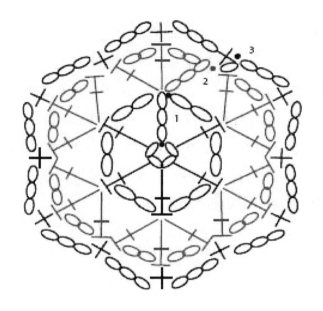

KEY
- sl st
- ch
- sc
- dc

Solid Circle

Make 4 ch and join with sl st to form a ring.

Rnd 1 1 ch, 8 sc into ring, sl st into first sdc.

Rnd 2 1 ch, 2 sc into each sc to end, sl st into first sc. 16 sc.

Rnd 3 1 ch, 1 sc into each sc to end, sl st into first sc.

Rnd 4 1 ch, 2 sc into each sc to end, sl st into first sc. 32 sc.

Rnd 5 1 ch, 1 sc into each of first 2 sc, 3 ch, (1 sc into each of next 2 sc, 3 ch) 15 times, sl st into first sc.

Fasten off.

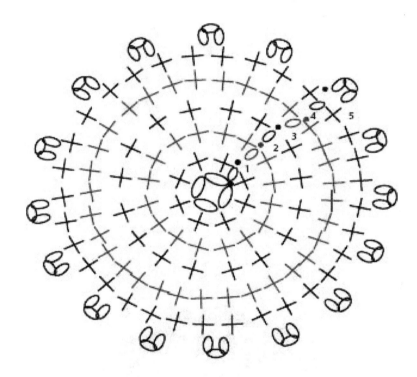

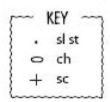

KEY
. sl st
o ch
+ sc